Gilles Deleuze and the Atheist Machine

# Gilles Deleuze and the Atheist Machine

The Achievement of Philosophy

F. LeRon Shults

Edinburgh University Press is one of the leading university presses in the UK. We publish academic books and journals in our selected subject areas across the humanities and social sciences, combining cutting-edge scholarship with high editorial and production values to produce academic works of lasting importance. For more information visit our website: edinburghuniversitypress.com

We are committed to making research available to a wide audience and are pleased to be publishing an Open Access ebook edition of this title.

© F. LeRon Shults, 2024, 2025, under a Creative Commons Attribution-NonCommercial licence

Edinburgh University Press Ltd
13 Infirmary Street, Edinburgh EH1 1LT

First published in hardback by Edinburgh University Press 2024

Typeset in Bembo
by Cheshire Typesetting Ltd, Cuddington, Cheshire

A CIP record for this book is available from the British Library

ISBN 978 1 3995 2959 4 (hardback)
ISBN 978 1 3995 2960 0 (paperback)
ISBN 978 1 3995 2961 7 (webready PDF)
ISBN 978 1 3995 2962 4 (epub)

The right of F. LeRon Shults to be identified as the author of this work has been asserted in accordance with the Copyright, Designs and Patents Act 1988, and the Copyright and Related Rights Regulations 2003 (SI No. 2498).

*To Justin E. Lane*

# Contents

*Preface* ix
*Abbreviations* x

1 Atheism as Philosophy's Achievement 1
   Achieving Atheism 3
   The Speculative and Practical Purposes of Philosophy 8
   Given Philosophy, What Machine Can Produce It? 12
   Given an Atheist Machine, What Can it be Used For? 17
   Philosophy and Computational Simulation Machines 21

2 Assembling the Atheist Machine 26
   Alliance and Fighters and Bias – Oh My! 27
   The Assemblage of (A)theism 33
   Deleuzian Social Machines and the Bio-cultural Sciences of Religion 38
   Becoming-atheist: Naturalism and Secularism 43
   10,000 Years of Non-linear, Social-machinic History 47

3 The Reversal of Platonism and the Rise of Simulation 52
   The Reversal of Platonism 53
   The Rise of Simulation 58
   DeLanda on Multiplicities and Mechanism-independence 61
   Virtual Phase Space and Actual Simulations 65
   The Achievement of Deleuze's Metaphysics 69

4 Assemblage Theory and Multi-agent Artificial Intelligence Modelling 73
   Theorising Assemblages in Human Geography 74
   A Thousand Abstract Machines 78
   DeLanda's Assemblage Theory and the Simulation of Emergence 82
   Emergent Social Assemblages in Multi-agent Artificial Intelligence Modelling 86
   Simulating Sustainable Social Assemblages 92

| | | |
|---|---|---|
| 5 | Simulating (Non-)Religion | 98 |
| | The Modelling Religion Project(s) | 99 |
| | The Causes and Consequences of 'Religion' | 103 |
| | Micro-, Meso-, and Macro-level Mechanisms in Religious Radicalisation | 108 |
| | Computational Models that Predict (and Prevent) Theism | 114 |
| | The Achievement of Deleuze's Meta-epistemology | 121 |
| 6 | Strategies for Promoting Safe Sects | 126 |
| | The (Mal)adaptiveness of Theism | 127 |
| | *Talking* about Safe Sects | 133 |
| | *Experimenting* with Safe Sects | 137 |
| | Prebunking Theism | 142 |
| | Sustainable Altruism in the Anthropocene | 146 |
| 7 | A Germ of Tranquil Atheism | 152 |
| | How Christ was Born(e) | 154 |
| | How Christianity Will Die | 157 |
| | Theist Credulity and Conformity Biases in Philosophy of Religion | 161 |
| | Computer Modelling and Philosophy of Religion | 165 |
| | The Achievement of Deleuze's Meta-ethics | 169 |
| 8 | How Do You Make Yourself an Atheist Body without Organs? | 174 |
| | To be Done with the Judgement of God | 176 |
| | A Joy Immanent to Desire | 180 |
| | Becoming-sorcerer | 184 |
| | The Brain-subject | 189 |
| | The Philosopher's Serenity | 193 |
| *References* | | 199 |
| *Index* | | 223 |

# Preface

I'm grateful to Carol Macdonald at Edinburgh University Press for her excellent help and advice throughout the process of producing this book. She made the experience as seamless and pleasant as my first time around with EUP, some ten years ago when I published my first monograph on Gilles Deleuze (Shults, 2014b). The current volume extends some of my arguments there and adds new ones, most of which are based on my work during the last decade on research projects related to simulating (non-)religious social assemblages using computer modelling (simulating machines). Some of the chapters that follow include ideas originally developed in various other essays, but these have been thoroughly disassembled and reassembled in a new and cohesive whole. Here I follow the convention, common in Deleuze scholarship, of simply referring to Deleuze even when citing or discussing works he co-authored with Félix Guattari. This is not meant to diminish the influence or importance of the latter, but merely to keep the focus on the former. In any case, I only follow this convention when the concepts being discussed have been clearly articulated by Deleuze elsewhere in his solo work prior to or in between his various publications with Guattari.

# Abbreviations

| | |
|---|---|
| AO | *Anti-Oedipus*, Deleuze and Guattari, 1983 |
| ATP | *A Thousand Plateaus*, Deleuze and Guattari, 1988 |
| DR | *Difference and Repetition*, Deleuze, 1995a |
| LOS | *The Logic of Sense*, Deleuze, 2004 |
| NP | *Nietzsche and Philosophy*, Deleuze, 1983 |
| WIP | *What is Philosophy?*, Deleuze and Guattari, 1996 |

# 1

# Atheism as Philosophy's Achievement

> Atheism is not a problem for philosophers, and nor is the death of God. Problems begin only afterward, when the atheism of the concept has been attained. It is surprising that so many philosophers still take the death of God as tragic. *Atheism is not a drama but the philosopher's serenity and philosophy's achievement.*
>
> (Deleuze and Guattari, 1996: 92; emphasis added, translation emended)

One of my main goals in this book is to explore the importance and function of atheism in Deleuze's philosophy, demonstrating its role in his contributions to metaphysics, epistemology, and ethics. I will construct and employ the concept of an 'atheist machine', the multiple uses and effects of which are expressed throughout Deleuze's writings. Using the language of *A Thousand Plateaus* (Deleuze and Guattari, 1988), we might say that the abstract machine of affirmative atheism produces rhizomatic lines of flight whose absolute deterritorialisation molecularises the transcendent pretences of monotheistic molarities. I will argue that the atheist machine is always at work wherever philosophy (schizoanalysis, rhizomatics, micropolitics, pragmatics, etc.) proceeds, as long as it proceeds. Given the consistent embrace and use of atheistic concepts throughout Deleuze's work, which we will examine in some detail below, his atheism has received surprisingly little attention in the secondary literature. I hope to show the creative power – and promote the philosophical use – of the Deleuzian atheist machine.

My other main goal is to bring Deleuze's philosophy into dialogue with recent advances in computational social simulation, especially multi-agent artificial intelligence modelling, which provide material warrant (and methodological weapons) for the task of articulating a flat ontology that can account for the morphogenesis of existing things (or the becoming of assemblages) through resources immanent to the world of matter and energy – without any appeal to transcendence. On the one hand, the successful development and deployment of computational methodologies that are capable of simulating the emergence and macro-level patterns of social (and other) assemblages from the micro-level behaviours and interactions of their component parts (a process involving both the production of a 'virtual' state space and the individuation of 'actual' events in simulation experiments) lend plausibility to Deleuze's philosophy of pure immanence. On the other hand, the use of such techniques, which is rapidly growing in popularity in disciplines such as biology, psychology, anthropology, sociology, and history, all of which play a role in Deleuze's work, can find more adequate philosophical moorings in the writings of the latter.

In pursuing these goals, I will rely heavily on a heuristic conceptual framework (outlined in Chapter 2) that integrates empirical findings and theoretical developments in the bio-cultural study of religion, including fields such as cognitive science of religion, evolutionary psychology of religion, anthropology of religion, and sociology of religion. This framework is meant to guide conversations about the causes and consequences of religious beliefs and behaviours, as well as about forces such as naturalism and secularism (not to mention nomadic war machines) that contribute to their dissolution in many contemporary social contexts. I sometimes refer to this as 'theogonic reproduction theory' because it attempts to explain how and why supernatural agents (or 'gods' in the broadest sense) are *born* in human minds and *borne* in human cultures through cognitive and coalitional biases that evolved for purposes of error management and risk management in relatively homogeneous small-scale societies in early human ancestral environments. The big question here is whether (or to what extent) these biases are now maladaptive in the pluralistic large-scale societies that populate our current socio-ecological environments.

That's a lot for one book. I'll back up, summarise, and provide previews as we go along and throw in some occasional autobiographical confessions to try and keep things interesting. In the remainder of this chapter, I introduce these themes in a bit more detail in order to set the stage for their explication and integration in the chapters that follow. The final subsection of this chapter explains why I am optimistic about a more intense dialogue between Deleuze-inspired philosophers and scholar-practitioners in the rapidly growing field of computational social simulation. It also offers a preview of the other chapters of the book, briefly outlining their relationships and roles in the overall argument. The central three sub-sections of this first chapter highlight Deleuze's emphasis on the speculative and practical objects of philosophy and begin to set out the concept of an 'atheist machine' that can be extracted from his work. I draw on several of his writings for this initial description but focus especially on *The Logic of Sense* (LOS) and his treatments of Spinoza and Nietzsche. I also spell out the rationale for utilising the machinic language of *A Thousand Plateaus* (ATP) in my attempt to clarify the role of atheism in Deleuze's philosophy. First, however, let's take a first crack at making sense of Deleuze's understanding of the relationship between philosophy and atheism.

## Achieving Atheism

The epigraph at the beginning of this chapter is from Deleuze and Guattari's final co-authored book *What is Philosophy?* (WIP). 'Atheism is not a drama but the philosopher's serenity and philosophy's achievement.' We'll return later to the sense in which atheism is the serenity of the philosopher, but our main focus here is on atheism as *the achievement of philosophy*. How are atheism and philosophy related for Deleuze? Atheism is the product of philosophy and, just as importantly, philosophy is the product of atheism. Atheism is not one possible product of philosophy, but the place (or event) where philosophy begins, the point at which it starts addressing 'problems' (in the positive sense of the 'problematic', which Deleuze develops in *The Logic of Sense* and *Difference and Repetition*). Moreover, for Deleuze, atheism is not one possible producer of philosophy, but the only machine that can produce it. These may seem like extreme claims but, as we will see, they make sense once we understand what Deleuze means by 'atheism' as well as by 'philosophy'.

This sub-section offers a first go at spelling out the sense in which Deleuze views atheism as philosophy's achievement. The context for the epigraph above is a discussion of some of the main differences between philosophy and religion. The sentence before this quote suggests that 'Perhaps Christianity does not produce concepts except through its atheism, through the atheism that it, more than any other religion, *secretes*.' The text in the epigraph is followed by the assertion that 'There is always an atheism to be *extracted* from a religion… It should be noted that religions do not arrive at the concept without denying themselves, just as philosophies do not arrive at the figure without betraying themselves' (WIP, 92, emphases added). Deleuze picks on Christianity here, for reasons we will examine in detail in Chapters 2, 7, and 8, but later in WIP he clearly distinguishes philosophy from 'religion' in general. Philosophy, science, and art are the 'daughters' of chaos, each 'bringing back' something from their struggle with chaos (variations, variables, and varieties, respectively).

These three are explicitly opposed to 'religion' because they are always and already bound up in the struggle against *opinion* – especially opinions woven into sacred canopies defended by religious hierarchies. 'Wherever there is *transcendence*, vertical Being, imperial State in the sky or on earth, there is *religion*; and there is *Philosophy* only where there is *immanence* … only friends can set out a plane of immanence as a ground from which idols have been cleared' (WIP, 43, emphases added). If religions secrete atheism, and atheism can always be extracted from religion, then we are clearly not dealing here with a simplistic or dualistic opposition (indeed, Deleuze consistently avoids such oppositions). Nevertheless, the claim in WIP that philosophy begins treating problems only after 'the atheism of the concept has been attained', and that religion is associated with opinion and transcendence, indicates that atheism – unlike religion – is inseparable from philosophy.

WIP is not unique. In his first co-authored book with Guattari, *Anti-Oedipus* (Deleuze and Guattari, 1983), Deleuze also linked atheism to the project of schizoanalysis. '[T]he unconscious of schizoanalysis is unaware of persons, aggregates, and laws, and of images, structures, and symbols. It is an orphan, just as it is an anarchist and an atheist' (AO, 342). In the critique of psychoanalysis, Deleuze identifies three errors concerning desire: lack, law, and the signifier. These are in fact the same error, an 'idealism that forms a pious conception of the unconscious'. But where did these errors come from? 'These notions cannot be prevented from dragging their *theological* cortege behind – insufficiency of being, guilt, signification ... But what water will cleanse these concepts of their background, their previous existences – *religiosity*?' (AO, 121, emphases added). The goal of schizoanalysis is 'to analyze the specific nature of the libidinal investments in the economic and political spheres, and thereby to show how, in the subject who desires, desire can be made to desire its own repression ... All this happens, not in ideology, but well beneath it...' (AO, 115). As we will see below, subjects come to desire their own *religious* repression as a result of evolved cognitive and coalitional mechanisms that surreptitiously regulate desiring-production by engendering god-conceptions in human minds and cultures. 'All this' does indeed occur 'well beneath' the surface of priestly ideology.

*Anti-Oedipus* emphasises that denying God is only a 'secondary thing' and accomplishes nothing if 'man' is straight away set in God's place. The person who realises that 'man' is no more central than 'God' does not even entertain the question of 'an alien being, a being placed above man and nature'. Such a person, Deleuze observes, no longer needs 'to go by way of this mediation – the negation of the existence of God – since he has attained those regions of an auto-production of the unconscious where the unconscious is no less atheist than orphan – immediately atheist, immediately orphan' (AO, 65–6). We will return below to the sense in which atheism is 'secondary' in our examination of Deleuze's reading of Nietzsche, but the key point at this stage is that for the schizoanalyst the unconscious is not mediated by Oedipus or Christ (or any other religious figure): it is *immediately* orphan *and* atheist. Atheism and schizoanalysis cannot be separated.

In the chapter on 'Nomadology' in *A Thousand Plateaus*, Deleuze explicitly links atheism to the creative war machine that was invented by the nomads. 'It may be observed that nomads do not provide a favorable terrain for religion; the man of war is always committing an offense against the priest or the god ... The nomads have a sense of the absolute, but a singularly *atheistic* one' (ATP, 422, emphasis added). In the plateau that deals in most detail with the 'Body without Organs', Deleuze highlights the triple curse cast on desire by 'the priest', the most recent figure of which is the psychoanalyst: 'the negative law, the extrinsic rule, and the transcendental ideal' (ATP, 171). The similarity between models of the Oedipal conflict that rely on privative, punitive, and palliative categories and traditional interpretations of the Genesis myth as a 'Fall' is hard to miss: both understand desire in terms of loss, guilt, and idealisation – as under the curse of anxiety, prohibition, and displacement from a desexualised paradise. Throughout the *Capitalism and Schizophrenia* project, which Deleuze saw as 'just plain old philosophy' (Deleuze, 2007: 176), he made it clear that schizoanalysis (pragmatics, rhizomatics, micropolitics, etc.) challenges the striations and segmentations of the socius effected by priestly figures, whether psychoanalytic or religious. Philosophy begins where religion ends – or starts secreting atheism.

This inherent link between atheism and philosophy ought to come as no surprise to those familiar with Deleuze's earlier single-authored works of philosophical portraiture, in which he consistently hammers away at religious ressentiment and traditional notions of God, and celebrates the atheistic effects of Nietzsche (Deleuze, 1983), Spinoza (Deleuze, 1992), Hume (Deleuze, 2001b), and even Kant (Deleuze, 1985). Atheism is also more or less explicit in his first two major constructive works. In *Difference and Repetition* (Deleuze, 1995a), he encourages us not to judge the atheist from the point of view of the belief that supposedly drives him, but to judge the believer 'by the violent atheist by which he is inhabited, the Antichrist eternally given "once and for all" within grace' (DR, 96). In *The Logic of Sense*, Deleuze insists that there has only ever been one ethics, the *amor fati* of the humour-actor who is 'an anti-God [*contradieu*]' – the Stoic sage who 'belongs to the Aion' and opposes the 'divine present of Chronos' (LOS, 170–1). As Deleuze put it an interview included in *Two Regimes of Madness*, '[R]eligions are worth much less than the nobility and the courage of the atheisms that they inspire' (Deleuze, 2007: 364).

We will have the opportunity to unpack Deleuze's understanding and use of atheism in more detail below, but the main point here is that he found atheism a somewhat obvious place to begin. Problems only begin afterwards. Instead of loitering around the starting line of philosophy, he encouraged us to get moving, to experiment on the plane of immanence by creating concepts. However, one of my main concerns throughout this book will be to explain why getting people to the starting line is harder than Deleuze seemed to realise. This is where research in the bio-cultural sciences of religion will play a role. Developments in these fields, as in the field of computer science, progressed rapidly in the last decade before – and even more rapidly in the decades following – Deleuze's death. Beginning in Chapter 2,

I explore ways in which empirical findings and theoretical developments in these disciplines can be productively connected to the Deleuzian atheist machine (philosophy). One of the most important effects (and uses) of an atheist machinic assemblage, I will argue, is the disassembling of the 'theist' machines that reproduce God-beliefs in the human Imaginarium and overtly (or covertly) pressure believers to keep nurturing them through regulated ritual behaviours.

Given the significant role that the critique of religion and the affirmation of atheism have played in Deleuze's work, it is perhaps surprising that these topics have received relatively little attention in the secondary literature. There are important exceptions, including the excellent expositions of aspects of Deleuze's atheism and 'anti-theology' in several chapters included in the edited volume on *Deleuze and Religion* (Bryden, 2001). However, one also finds in that volume instances of another, quite common strategy among *religious* scholars of religion (or theologians) who also fancy Deleuze, namely, downplaying or even denying his atheism while attempting to show that aspects of his philosophy can be attached to *theological* machines in order to support some religious (usually Christian) set of beliefs or ritual practices. Indeed, entire books have been devoted to this sort of apologetic use of Deleuze (e.g., Justaert, 2012; Simpson, 2012).

This brings me to my first confession, which has to do with my own achieving of atheism. For most of my educational and professional career, from 1981 to 2011, I was being trained in or teaching Christian theology. My encounter with Deleuze towards the end of this period was a decisive turning point in my becoming-atheist. However, my first publication on Deleuze (Shults, 2011) engaged in precisely the way of using his philosophy about which I was complaining in the previous paragraph. As a self-identified theologian, all those many years ago, I tried to do what (relatively liberal) Christian theologians have always done with non-Christian philosophers whom they find fascinating: borrow insights from his corpus that could be adopted and adapted to fit into – or 'reform' – the version of Christianity maintained in the social networks within which I found myself (American evangelicalism). The more I read Deleuze, however, the more I realised that the atheist force of his philosophy cannot be so easily tamed. His work resists the domestication of sacerdotal theology, breaks transcendent images that shackle thought, and escapes the priestly curse on desire. Or, at least, it motivated me to do so.

And so I wrote a book about it. This was my first single-authored book on Deleuze, published ten years ago: *Iconoclastic Theology: Gilles Deleuze and the Secretion of Atheism* (Shults, 2014b). As you might imagine, a lot happened between 2011 and 2014. When I published that book, I was already an atheist (obviously) but was also still a professor of theology (perhaps not so obviously). At that stage, I was naïve enough to think that I could get away with using 'theology' in the title, and throughout the book, by appealing to Aristotle's uses of the Greek term *theologia* as a description of 'first philosophy', or what would later be called metaphysics, and to some of Deleuze's own ambiguous uses of the term.

I realise now that calling it 'theology' (however iconoclastic it might be) was distracting; the term simply has too much baggage in our late modern context. I stand by my claims about both Deleuze and atheism in that book, but I now wish I had simply made a distinction between (sacerdotal) *theology* and (iconoclastic) *philosophy*. This is the approach I take in the current book. It is not likely that my erstwhile theological colleagues will stop borrowing from Deleuze as they try to find ways to postpone the dissolution of (their favoured denomination of) Christianity. Nor is my goal to convince them to stop. Such borrowing actually increases the secretion of atheism, so I increasingly find myself rooting for them. Nevertheless, I do think it is worthwhile explaining why this sort of attempt at the apologetic absorption of Deleuzian concepts into Christianity is self-defeating. I make this argument most explicitly in Chapters 2, 6, and 7.

As strange as it might initially sound, I am not claiming that atheism is 'better' than theism in some abstract, transcendent, or even moral sense. Like all machines, theist and atheist machines produce, register, and consume in relation to other machines on the plane of immanence (or within and across the strata). Insofar as they are related to the despotic and nomadic social-machines (respectively), theism and atheism are always interacting, and their 'use' in any context may be more or less (and always both) arboreal and rhizomatic, molar and molecular, striated and smooth, etc. I spell this out in more detail in Chapter 2. I do argue that in the contexts in which most of my readers live, the atheist machine has more creative, liberating power than the theist machine, but there is no 'moral' judgement here. I explain what I mean by this when discussing Deleuze's ethics in later chapters.

One more qualification for now. I am not claiming that readers 'ought' to be doing philosophy (some will prefer art or science or something else, perhaps sorcery), nor that those who pursue philosophy 'ought' to be Deleuzian. I am claiming that conceiving of atheism as philosophy's achievement (and using the atheist machine to produce philosophy) is one way to liberate feeling, thinking, and acting from the repressive anxiety and oppressive constraints of theism. Believe it or not, computer simulation can also help. But we'll get back to that. Our next step is to further clarify Deleuze's understanding of philosophy in general and of machinic assemblages in particular.

## The Speculative and Practical Purposes of Philosophy

In these next three sub-sections I will outline Deleuze's view, adopted and adapted from a line of philosophers he traces from the ancient Greeks through Spinoza and Nietzsche, of the speculative and practical purposes (or objects, tasks, moments) of philosophy. In an appendix to *The Logic of Sense* that deals with the simulacrum and ancient philosophy, Deleuze spells out the impact of Lucretius' (and Epicurus') understanding of philosophy as Naturalism.

> The *speculative* purpose and the *practical* purpose of philosophy as Naturalism, science and pleasure, coincide on this point: it is always a matter of *denouncing* the illusion, the false infinite, the *infinity of religion* and all of the theologico-erotic-oneiric myths in which it is expressed. To the question 'what is the use of philosophy?' the answer must be: what other subject would have an interest in *erecting* the image of a *free person*, and in denouncing all of the forces which need myth and troubled spirit in order to establish their power? (LOS, 314, emphases added, translation emended)

For Lucretius (and Deleuze), Naturalism is the philosophy of affirmation, of joy in the truly infinite diverse production of Nature, rather than a philosophy of anxiety tied to the false infinite of myth, 'the myth of a false philosophy totally impregnated by theology' (LOS, 315).

For our current purpose, which is to highlight the 'speculative' and 'practical' aspects of Deleuze's philosophy, it is not necessary to go into the details of the Lucretian understanding of the true infinite in physics (which has to do with his atomism and the idea of the clinamen) or of happiness (which has to do with affirming the multiple as multiple and taking joy in the diverse as diverse in Nature). These themes have been helpfully exposited elsewhere (e.g., Bennett, 2019). In this context, the important point is the way in which the tasks of philosophy are framed by Deleuze as denouncing the 'infinity of religion' and holding forth the image of a 'free person'. 'To distinguish in men what amounts to myth and what amounts to Nature, and in Nature itself, to distinguish what is truly infinite from what is not – such is the practical and speculative object of Naturalism' (LOS, 315).

These tasks of philosophy are linked because determining the distinction between the true infinite and the false infinite is 'the necessary means of ethics and practice'. The 'religious man' is characterised by avidity and anguish, covetousness and culpability, a 'strange complex that generates crimes'. This complex itself is generated by the simulacra, which themselves move below the minimum of sensible time, but produce theological, erotic, and oneiric phantasms. When taken seriously, these lead to two illusions (images): of an infinite capacity for bodily pleasure and an infinite duration of the soul, which in turn lead to the idea of an infinite suffering after death. 'And the two illusions are linked: the idea of infinite punishment is the natural price to be paid for having unlimited desires' (LOS, 309).

In the same appendix Deleuze explores Nietzsche's description of the task of philosophy as 'the reversal of Platonism'. Earlier in *The Logic of Sense*, Deleuze had identified the Stoics as the first to reverse Platonism, to 'bring about a radical inversion' (LOS, 9) of the dualism between the intelligible and the sensible. We will return to the Stoics later, but at this stage I want to emphasise Deleuze's interpretation of Nietzsche's call to reverse Platonism as a call to track down the motivation for formulating the theory of Ideas in the first place. Using examples from several of Plato's Dialogues, Deleuze argues that the former's real motivation had to do 'with selecting among the pretenders, distinguishing good and bad copies or, rather, copies (always well-founded) and simulacra (always engulfed in dissimilarity)'. Knowledge requires 'assuring the triumph of the copies over simulacra, of repressing simulacra, keeping them completely submerged, preventing them from climbing to the surface and "insinuating themselves" everywhere' (LOS, 294).

Why is this important? Because through his attempt to ensure the triumph of icons over simulacra, Plato set up the domain of 'representation', which privileged the Same (model) and the Similar (copy) and repressed the unlimited becoming of the simulacra, as the domain within which most philosophers would work for the next two millennia. Aristotle takes a second step by deploying representation as limited and finite, covering the whole domain from the highest genera to the lowest species, as the foundation for knowledge. However, Deleuze then points to a third moment, 'under the influence of Christianity', in which philosophers moved beyond the attempt to establish a foundation for representation that made it possible (Plato) and to specify its determinations (Aristotle). In the wake of Christianity, philosophers tried 'to *render it infinite*, to endow it with a valid claim to the unlimited, to make it conquer the infinitely great as well as the infinitely small, opening it up to Being beyond the highest genera and to the singular beneath the smallest species'. Through this sort of conquest of the infinite, whether focused on the infinitely small or the infinitely large (Leibniz and Hegel are Deleuze's key examples of these, respectively), philosophy remains trapped within the domain of representation, as it pursues 'the same task, Iconology, and adapts it to the speculative needs of Christianity. Always the selection among pretenders, the exclusion of the eccentric and the divergent, in the name of a superior finality, an essential reality, or even a meaning of history' (LOS, 297).

We will go into a detailed discussion of the task of philosophy as the 'reversal of Platonism', and its relation to the rise of computer simulation, in Chapter 3 below. The main point at this early stage is that philosophy (so conceived) is atheistic in the sense that it denounces the infinity of religion in general and the iconological 'representation' of the Infinite in Christianity in particular. This does not mean philosophy's tasks are only negative and destructive; in the next section, we will see that philosophy for Deleuze is inherently positive and creative (even in its destructiveness). However, it does mean that philosophy only gets to its creative work after (or as) atheism is achieved. As Deleuze put it when describing the 'quietly godless philosopher' François Chatelet, the latter's was 'a tranquil atheism, that is, a philosophy in which God is not a problem – the nonexistence and even the death of God are not problems, but rather conditions that should be treated as givens so that the real problems can then emerge: this is the only humility' (Deleuze, 2005a: 716).

The Stoics and Epicureans may have had a privileged place in *The Logic of Sense* but, as noted briefly above, Deleuze found atheist machines at work in the writings of all of the authors he engaged in his early books on the history of philosophy. Spinoza and Nietzsche, however, seem to play a special role. As Deleuze notes in an interview reported in *Negotiations* 'I did begin with books on the history of philosophy, but all the authors I dealt with had for me something in common. And it all tended toward the great Spinoza–Nietzsche equation' (Deleuze, 1995b: 135).

Spinoza's importance for Deleuze is well known, and the former is the only philosopher on which the latter wrote two books. The first and larger book exposited Spinoza's *Expressionism* (Deleuze, 1992) in dialogue with the medieval theological and philosophical sources against which his 'atheism' was a revolt. The second, smaller volume – *Spinoza: Practical Philosophy* (Deleuze, 2001a) – even more explicitly emphasises the link between the speculative and the practical in philosophy. On the one hand, the 'sad passions' of religion, which are based on illusions such as divine punishment, have led to a confusion between two orders (the truths of Nature and the moral laws of institutions) that Spinoza works to distinguish. For Spinoza, the 'tragedy of theology and its harmfulness', explains Deleuze, are not only 'speculative' but also 'practical', leading to the resentment against life that is characteristic of the slave, the tyrant, and the priest (2001a: 24). Instead, Spinoza pursues philosophy, especially in the *Ethics*, as a 'voyage in immanence' that is simultaneously the 'conquest of the unconscious', a philosophy in which '[e]thical *joy* is the correlate of speculative affirmation' (2001a: 29).

For Deleuze, however, even Spinoza did not go far enough in his atheism. Spinoza leaves substance independent of the modes, with the latter dependent on the former. There are still traces of transcendence in this philosophy. To achieve univocity of being (pure immanence), 'Substance must itself be said *of* the modes and only *of* the modes.' This requires 'a more general categorical reversal according to which being is said of becoming, identity of that which is different, the one of the multiple, etc.' (DR, 40). This, Deleuze argues, is exactly what Nietzsche meant by the eternal return (of the different). Whether Nietzsche really meant this is beside the point. The point is that Deleuze extracts from Nietzsche's writings what I am calling an 'atheist machine' that denounces all appeals to transcendence and joyfully embraces the repetition of difference.

As with Lucretius, Deleuze finds a *speculative* and a *practical* aspect of Nietzsche's philosophy, which are mutually reinforcing. These are summarised in *Nietzsche and Philosophy*:

> Nietzsche's speculative teaching is as follows: becoming, multiplicity and chance do not contain any negation; difference is pure affirmation; return is the being of difference excluding the whole of the negative … Nietzsche's practical teaching is that difference is happy; that multiplicity, becoming and chance are adequate objects of joy by themselves and that only joy returns. Multiplicity, becoming and chance are the properly philosophical joy in which unity rejoices in itself and also in being and necessity. (NP, 190)

Here we can begin to see the sense in which, for Deleuze, atheism is 'the serenity of the philosopher' as well as 'philosophy's achievement'. Nietzsche's atheism is obviously destructive (doing philosophy with a hammer), but it is also affirmative. To affirm, for Nietzsche, is '*to release, to set free what lives*' (NP, 185). Nietzsche's philosophy is 'anti-religious' but only as a 'logic of pure affirmation and a corresponding ethic of joy' (NP, 17).

Two other aspects of Nietzsche's atheist philosophy, as reconstructed by Deleuze, are important to introduce at this stage. First, the 'death of God' is of no consequence if humans killed God only 'to take his still warm seat' (NP, 151). One does not achieve the freedom of pure immanence by replacing the God-Man with the reactive Man-God of bad conscience and *ressentiment*. The atheist machine disassembles Oedipal Man as well as Oedipalising God. Second, Christianity plays a special role for both Nietzsche and Deleuze in the production of atheism as the achievement of philosophy. The reactive life of Christianity, with its pitiful slave morality, is rooted in the idea that 'we put God to death. In this way it *secretes its own atheism*, an atheism of bad conscience and *ressentiment*' (NP, 154, first emphasis added). As we will see in the chapters that follow, these two Nietzschean proclamations echo throughout Deleuze's own atheist philosophical achievements.

If, as Deleuze argued in *The Logic of Sense*, philosophy is 'always a matter' of denouncing the infinity of religion and of joyfully affirming freedom, then we need to be clear on exactly what we mean by religion as well as by freedom. I'll return to the latter below, but it is important at this stage to provide an initial clarification of the senses in which I will be using the terms 'religion' and 'theism'. Although Deleuze engages a wide variety of sciences in his philosophical experimentation, he was writing before the emergence or at least before the explosion of empirical research into the cognitive and evolutionary sciences of religion. As noted above, my book *Iconoclastic Theology* exposited and expanded Deleuzian atheism by bringing it into dialogue with recent developments in this literature. Scholars in these fields operationalise 'religion' in ways with which Deleuze was not (and could not have been) familiar. Although Deleuze heavily engages with medieval theology throughout his work, he rarely concerns himself with definitions of 'theism'. However, for the most part, when Deleuze writes about *religion* he seems to mean roughly what contemporary philosophers of religion usually mean by *theism*.

Because I am interested here in bringing Deleuze into dialogue with the philosophy of religion as well as the cognitive and computational sciences of religion, in the current context I will use the terms religion and theism differently than I have in other contexts. I will continue to operationalise *religion* as 'shared imaginative engagement with axiologically relevant supernatural agents' (e.g., Shults, 2014c; 2018b), a definition that will be parsed in detail in Chapter 2. However, I will reserve the term *theism* – or 'the *theistic* machine' – for expressions of religion of the sort that Deleuze links to the despotic social machine (especially monotheisms such as Christianity). Theistic machines are social assemblages whose cohesion relies primarily on sacerdotally mediated imaginative engagement with axiologically relevant supernatural agents *and* an Infinite Supernatural Agent whose representation is authorised and policed by priests and theological elites. This is what Deleuze has in mind when he identifies 'the infinity of religion' as the target of the speculative and practical tasks of philosophy, and identifies 'atheism' as the achievement of philosophy.

### Given Philosophy, What Machine Can Produce It?

Spoiler alert. The answer is the atheist machine. It is the atheist machine that produces philosophy. The atheist machine denounces the infinity of religion and joyfully erects an image of the free affirmation of multiplicity. But we need to back up. In what sense is atheism a 'machine'? And how does it 'produce' philosophy? All of this will be explicated in later chapters; the goal here is simply to provide an introduction to the relevant Deleuzian terminology that is necessary for understanding the concept of an atheist machine. The first step is to outline the concepts of desiring-machines and social machines, as well as machinic assemblages and abstract machines, which Deleuze created in his work with Guattari in the *Capitalism and Schizophrenia* project. The first chapter of *Anti-Oedipus* – 'The Desiring-Machines' – famously begins:

> It is at work everywhere, functioning smoothly at times, at other times in fits and starts. It breathes, it heats, it eats. It shits and fucks. What a mistake to have ever said *the* id. Everywhere *it* is machines – real ones, not figurative ones: machines driving other machines, machines being driven by other machines, with all the necessary couplings and connections. (AO, 1)

Everything is a machine. Desiring-machines everywhere. '*There is only desire and the social, and nothing else*' (AO, 31). Desiring-machines are not Imaginary, as some psychoanalysts would have it, but Real: 'There is only desire and environments, fields, forms of herd instinct' (AO, 316). It is important to emphasise at the outset that this is not 'mechanism' in the sense typically opposed to 'vitalism'. The latter is precisely the sort of dualism that *Anti-Oedipus* (e.g., AO, 312), and later *A Thousand Plateaus* (e.g., ATP, 22) struggle to overcome or dissolve.

The basic metaphysical claim of these volumes is that all that exists (all becoming) is machinic: desiring-machines consuming, producing, and registering on the plane of immanence, and the social machines that 'fall back upon' them. The third major section of *Anti-Oedipus* introduces and outlines three 'social machines', which the authors provocatively call the 'primitive territorial machine', the 'barbarian despotic machine', and the 'civilized capitalist machine'. They also hint at a 'revolutionary' machine (e.g., AO, 323), a concept they spell out later in *A Thousand Plateaus* as the 'nomadic war machine'. We will return to these social machines in Chapter 2 and explore their relationships with what I am calling the 'atheist machine'. Here the key point to remember is that the distinction between desiring-machines and social machines is not a dualism: 'There are no desiring-machines that exist outside the social machines that they form on a large scale; and no social machines without the desiring-machines that inhabit them on a small scale' (AO, 373).

Instead of asking psychoanalytic questions about the Oedipal triangle (daddy–mummy–me), schizoanalysis poses the 'more important' questions: '*Given a certain effect, what machine is capable of producing it? And given a certain machine, what can it be used for?*' (AO, 3, emphasis added). In this section, we are setting up the context for answering the first question (in relation to the effect called 'philosophy') and in the next section we will begin spelling out the answer to the second question (in relation to a certain machine called 'atheism'). In both cases, I rely more heavily on the language of machinic assemblages and abstract machines developed in *A Thousand Plateaus*. In their discussion of those concepts in the latter, Deleuze and Guattari pose a pair of questions very similar to those just cited above from *Anti-Oedipus*.

> In every respect, machinic assemblages effectuate the abstract machine insofar as it is developed on the plane of consistency or enveloped in a stratum. The most important problem of all: *given a certain machinic assemblage, what is the relation of effectuation with the abstract machine? How does it effectuate it, with what adequation?* Classify assemblages. What we call the mechanosphere is the set of all abstract machines and machinic assemblages outside the strata, on the strata, or between strata. (ATP, 79–80, emphasis added)

Mechanosphere. This is Deleuze and Guattari's last word in *A Thousand Plateaus*. Literally. The book ends by emphasising that 'Every abstract machine is linked to other abstract machines, not only because they are inseparably political, economic, scientific, artistic, ecological, cosmic – perceptive, affective, active, thinking, physical, and semiotic – but because their various types are as intertwined as their operations are convergent. Mechanosphere' (ATP, 566).

Deleuze and Guattari adopt (and adapt) Gregory Bateson's use of the term 'plateau', which they describe in the Introduction as 'a continuous, self-vibrating region of intensities whose development avoids any orientation toward a culmination point or external end ... any multiplicity connected to other multiplicities by superficial underground stems in such a way as to form or extend a rhizome' (ATP, 24). By the end of the book, they have explicitly linked 'plateau' to the concept of 'abstract machine'. In relation to the plane of consistency, '*each abstract machine can be considered a "plateau" of variation* that places variables of content and expression in continuity' (ATP, 563, emphasis added). Given their centrality within – or rhizomatic extension across – *A Thousand Plateaus* it is not surprising that the secondary literature contains several robust scholarly analyses of these concepts (abstract machines, machinic assemblages, etc.) and the relation between them (e.g., Adkins, 2015; Nail, 2017; Somers-Hall et al., 2018; Buchanan, 2020). One of my goals in the current book is to clarify the 'simulating' function of concepts such as machinic assemblage and abstract machine in *A Thousand Plateaus*, and the role these can play in the construction of a metaphysics of pure immanence (and so in the reversal of Platonism).

When asked in a 1980 interview about what (if anything) functioned as the unity of the recently published *A Thousand Plateaus*, Deleuze responded, 'I think it is the idea of an assemblage' (Deleuze, 2007: 177). He went on to explain that this new concept was meant to replace the idea of 'desiring-machines' in *Anti-Oedipus*, which he and Guattari had co-authored a few years earlier. As Daniel Smith has pointed out, the concept of 'assemblage' also seems to have taken over the role that the concept of 'simulacrum' had played in some of Deleuze's earlier single-author works (Smith, 2012: 26), especially *Difference and Repetition* and *The Logic of Sense*. In the latter, Deleuze argued for a 'reversal of Platonism' that involves an affirmation of the productive power of the simulacra to deny or overthrow both '*the original and the copy, the model and the reproduction*', thereby leaving the same and the similar with no essence 'except as *simulated*, that is as expressing the function of the simulacrum' (LOS, 271).

In practice, if not in name, Deleuze is clearly pursuing the 'reversal of Platonism' in *A Thousand Plateaus* as well. For example, in discussing the 'war machine' he argues that thought can be extricated from the State model (or image of thought) by the form of exteriority of thought, which is 'not at all *another image* in opposition to the image inspired by the State apparatus. It is, rather, a force that destroys both the image *and* its copies, the model *and* its reproductions...' (ATP, 416). In his critical introduction and guide to *A Thousand Plateaus*, Brent Adkins explicitly links Deleuze and Guattari's creation of a theory of assemblages to Deleuze's earlier call for the reversal of Platonism. The philosophy of the book, he argues, 'is predicated on the continuity of the sensible and the intelligible', in contrast to the discontinuity proposed by Plato and his followers (Adkins, 2015: 11–12). This is also crucial for understanding the concept of abstract machines since, as Adkins points out, the adjective 'abstract' must be taken in the sense of 'continuous' – that is, the opposite of 'discrete' rather than the opposite of 'concrete' (Adkins, 2015: 61–2). For Deleuze there are no discrete transcendent models or Ideas in relation to which copies must be compared and beings must be judged; there is only univocal being articulated in complex and continuous relations among assemblages, abstract machines, the strata, and the mutually immanent planes of consistency and organisation.

Much like the 'paradoxical element' or 'aleatory point' in *The Logic of Sense*, the abstract machine in *A Thousand Plateaus* 'exists *simultaneously* developed on the destratified plane it draws and enveloped in each stratum whose unity of composition it defines' (ATP, 78). The metaphysical dualism between the intelligible and the sensible is overcome by the concept of abstract machines, which exist both on the plane of consistency and in the strata, diagrammatically 'drawing' the former and compositionally 'defining' the latter. Deleuze emphasises that the plane of consistency (or immanence) 'does *not preexist* the movements of deterritorialization that unravel it, the lines of flight that draw it and *cause it to rise to the surface*, the becomings that compose it' (ATP, 297, emphasis added). This 'rising to the surface' reminds us of his discussion of the simulacra in *The Logic of Sense*. Everything happens on the surface in *A Thousand Plateaus*, but here the surface is constituted as a double articulation coordinated by the abstract machine, which 'constructs continuums of intensity, emits and combines particle-signs and performs conjunctions of flows of deterritorialization' (ATP, 78).

But how is all of this related to the 'most important' problem noted above: what is the relation of effectuation between an assemblage and an abstract machine? In *A Thousand Plateaus*, the concept of assemblage is defined as a 'two-sided' entity. One side of the assemblage 'has to do with enunciation or formalizes expression', while on its other side, 'inseparable from the first, it formalizes contents, it is a machinic assemblage or an assemblage of bodies' (ATP, 155). All assemblages are both 'machinic assemblages' in which bodies are intermingling and reacting to one another and 'collective assemblages of enunciation' through which incorporeal transformations (e.g., propositions about states of affairs) can be attributed to bodies (ATP, 97–8). Because the two sides of an assemblage are 'in reciprocal presupposition', Deleuze argues that there must be 'something in the assemblage itself that is still more profound than these sides and can account for both ... This is what we call the *abstract machine*, which constitutes and conjugates all of the assemblage's cutting edges of deterritorialization' (ATP, 155). So, in a sense, the assemblage is doubly two-sided. The machinic/enunciative distinction can be conceived on a 'horizontal axis', but on a 'vertical axis' the assemblage 'has both *territorial sides*, or reterritorialized sides, which stabilize it, and *cutting edges of deterritorialization*, which carry it away ... The tetravalence of the assemblage' (ATP, 97–8).

All of these concepts are relevant for understanding the atheist machine. On the one hand, we can speak of the *abstract machine of atheism*, whose construction of continuums of intensity and emissions of singularities performs conjunctions of flows that deterritorialise theism (in the sense defined above) and (re)territorialise philosophy, science, and art, as well as naturalism and secularism (in a sense defined below). On the other hand, we can also speak of *atheist assemblages*, which are simultaneously machinic assemblages of intermingled and interacting bodies and collective assemblages of enunciation transforming propositions attributed to bodies. Atheist assemblages are *effectuations* of the abstract machine of atheism. The adequation of their effectuation, their classification as atheist assemblages, depends on the extent to which they produce the relevant interminglings of bodies and incorporeal transformations. As we will see in Chapter 3, this can all be articulated using Deleuze's distinction between the virtual and the actual as well. The main point at this stage is that my use of the phrase 'atheist machine' in what follows is an attempt to 'classify assemblages', namely, atheist assemblages that effectuate the abstract machine of atheism, and to articulate the criteria by which to evaluate their adequation.

## Given an Atheist Machine, What Can it be Used For?

I'll return to all these concepts below, but for now let's take another step back. What is it that the atheist machine allegedly produces? Philosophy (among other things). And what is philosophy? In his book with Guattari with that question as its title, Deleuze writes that:

> Philosophy presents three elements, each of which fits with the other two but must be considered for itself: *the prephilosophical plane it must lay out (immanence), the persona or personae it must invent and bring to life (insistence), and the philosophical concepts it must create (consistency)*. Laying out, inventing, and creating constitute the philosophical trinity – diagrammatic, personalistic, and intensive features. (WIP, 76–7)

I will argue that these elements or features of philosophy are produced (and can only be produced) by the atheist machine, that is, by atheist assemblages whose edges of deterritorialisation are conjugated by the abstract machine of atheism (a plateau of variation placing variables of godless content and godless expression in continuity) as they liberate atheist bodies and achieve the atheism of the concept.

In this penultimate section of this introductory chapter, I want to make three points about the uses of the atheist machine that will be important to remember as we go along. First, the atheist machine can be used for more than the production of philosophy. As noted above, Deleuze makes a clear distinction between *religions*, on the one hand, which invoke gods to 'paint a firmament' with figures of an *Urdoxa* to protect us from chaos, making opinions (*doxa*) 'like a sort of umbrella', and *philosophy, science, and art*, which 'cast planes' over the chaos, on the other. These latter three disciplines 'tear open the firmament and plunge into the chaos' (WIP, 202). What do they bring back from this plunging? The philosopher brings back *variations*, which are 'still infinite but that have become inseparable on the absolute surfaces or in the absolute volumes that lay out a secant plane of immanence'. The scientist, on the other hand, brings back *variables* 'that have become independent by slowing down, that is to say, by the elimination of whatever other variabilities are liable to interfere'. Finally, the artist brings back *varieties* 'that no longer constitute a reproduction of the sensory in the organ but set up a being of the sensory, a being of sensation, on an inorganic plane of composition' (WIP, 202).

Unlike philosophy, religions cannot arrive at the concept without 'betraying themselves', because their very relation to the plane of immanence is to ward off 'philosophy in advance from the point of view of its very possibility' (WIP, 93). Unlike science, which is 'opposed to all religion' and casts planes of reference, religions (or to be more precise, Deleuze should have said theistic religions) attempt an 'infinite religious utilization of the figure' (WIP, 125). Unlike art, which is in 'opposition to the suprasensory transcendence of religion' (WIP, 193) and casts planes of composition, (theistic) religion fabulates an infinite Figure painted on a firmament pretending to represent a plane of transcendence. My point at this early stage is that the atheist machine – atheist assemblages that pull down or break through painted firmaments of a religious Figure – plays a role in the production of science and art as well as philosophy. I'll return to science, especially computer science, in several of the chapters that follow, and more briefly to art in Chapters 7 and 8. Throughout the book we will also observe how atheism is related to what I'm calling the naturalist and secularist machines (introduced below), which of course have many uses beyond the production of philosophy.

The second introductory point I'd like to make is that the atheist machine has creative as well as destructive uses or, better, its destructive use is simultaneously a creative use and vice versa. So far I have been mostly focused on the destructive aspect of its use, its iconoclastic clearing the ground of the idols of religious transcendence. As Deleuze put it: 'Wherever there is transcendence, vertical Being, imperial State in the sky or on earth, there is *religion*; and there is Philosophy only where there is immanence ... only friends can set out a plane of immanence as *a ground from which idols have been cleared*' (WIP, 43, emphases added). However, this negative clearing of the ground is simultaneously a positive setting out of a plane of immanence. As we noted above, for Deleuze, philosophy both denounces the infinity of religion and erects the image of the joyfully free person. Philosophy tears down the myths of Being, the One, and a 'false philosophy totally impregnated by theology'. It attacks the negative, which linked the intelligible to the One, and establishes the 'multiple as multiple' as the object of affirmation and the 'diverse as diverse' as the object of joy (LOS, 315).

Sometimes destruction simply conserves and perpetuates the 'established order of representation, models, and copies', but there is another productive mode of destruction in which the models and copies are destroyed 'in order to institute the chaos which creates, making the simulacra function and raising a phantasm – the most innocent of all destructions, the destruction of Platonism' (LOS, 303). We find a similar emphasis in the depiction of schizoanalysis in *Anti-Oedipus*. 'Destroy, destroy. The task of schizoanalysis goes by way of destruction – a whole scouring of the unconscious, a complete curettage. Destroy Oedipus, the illusion of the ego, the puppet of the superego, guilt, the law, castration' (AO, 342). However, schizoanalysis simultaneously performs its positive tasks of ensuring 'the machinic conversion of primal repression ... into a condition of real functioning ... causing the desiring machines to start up again' (AO, 373), and attaining 'a nonfigurative and nonsymbolic unconscious … flows-schizzes or real-desire, apprehended below the minimum conditions of identity' (AO, 385). The creative–affirmative function of philosophy (schizoanalysis, micropolitics, rhizomatics, etc.) is always on the other side of the iconoclastic–destructive function of philosophy – and vice versa.

All of this is based on an affirmative understanding of 'atheism' which, despite its negative etymology (a-theism), is in fact a positive concept (somewhat like non-violent, unbiased, or fearless). Atheism and atheists have had a bad rap for a long time, partly due to the evolved fear-based and violence-amplifying religious biases that we will explore beginning in the next chapter. This is not to deny that some militant atheists are fearful, biased, and violent. No doubt this is the case. However, empirical research has increasingly shown that non-religious people tend to be more altruistic and open and non-religious populations tend to be safer and freer than their religious counterparts (for a summary of some of this research, see Zuckerman, 2010; Shults, Gore et al., 2018a; Shults, 2018b). And as the anti-atheist bias fades, historical research is uncovering the positive origins and contributions of atheism in the unfolding of modern science, art, psychology, politics and other fields (Hecht, 2004; Stephens, 2014; Watson, 2014; Devellennes, 2021). Moreover, as we will see in Chapter 7, most contemporary philosophers now embrace some form of atheism. Indeed, the bias against atheism is diminishing worldwide as societies secularise and as science provides ever more naturalist explanations of the world.

And this brings us to my third introductory point about the uses of the atheist machine. Throughout this book I will spell out the creative power of atheist assemblages in relation to naturalism and secularism, linking them all together within the context of the conceptual framework (based on findings within the bio-cultural sciences of religion) that I mentioned above and will outline in detail in the chapters that follow. So, here at the beginning, I want to take a first crack at explaining what I mean by these terms and their methodological and metaphysical manifestations.

There are many varieties of *naturalism*, but most share a resistance to appeals to supernatural agency in theoretical explanations of the natural world, especially in the academic sphere. Individual scholars might continue to harbour religious beliefs in their personal lives, but most are (at least) methodologically naturalistic in the sense that they exclude god-concepts from their scientific hypotheses. There are also many varieties of *secularism*, but most share a resistance to appeals to supernatural authority in practical inscriptions of social worlds, especially in the public sphere. Individual civil leaders in complex, democratic contexts might maintain membership in religious in-groups, but a growing number are (at least) methodologically secularist in the sense that they exclude divine sanctions as grounds for their political proposals.

However, naturalism and secularism are often embraced primarily as pragmatic strategies, not as claims about reality. As *religious* philosophers like to point out, accepting the importance or even the necessity of *methodological* naturalism in science does not require philosophers (or scientists) to affirm *metaphysical* naturalism (or atheism). It is true that the latter is not logically entailed by the former, but after centuries of watching trans-communally verifiable naturalistic explanations consistently outperform idiosyncratic and parochial supernaturalistic interpretations of the causes of events, it is not surprising that one finds the burden of proof increasingly being shifted on to theologians and religious philosophers. Every successful scientific endeavour contributes to the growing implausibility of 'religion' (in the sense defined above) in the spheres of public and academic discourse. As we will see below, developments in computer modelling and social simulation have a unique contribution to make here.

What about secularism? Today most people in pluralistic, Western, democratic societies – including (non-fundamentalist) theistic philosophers of religion – are *methodological* secularists. That is, even if they are religiously affiliated, they typically accept that the organisation and regulation of the social field (at least in the legal and public spheres) should not be authorised solely or even primarily by appeals to norms that are allegedly revealed by the supernatural agents ritually engaged by a particular religious in-group. Increasingly, however, people (and especially young people) in these contexts are adopting *metaphysical secularism*: explicitly eliminating supernatural authorities from their list of ontological inventory items, and so from the list of resources available for constructing and maintaining social norms. In other words, more and more people are secular in their meta-ethics: the way in which they think about the conditions for acting sensibly in society and the feasibility of pragmatic strategies for coordinating social forces involves no reference to transcendent supernatural authorities.

What does this have to do with Deleuze? We already noted above his enthusiasm for the Naturalism of Lucretius (and Spinoza, Nietzsche, etc.). His philosophy is clearly metaphysically naturalist in the sense outlined above. Is he also enthusiastic about secularism? No doubt there are uses of this latter term against which Deleuze would revolt, as readers of the *Capitalism and Schizophrenia* project and his other contributions to political philosophy are well aware. However, in the sense in which I am using the terms, it is equally clear that Deleuze is a metaphysical as well as a methodological secularist. Deleuze attempts to cast a plane of immanence on (or in) which the problem is not about belief (or non-belief) in the existence of God, but about the one who *believes in the world*, and not even in the existence of the world but in its possibilities of movements and intensities, so as once again to give birth to new modes of existence, closer to animals and rocks. It may be that *believing in this world*, in this life, becomes our most difficult task, or the task of a mode of existence still to be discovered on our plane of immanence today. (WIP, 74–5, emphases added)

In the sense of affirming the worldly (*saecularis*), rather than the godly (*caelestis*), as providing immanent criteria for micropolitics, for making oneself a Body without Organs, and for the creative use of the nomadic war machine, Deleuze's philosophy is wholeheartedly secular or perhaps, as Marie Chabbert puts it, a 'becoming-secular' (2018).

What can the atheist machine be used for? I've begun to outline some of its many uses, and we'll spell these out in the chapters that follow with reference to a variety of Deleuzian concepts. However, given that many readers will be more familiar with Deleuze than they are with computer modelling, I first want to make an initial case for the value of the latter in philosophy in general in order to ease the doubts some might have about my chances of succeeding in the second main goal of this book.

### Philosophy and Computational Simulation Machines

As noted above, this goal is to bring Deleuze's atheist philosophy into explicit dialogue with recent advances in computational modelling and simulation (CMS), showing how the latter provides empirical tools for bolstering the plausibility of the former and how the former provides conceptual tools for making sense of the latter. Here I am writing mostly for philosophers, and readers do not need to be computer scientists or familiar with social simulation in order to follow the arguments. This book is about philosophy as an atheist machine. Nevertheless, CMS plays a crucial role in the argument and so a brief introduction will help to pave the way for the discussions in the following chapters.

Like most normal people, computer scientists have typically had little interest in the apparently arcane arguments of philosophers about the nature of being(s) and non-being or the metaphysical conditions for any and all human experience whatsoever. Such debates have seemed wholly irrelevant to their work. Like most scholars in the humanities, philosophers have typically had little interest in the apparently arcane algorithms used by computer scientists to model and simulate the behaviour of complex adaptive systems. Such tools have seemed wholly irrelevant to their work. In recent years, however, all of this has begun to change. On the one hand, a growing number of scientists in the CMS community are exploring ways in which developments in their field bear on philosophical issues related to ethics, epistemology, and ontology (e.g., Tolk, 2013; Elsenbroich and Gilbert, 2014; Gräbner, 2018; Kirchner et al., 2019; Weisberg, 2012; Wolfram, 2002; Winsberg, 2010). On the other hand, a growing number of philosophers are recognising the value of computational models and social simulation for guiding reflection on and providing insight into some of these classical philosophical issues (e.g., Mascaro, 2010; Grim et al., 2016; Shults and Wildman, 2019; Grim, 2002; 2019a; Shults and Wildman, 2020b; Develaki, 2019; Bankes et al., 2002).

Before going further, let's acknowledge that this scientific field is not the most obvious candidate for dialogue with Deleuzian philosophy. The way in which Deleuze's philosophical creation of concepts was deeply informed by his engagement with a wide variety of sciences is well known (De Beistegui, 2004; Jensen and Rödje, 2010; Protevi, 2013). However, in the early pages of *A Thousand Plateaus*, Deleuze singles out the discipline of 'computer science' for critique, noting that it clings 'to the oldest modes of thought', relying on hierarchical 'command trees', which are all too arborescent and grant 'all power to a memory or central organ'. This makes it difficult, Deleuze argues, to reach multiplicities or make rhizomes (ATP, 18). On the next page, however, he points hopefully to the work of some authors in this field who (in the mid-1970s) were emphasising the importance of

> acentered systems, finite networks of automata in which communication runs from any neighbor to any other ... such that the local operations are coordinated and the final, global result synchronized without a central agency ... [T]his kind of machinic multiplicity, assemblage, or society rejects any centralizing or unifying automaton as an 'asocial intrusion'. (ATP, 19)

A lot has happened in computer science since *A Thousand Plateaus* was published in 1980. As Manuel DeLanda notes, most old programming languages did indeed control computational processes in a rigid, 'hierarchical' way, always eventually deferring to a 'master program'. However, in 'object-oriented' programming languages, far more popular today especially in the computational social sciences, 'control is always decentralized as software objects encapsulating a set of operators are called into action by patterns in the very data they operate on' (DeLanda, 2011: 202). As we will see, this means that computational modelling in general, and simulations of psychological and social phenomena in particular, are susceptible to being understood in terms of assemblages of assemblages. This opens up new possibilities for experimental philosophy within the Mechanosphere.

The illuminative and explanatory power of CMS techniques have had such a profound effect on a wide variety of scientific disciplines (Humphreys, 2006) that they have been called the 'third pillar' of science, alongside theory and experimentation (Benioff and Lazowska, 2005; Yilmaz, 2015). Such analytical and predictive approaches have been a methodological staple for decades in the natural sciences, and have been adopted by businesses, military agencies, disease control organisations, and similar institutions to simulate the probable impact of different policies on alternative future scenarios (Ahrweiler et al., 2016; Badham et al., 2021; Currie et al., 2020; Desai, 2012; Diallo et al., 2021; Gilbert et al., 2018; Law and Kelton, 1991; Tolk, 2012).

However, computational tools have also become increasingly popular in the social sciences in the last couple of decades. Social simulation has matured significantly as a sub-field (Hauke, Lorscheid, and Meyer, 2017). CMS methods have also been making inroads in the humanities, generating new insights in history, literature, philosophy, and other fields (DeLanda, 2011; Elsenbroich and Gilbert, 2014; Youngman and Hadzikadic, 2014; Shults, 2019a). As I will illustrate in some detail below, the use of these tools among researchers interested in (non-)religion has also been growing quite rapidly in the last decade. The success of this approach has contributed to the emergence of what some scholars call 'computational social science' (Epstein, 2006; Alvarez, 2016; Squazzoni, 2012). We'll return to this 'rise of simulation' in Chapter 3, and provide several examples of the explanatory power and philosophical relevance of simulation (focusing on an approach called multi-agent artificial intelligence modelling) in Chapters 4 and 5.

In his editorial introduction to a special issue of *Open Philosophy* on 'Computer Modeling in Philosophy', Patrick Grim suggested that computer modelling may come to play a role in twenty-first-century philosophy analogous to that traditionally played by logic (Grim, 2019b). As historians of philosophy know, logic had a powerful generative and regulative function in the work of nineteenth-century thinkers such as Hegel, Frege, Cantor, Meinong, and Peirce (albeit in vastly different ways), which would have ramifications for the split between analytic and continental philosophy in the twentieth century. Given the analytic and synthetic capacities of computational methods in general, and the productivity of social simulation in particular, these new tools for thinking could well have a similarly transformative effect on twenty-first-century philosophy.

What can CMS (and especially multi-agent artificial intelligence modelling) methodologies provide that other more traditional methodological approaches do not? Such approaches have many virtues that set them apart from other methods. The process of constructing a computer model forces researchers to be exceptionally precise in the conceptualisation and operationalisation of their variables and to formalise their assumptions about the causal interactions among them. After quantifying this information within algorithms that drive computational architectures (usually structured by state charts or stock-and-flow diagrams), high-powered computers or high-performance computing clusters can explore the multi-dimensional parameter space and produce simulations of social dynamics far more efficiently and rapidly than the human mind. But what exactly is new and distinctive here? These methods enable scholars to

- achieve higher levels of *conceptual clarity* as they formalise or operationalise elements of their theories (thereby surfacing their assumptions about the nature of – and relational interactions among – the variables in the social systems they study);
- explain the *emergence* of a complex macro-level social phenomenon by 'growing' it bottom-up from micro-level agent behaviours and meso-level interactions (thereby shedding light on plausible *causal* factors rather than merely establishing statistical correlation); and
- explore the multi-dimensional phase space of a social system in order to determine the parametric *conditions* under which – and the *mechanisms* by which – specific configurations are likely to emerge (thereby enabling policy-relevant *experiments* in artificial societies that would not be feasible or ethical in real-world societies).

My main interest here is in explaining the value of social simulation for *philosophers*, and so I've listed these capacities of CMS methods in roughly the order in which I think most philosophers are likely to find them attractive.

The desideratum of conceptual clarity should be the least controversial. As those who have attempted to implement and integrate their theories within a complex computational architecture can attest, the process can be both dizzying and delightful. CMS techniques provide philosophers with a way of constructing a conceptual scaffolding for their mind palaces, which not only makes them easier to build and keep clear of clutter but also makes them easier for others to critically engage with. Not all philosophers are interested in emergence and causality, but for those who are I spell out the potential metaphysical and epistemological implications of CMS (interpreted in light of Deleuze's concept of assemblages) in Chapters 2–5. Not all philosophers are interested in addressing contemporary issues of societal relevance, but for those who are I outline the capacity of CMS to contribute to some of the major ethical debates currently facing humanity in Chapters 6 and 7.

This might be enough to get some philosophers more interested in exploring the uses of simulation machines. However, one of the main claims I want to defend in the following chapters is that CMS ought to be particularly interesting for Deleuze scholars or other philosophers interested in the reversal of Platonism. As I will explain in more detail below, the most interesting reason to bring CMS into dialogue with Deleuzian-inspired philosophy is that it enables us to

- articulate the mutual conditioning of the *virtual* phase space of a computational model and the alterable variables and relations expressed in *actual* simulations in a way that clarifies and bolsters Deleuze's metaphysics (and meta-epistemology and meta-ethics) of pure immanence.

To reciprocate, Deleuzian philosophy can clarify and bolster the relative successes of CMS methodologies, especially multi-agent artificial intelligence modelling.

The overall flow of the argument will go as follows. Chapter 3 will begin to spell out the claim that Deleuzian philosophy and computer modelling and simulation can be productively brought into dialogue. It ends with a discussion of the achievement of Deleuze's atheist *metaphysics*. The fourth chapter returns more explicitly to the language of assemblages, borrowing heavily from Manuel DeLanda's interpretation and use of Deleuze, in part because of the former's own contributions to the philosophy of computer simulation. Chapter 5 provides more examples of the fruitful collaboration between computer modelling and the atheist machine, concluding with a summary of the achievement of Deleuze's atheist *meta-epistemology*. The sixth chapter responds to some friendly critics of my earlier arguments about the implications of findings in the bio-cultural sciences and describes some strategies for prebunking theism and fostering sustainable altruism in the Anthropocene. Chapter 7 tackles the concrete case of the role of religious (or theist) bias in the sub-discipline of the philosophy of religion, in the context of Deleuze's claim that Christianity secretes atheism more than any other religion. That chapter concludes with a summary of the achievement of Deleuze's atheist *meta-ethics*. The final chapter summarises the argument as a whole and uses it to explicate some of the pragmatic implications of conceptualising atheism as the serenity of the philosopher. First, however, Chapter 2 explains how all these claims can be integrated within the conceptual framework that I've been hinting at throughout this introductory chapter.

# 2

# Assembling the Atheist Machine

Where do babies come from? Why do parents keep them around? For those of you wondering what this has to do with the atheist machine, hang in there for a couple of paragraphs. Archaeologists working at ancient sites do not have to dig around for answers to such questions. As they unearth skeletons and artefacts, they can confidently assume that the regular arrival and continued nurture of the infants in that community were the result of the same basic sort of coital procedures and mating strategies that were naturally selected during the evolution of *Homo sapiens* in the Upper Palaeolithic and that continue to replenish the human population today. Although research on these practices in contemporary contexts might yield insight into some interesting variations, cultural anthropologists know enough about biological and human evolution, psychological attachment dynamics, and social entrainment practices to explain, without additional field work, where *babies* come from and why adults usually keep them around.

A similar confidence has emerged among scholars in the bio-cultural sciences of religion about the mechanisms by which *gods* are born in human minds and borne in human cultures. During the last three decades or so, theoretical proposals based on empirical research within a wide variety of fields such as evolutionary biology, archaeology, cognitive science, moral psychology, historical sociology, and cultural anthropology have been converging around the claim that religious phenomena can be explained by the evolution of *cognitive* processes that *hyper-detect* human-like forms in the natural world and *coalitional* processes that *hyper-protect* culturally inscribed norms in the social world. Elsewhere I have summarised many of the major theories within the bio-cultural study of religion that shed light on these god-bearing mechanisms, consolidating them in what I call theogonic reproduction theory (see Shults, 2014c; 2018b, for a more detailed outline and defence of the theory). In the first section of this chapter, I introduce this conceptual framework to serve as a guide for discussing these cognitive and coalitional mechanisms that lead to shared imaginative engagement with supernatural agents in human populations.

The second section describes some of the historical contingencies surrounding the emergence of the (Western) monotheistic idea of 'God' – an infinite supernatural agent who has a special plan for a particular group.

It explains how the advent of this conception, which turns out to be logically, psychologically, and politically unbearable, contributed to the assemblage of the atheist machine during the axial age. In the third section, I utilise the framework outlined in the first two sections as a heuristic tool for clarifying the dynamics at work within and among the four main social machines treated in the *Capitalism and Schizophrenia* project (i.e., the territorial, despotic, capitalist, and war machines). As we will see, the atheist machine plays a special role in the creative production of the (revolutionary) war machine. The fourth section explores the process of becoming-atheist, with special attention paid to the relation between naturalism and secularism in many contemporary contexts. The final section briefly demonstrates the explanatory power of this integrated model by examining how these four social machines have overlapped and exerted influence on each other during the Holocene, setting the stage for later discussions of the (mal)adaptiveness of theism and the potentially productive use of the atheist machine in the Anthropocene (the relatively recent time period in which human behaviour has deeply affected the geological environment).

### Alliance and Fighters and Bias – Oh My!

In what follows, I will often refer to religious (and theist) *biases*. It is important to begin by emphasising that biases, in the most general sense of the term, are not necessarily bad. In fact, many human biases are good, and some, perhaps most, are even necessary for our survival. Naturally evolved cognitive dispositions often serve us well when we need to act fast, to access or process memories quickly, or to interact in contexts where there is not enough (or too much) information. For example, most of us are 'biased' towards eating when we feel hunger, avoiding dangerous predators when we see them, and pursuing sex when we feel aroused. If our ancestors had not evolved these kinds of relatively automatic self-preserving (and species-preserving) proclivities, we would not be here to discuss them. It is possible to resist these sorts of tendencies, at least up to a point. One might, for example, go on a diet, learn how to tame lions, or become a celibate monk. However, if an entire generation of human offspring somehow completely failed to inherit (and act on) these kinds of naturally selected biases, it would likely be the end of the species.

Biases towards feeding, fleeing, and fucking have contributed to our survival. But what about fighting? Humans also have an evolved tendency to form strong alliances and work hard to protect them. In fact, the capacities for cooperating, coordinating, and competing within and across groups served our ancestors well. And, to a certain extent, they continue to serve us well today. Few of us would judge a mother for impulsively prioritising the care (or defence) of her newborn child over the care of others, especially under stressful conditions. Some of us even encourage skirmishes between fortuitously formed, non-kin-based alliances, such as those that make up youth sports leagues. These predilections towards finding allies and fighting outgroups are examples of the sort of evolved biases that helped our progenitors survive, and so it is no surprise to find them widely distributed in the human population today. Such tendencies were naturally selected because they facilitated survival within a specific ecological environment, and now they have been transmitted over the generations to us.

However, most of us no longer live in the same kind of natural and cultural environments as our hunter-gatherer ancestors. Biases that were adaptive (or improved the quality of life for some individuals) in one context may well be maladaptive (or decrease the quality of life for other individuals) in another context. For example, a strong desire for sugar or fat would have motivated early mammals to ingest as much as possible when these relatively rare commodities were available. Today, in contexts with inexpensive supermarket ice cream, those urges can be seriously bad for our health. This can also be true of biases related to individuals' formation of alliances and willingness to fight for them. Warriors with a hair-trigger predisposition to kill (or die) for their in-group would have come in handy when one small band of *Homo sapiens* bumped into another in the Upper Palaeolithic, especially if they were competing for scarce resources. However, this kind of instinctive, hyper-sensitive, violent, xenophobic reaction causes more harm than good in contemporary, densely populated, pluralistic urban contexts.

The same can be said of racist, sexist, and classist biases. Many of us find these latter prejudices noxious and do what we can to draw attention to their deleterious effects, especially on minorities, women, and those with scarce material resources. In our efforts to contest such biases, however, it is important to acknowledge that the tendencies that help to maintain these inequalities did not come out of nowhere. As human populations grew in size and diversity in the Neolithic, they increasingly domesticated plants and animals and experimented with more complex, sedentary forms of social organisation. The larger-scale societies that emerged and survived were those in which individuals were willing to accept (or had imposed upon them) new and more differentiated ways of managing the means of production and reproduction. During the Bronze and Iron Ages, empires were forged and maintained through the forced servitude of conquered ethnic groups, the conjugal constraint of women, and the emergence of complex civilisational forms in which wealth was constantly redistributed upwards through bureaucratic and priestly hierarchies to subsidise the militaries, monuments, and myths that supported despotic regimes.

However unpleasant all of that was (and still is) for some individuals, it 'worked'. Over long periods of time, large numbers of human beings were able to capture enough energy and survive long enough to reproduce – and here we are. All of this must be taken into consideration when we turn to the exploration (and contestation) of *religious* biases. The role of religion in sanctioning the attitudes and norms that reinforce racism, classism, and sexism is well-known to professional historians, as well as to casual readers of the Hebrew Bible, the New Testament, and the Qur'an. In recent decades, however, empirical findings and theoretical developments within a wide range of disciplines in the scientific study of religion have shed new light on the cognitive and coalitional mechanisms behind this sanctioning. The key question today is whether these biases are still 'good for us'. We will return to this question throughout this book.

It is important to acknowledge that phenomena associated with 'religion' are complex and contested (like the term itself). For the purpose of this interdisciplinary philosophical experiment, however, I use the term to indicate an aggregate of features that have in fact been found in every known culture, past and present, namely, *shared imaginative engagement with axiologically relevant supernatural agents*. Here 'supernatural agents' refers to entities that are attributed human-like intentions, emotions, and agency, but whose alleged existence does not require embodiment within naturally evolved biological systems (as human intentionality, emotion, and agency do). To qualify as religious, such entities must also be taken by members of an in-group to be relevant for the normative and valuational (axiological) structures that guide the group's attitudes and behaviour. This applies to entities as diverse as totem animal spirits and punitive divine beings. It is not uncommon in the bio-cultural study of religion to use the term 'gods' to refer to any kind of supernatural agent (e.g., Atran, 2002; Lewis-Williams, 2010; Tremlin, 2010), an approach I will follow here. To qualify as 'religious' in the sense intended throughout this book, imaginative engagement with such coalition-favouring entities must be communally shared and expressed in the context of mediated in-group ritual practices designed to honour, assuage, or manipulate them in some other way.

The basic empirical claim of theogonic reproduction theory is that gods (supernatural agent conceptions) are *born* in human minds and *borne* in human cultures as a result of a complex set of reciprocally reinforcing, phylogenetically inherited, and socially sustained cognitive and coalitional biases. The evolutionary roots of theogonic (god-bearing) mechanisms help to explain why gods are so easily born(e) in the mental and social Imaginarium of human life. Most contemporary *Homo sapiens* are naturally drawn into the bio-cultural attractor space created by the integration of two mutually intensifying aggregates of evolved tendencies that I call anthropomorphic promiscuity and sociographic prudery. These cognitive and coalitional dispositions are part of our phylogenetic inheritance and have been reinforced by millennia of social entrainment practices. In the environment of our early ancestors the selective advantage went to hominids who were able to quickly detect relevant agents in the natural environment and whose groups were adequately protected from dissolution by reducing the number of cheaters and freeloaders in the social environment, both of which were buttressed by 'religion'. The coordinate grid in Figure 1 represents a conceptual framework for discussing the possible correlations between these types of cognitive and coalitional dispositions – and their contestation.

The horizontal line in Figure 1 represents a continuum on which one can mark a person's tendency to guess 'hidden human-like supernatural force' when confronted with ambiguous or frightening phenomena in the natural environment. This general tendency can be fractionated into a host of evolved biases and personality factors that are distributed differently among individuals, such as ontological confusion, teleological reasoning, agency detection, magical thinking, and schizotypy (e.g., Guthrie, 1993; Kelemen, 1999; Caldwell-Harris et al., 2011; Talmont-Kaminski, 2014; Breslin and Lewis, 2015; Lindeman et al., 2015) An anthropomorphically promiscuous person will always be on the lookout for intentional causes, jumping at explanations that appeal to 'agency' even – or especially – when such inferences are not verifiable. Individuals leaning towards the left end of the spectrum are more likely to commit errors when making judgements about the presence of other minds or the purposiveness of apparent patterns, especially under stressful conditions. The anthropomorphically prudish, on the other hand, are suspicious about hypotheses that appeal to disembodied intentional forces. They prefer to reflect more carefully before grabbing on to supernatural agent interpretations.

Think of the vertical line as representing a continuum on which one can register how tightly a person tends to bind him or herself to conventional religious modes of inscribing the social field, that is, to the proscriptions and prescriptions that regulate the practices and boundaries of the coalition with which he or she primarily identifies. This general tendency may be shaped by a variety of other differentially distributed biases and personality factors, such as risk-aversion, susceptibility to charismatic leaders, and out-group prejudice, which can be ratcheted up by stressful contextual conditions (e.g., Bulbulia, 2012; Bulbulia and Schjoedt, 2010; Etengoff and Lefevor, 2021; Ng and Gervais, 2017; Schjoedt et al., 2011; Sekerdej et al., 2018).

Sociographic prudes are strongly committed to the divinely sanctioned social norms of their in-group, following and protecting them even at great cost to themselves. Individuals at the low end of this spectrum are more likely to be suspicious of outsiders and to accept claims or demands that appeal to the allegedly supernatural authorities of their own in-group. On the other hand, the sociographic promiscuity of those oriented towards the top of the spectrum renders them more open to intercourse with out-groups about alternate normativities and to the pursuit of innovative modes of creative social inscription. Such persons are also less likely to accept restrictions or assertions that are based only (or even primarily) on appeals to religious authority.

It is important to emphasise that anthropomorphic promiscuity and sociographic prudery are *reciprocally reinforcing*. Conceptions of gods may be easily born in human minds but it takes a village to raise them. Supernatural agents who are cared for and ritually engaged with in a coalition then become easy imaginative targets for the hair-trigger agency detection mechanisms of each new generation. The mutual intensification of god-bearing mechanisms, which increases the stability and reproductive capacity of complex adaptive religious systems, helps to explain why shared imaginative engagement with supernatural agents has been so prevalent across human cultures throughout history. In the environment of our early ancestors the selective advantage went to hominids who developed cognitive capacities that quickly *detected* relevant agents in the natural milieu and whose groups were adequately *protected* from the disruption that could result from too many cheaters in the social milieu.

Although scholars in the bio-cultural evolutionary sciences of religion often disagree about the role or significance of particular mechanisms, the general consensus is that shared imaginative engagement with 'gods' (whether animal spirits, ancestor ghosts or, eventually, 'higher' deities) would have provided a survival advantage insofar as beliefs about potentially punitive, contingently embodied intentional forces (who might be watching), and emotionally arousing, communal ritual behaviours intended to please or appease them, tend to amplify *inferences* about hidden agents and *preferences* for in-group norms (e.g., Atran, 1993; 2002; Boyer, 1994; 2002; Teehan, 2010; Rossano, 2010; Pyysiainen, 2009; Lewis-Williams, 2010; McCauley, 2013; Slone and Slyke, 2015; Voland and Schiefenhövel, 2009; Turner et al., 2017). All living human beings share a phylogenetic inheritance shaped by the integration of these god-bearing biases, which explains why we are so easily swayed by the integrated theogonic forces in the lower left quadrant of Figure 1.

If these hypotheses were true, we would expect the available data to provide evidence of the phylogenetically ancient emergence of these god-bearing

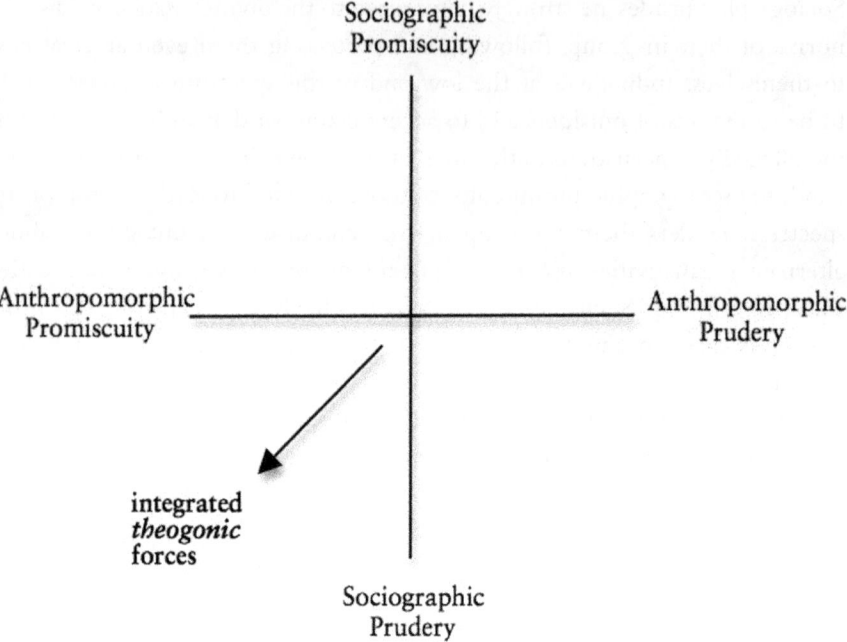

Figure 1. Theogonic forces

mechanisms, of their relatively early ontogenetic emergence across cultures, and of individual and contextual variance in their distribution across human populations. We would also expect to find statistical correlations between levels of anthropomorphic promiscuity and sociographic prudery (and their component mechanisms), empirical evidence of the mutual amplification of these mechanisms under relevant conditions, and individual and contextual variation in the reciprocal intensification of these evolved biases. And this is indeed what we do find (see Shults 2014a; 2014b; 2015b; 2018c for expositions and analyses of the evidence). Given religion, what machine can produce it? The integrated theogonic mechanisms of anthropomorphic promiscuity and sociographic prudery. Given a religious machine, what can it be used for? Many things, including virtue cultivation and social cohesion. However, such social assemblages can also amplify superstitious thinking and segregative behaviours that are highly problematic in many contemporary contexts.

As we will see below, the (relative) success of science and the (relatively) peaceful cohesion of democratic, pluralistic societies require that those who want to participate in the academic and public spheres learn how to challenge the cognitive and coalitional defaults that promote religious superstition and segregation. But if the biases that lead to shared imaginative engagement with axiologically relevant supernatural agents were so deeply woven into the genetic and memetic structures of human life, why and how did they come to be challenged in the first place? Scientific naturalism and political secularism are expanding in many parts of the world. A growing number of us do not think we need gods to make sense of the natural world or to act sensibly in the social world. Where did such 'atheistic' ideas come from? They were already gestating during the axial age.

## The Assemblage of (A)theism

So far, we have mostly been discussing that (really) old-time religion, which resulted from cognitive and coalitional mechanisms that naturally evolved and became integrated in early ancestral environments, probably over one hundred thousand years ago. What I am calling the atheist machine, however, emerged in earnest only within the last few thousand years. Ironically, bearing atheism became easier and easier as theistic machines took over large-scale social assemblages, especially in the wake of the axial age in west Asia (discussed below). As noted in Chapter 1, I am distinguishing here between religion in general and theism as a particular expression of religion. As we will see, theism follows religious biases to infinity. Denouncing this 'infinity of religion', as Deleuze put it, is a constitutive task of philosophy. My main interest in this book is to promote the use of the atheist machine in contemporary philosophy. In order to succeed in such a task, however, it is important to understand the origin of 'theism' as distinct from 'religion'. Linking Deleuze's understanding of social machines to the conceptual framework introduced in the previous section can help. In what follows, I incorporate aspects of arguments originally formulated in chapter 5 of *Iconoclastic Theology: Gilles Deleuze and the Secretion of Atheism* (Shults, 2014b).

For most of the history of *Homo sapiens*, shared belief in local animal spirits or limited ancestor ghosts was enough to hold together small-scale societies of hunter-gatherers. Local totemic rituals involving such finite supernatural agents sufficed for the sedentary collectives that began to form during the Neolithic. Over the millennia, however, in many contexts across the most fertile areas of east, south, and west Asia, human groups grew in size and complexity and claimed ever larger plots of land for themselves. So did their gods. As coalitions were amalgamated or assimilated by one another, smarter and more powerful supernatural agents were needed – 'high gods' who could monitor the behaviour of more human agents and trump the local spirits or ancestral authorities of the newly merged coalitions. Ever bigger groups required ever bigger and ever more punitive (or at least moralistic) gods in order to ensure that everyone cooperated and stayed committed (Norenzayan,

2013; 2015; Watts et al., 2015; Purzycki et al., 2016; Whitehouse et al., 2019; McCaffree and Abrutyn, 2020; Beheim et al., 2021).

During the first millennium BCE, in the largest and most complex literate states across east, south, and west Asia, a new sort of god-concept was born in the minds of intellectual and priestly elites: an all-encompassing supernatural agency whose influence was universal and in relation to whom all behaviour was punished (or rewarded). The period from approximately 800 to 200 BCE is commonly called the 'axial age' because it represents a turning point, or axis, in the transformation of civilisational forms in human history. The most common ideas about an ultimate Reality that emerged in east and south Asia during this period did not explicitly (or unambiguously) involve the attribution of intentionality to an infinite force. Dao and Dharma, for example, were supposed to be morally relevant for any and all groups, but most Chinese and Indian religious scholars seriously questioned whether such realities should be primarily conceived as person-like and coalition-favouring.

There was far less doubt in the monotheist traditions that emerged in the wake of the west Asian axial age: we are made in the *image* of God and God has a special plan for *our* group. The identity of Jewish – and eventually Christian and then Muslim – coalitions was tied to narratives about the creation of Adam and the call of Abraham to a promised land (paradise lost, and found, in west Asia). Theological debates among these religious in-groups centre around questions about the extent to which (or whether) Moses, Jesus, or Muhammad mediate divine law-giving and care-giving. Which group has the definitive revelation of – and ritual access to – the one true God who will personally punish (or reward) everyone for all eternity? Monotheism is anthropomorphic promiscuity and sociographic prudery gone wild – superstition and segregation applied to infinity.

As we will see in more detail in the next section, Deleuze often noted a special relation between monotheism and what he called the *despotic* machine. When the coding of flows in the 'primitive' territorial socius are overcoded in the despotic socius, then 'the ancestor – the master of the mobile and finite blocks – finds himself dismissed by the deity, the immobile organizer of the bricks and their infinite circuit' (AO, 217). For Deleuze, the main role of the deity seems to be the inscription of debt into the very existence of the despot's subjects, who now owe their very being to the despot-god. '*There is always a monotheism on the horizon of despotism*: the debt becomes a debt of existence, a debt of the existence of the subjects themselves' (AO, 215, emphasis added). Even if the priest (or the prophet) connected to the king-despot does not see the disobedient actions or disrespectful attitudes of the people, the inescapable Eye of God will – and no sinner can hide from his judgemental voice and punitive hand.

Among the despot's bureaucrats, the monotheistic priest has a special role: administering the face of God and interpreting his intentions. 'A new aspect of deception arises, the deception of the priest: interpretation is carried to infinity and never encounters anything to interpret that is not already itself an interpretation' (ATP, 126–8). The revelation that is allegedly encountered in holy texts and engaged with in rituals is ambiguous; it can be (and must be) endlessly interpreted in new ways because ideas about counter-intuitive discarnate forces are not empirically constrained. What does the Torah (Bible, Qur'an) *mean*? What does God *want* us to do *now*? The transcendent God of monotheism, Deleuze notes, 'would remain empty, or at least *absconditus*, if it were not projected on a plane of immanence of creation where it traces the stages of its theophany'. Whether it takes the form of imperial unity or spiritual empire, 'this transcendence that is projected on the plane of immanence paves it or populates it with Figures' (WIP, 88–9).

On the one hand, the intellectual and priestly elites of monotheistic coalitions insist that their supernatural agent has appeared and will continue to appear in the finite world. On the other hand, they also insist that his glorious nature is infinitely transcendent and beyond comprehension – even the despot may misinterpret God (Arnason et al., 2004; Bellah, 2011; Eisenstadt, 1986). This tension has always characterised *theology*, which was also born during the axial age. Broadly speaking, theology is the construction and critique of hypotheses about the existential conditions for axiological engagement (Shults, 2014c). What is it that makes possible – or actual – the real, finite human experience of valuing and being valued? In their attempts to answer this sort of question, the majority of theological hypotheses within the monotheistic coalitions that eventually came to dominate most of west Asia and Europe (and much of the rest of the globe) followed the theogonic trajectory depicted in Figure 1.

Even among theologians (as well as priests and prophets) who were committed to the sacerdotal regulation of religious minds and groups within particular monotheistic in-groups, however, one can also find minority reports that contest the idea of God conceived as a person-like, coalition-favouring, punitive disembodied entity. We have already alluded to the first reason the intellectual elites in such religious groups might have had for resisting finite images of God as, for example, a 'Father' or 'Judge': whether material or semiotic, such images (icons) are all too easily taken by regular religious people as actual representations of an infinitely glorious and holy divine Reality that ought not to be represented. This is (part of) the motivation behind warnings against idolatry and occasional acts of physical iconoclasm. An infinite God *must not* be represented for doxological reasons.

Moreover, an infinite God *cannot* be represented for logical reasons. One of the existential requirements for intentionality is being in relation to something not identical to oneself, that is, to an object of intention. This is the case even if one is intentionally relating to one's imagined, future self – intending, for example, to become a better person. Intentionality presupposes an in-tensional relation to that which one is not, or that which one does not yet have. In other words, it requires being-limited, which is the definition of finitude. This is why absolute or true infinity cannot be intentional: to conceive it as such would be to imagine it as *related* to an object that it was not (such as a finite creation), in which case it would not be *absolutely* unlimited. Moreover, cognitive and coalitional defaults evolved to engage *finite* supernatural agents, and the pressure exerted by the notion of an all-knowing and all-powerful *infinite* despot-God is simply psychologically and politically unbearable (Shults, 2014c). People might memorise and repeat orthodox doctrinal formulations about God's omniscience, omnipotence, and impassibility, but in everyday life, and especially under stress, they immediately fall back into their default tendencies and imagine a finite, temporal god who is interested in their kith and kin (Slone, 2007).

The idea of 'God' as an infinite disembodied intentional force was tentatively born(e) in the minds of theologians who pressed the evolved defaults towards anthropomorphic promiscuity and sociographic prudery as far as they would go – which turned out to be too far. If God is so transcendent that he cannot be represented, then he cannot be conceived (or perceived) as a human-like agent (or anything else). If God eternally foreknows and pre-ordains *everything*, then it is hard to understand the point of praying to or ritually engaging with him. Throughout the centuries, monotheistic theologians have worked hard to defend hypotheses about the conditions for axiological engagement that utilise images (icons) of God as a person who cares about a group while simultaneously emphasising that such images must be broken.

Evolved cognitive defaults for detecting finite agents crumple under the pressure of trying to think an infinite intentional entity. Evolved coalitional defaults for protecting in-groups implode (or explode) under the stress of trying to live in complex literate states. It is not hard to imagine why and how atheism would emerge as an increasingly viable option (albeit rarely, slowly and tentatively) as monotheism took over in large-scale, pluralistic societies. The abstract, transcendent God described by the priest does not seem to have any relevance for daily life. All these people around me have different views of gods whom they think care about their group. They try to explain the natural world in superstitious ways that make no sense to me. They try to regulate the social world in segregative ways that make it difficult for me and those I love. Perhaps we can make sense of the cosmos and behave sensibly in society without bearing God – or any other finite supernatural agents preferred by particular in-groups.

In other words, the rise of relatively (in)credulous and relatively (non)conformist priestly elites, who were central to the construction of theist machines, provided the conditions for the intensification of incredulity and nonconformity that would come to characterise atheist machines. As noted above, 'religion' is engendered by the integration of a set of credulity biases (anthropomorphic promiscuity) and a set of conformity biases (sociographic prudery). These evolved tendencies functioned as social glue for early human societies, including the large-scale, literate societies that eventually launched the 'axial age'. Theism pressed these biases to infinity (and eternity), which led to what Deleuze calls the 'secretion' of atheism. In Chapter 7 we will return to the question of why Deleuze thought Christianity secreted atheism more than any other religion.

The assemblage of the atheist machine involved the contestation of the evolved theogonic mechanisms depicted in Figure 1, a contestation that opened up lines of flight that were previously unimaginable. Although its use in and effect on the mental and social fields of the civilisations that emerged out of the west Asian axial age were initially quite limited, the atheist machine began to unveil the implausibility of the various (contradictory) ideas and the unfeasibility of the various (contradictory) ritual strategies for organising normativity. Even when contesting the relevant cognitive and coalitional biases is not consciously oriented towards clearing the ground of religious icons, it automatically has a theolytic (god-dissolving) effect. The intensification and integration of the forces of anthropomorphic prudery and sociographic promiscuity are part of the actualisation of atheist machinic assemblages (Figure 2).

We will return below to the upper left and lower right quadrants, but for now let's focus on the god-dissolving (theolytic) mechanisms that are integrated in the upper right quadrant. Anthropomorphic prudery can be fostered by critical reflection and especially by training in the sciences, which are naturalistic (at least methodologically). Sociographic promiscuity can be fostered by encounters within pluralistic societies and especially by relatively transparent democratic states, which are secularistic (at least methodologically). The good news, from my perspective, is that as *naturalist* explanations of the world and *secularist* inscriptions of society take root and grow within a population, people start to lose interest in engaging in theistic sects. They become better at making sense of the world without relying on supernatural agents and better at acting sensibly in society without complying with supernatural authorities. This, in turn, makes it easier to discuss and explore solutions to the contemporary global challenges we all face today.

I'll return to the role of naturalism and secularism in the assemblage of the atheist machine later in this chapter and throughout the book, but first let's

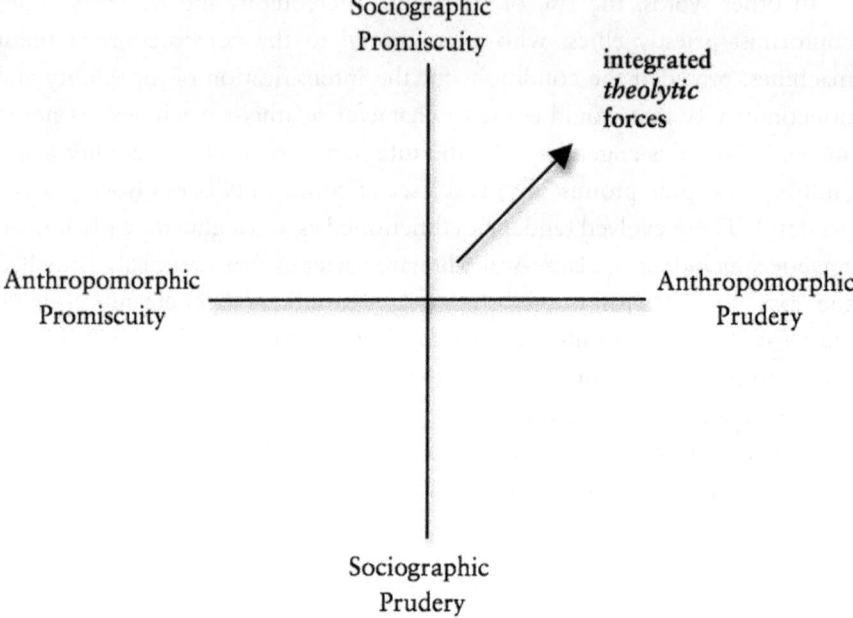

**Figure 2.** Theolytic forces

bring this heuristic conceptual framework into more explicit dialogue with Deleuze's distinctive social machines.

## Deleuzian Social Machines and the Bio-cultural Sciences of Religion

It is important to remember that Deleuze does not think of the social machines described below as concrete, historical formations of the socius that were (or will be) realised in a particular order. Rather, they are abstract machines that are actualised in diverse ways within all complex social assemblages, precisely in their intensive mutual interactions. The territorial, despotic, and capitalist machines are all social productions that 'fall back' on desiring-production; each in its own way creates a 'full body', a 'recording surface' that inscribes the desiring-machines and schiz-flows (pure becoming) of the Real. As we will see, although the war machine can be captured by the State, in itself it is the creative element or productive force of rhizomatic lines of flight that escape repressive representations.

The *territorial* (or primitive) machine is the 'first form of socius, the machine of primitive inscription' (AO, 155). A socius is produced whenever there is a coding (inscription) of stock (consumption) that falls back upon the flow (production) of desire. The first mode of representation organises itself at the surface by the coding of filial flows through alliances, thereby creating a 'territory'. The unit of alliance is debt, and alliance, suggests Deleuze, is 'representation' itself. When it falls back on the desiring-production of human bodies, the territorial machine constitutes a debt system involving 'a voice that speaks or intones, a sign marked in bare flesh, an eye that extracts enjoyment from the pain'. An element of transcendence (representation of an ideal) is introduced, but it remains 'quite close to a desiring machine of eye-hand-voice' (AO, 207). The territorial assemblage is declined on the full body of 'the earth' through the *coding* of lateral alliances and extended filiations.

The *despotic* (or barbarian) machine, on the other hand, appears with the force of a 'projection that defines paranoia', in which a 'subject leaps outside the intersections of alliance-filiation, installs himself at the limit, at the horizon, in the desert, the subject of a deterritorialized knowledge that links him directly to God and connects him to the people' (AO, 211). Deleuze describes despotism as the first principle of a paranoiac knowledge that withdraws from life and from the earth, producing a judgement of both. The socius will now be inscribed on a new surface, not the earth, but the full body of 'the despot' (or his god). The savage system of *cruelty* is replaced by the barbarian system of *terror*. The voice is no longer one of alliance across filiations, but 'a fictitious voice from on high'. In *A Thousand Plateaus*, this is also spelled out in relation to the 'facialization machine', which effects an overcoding wrought by the signifying despotic Face, irradiating a surveillance that reproduces paranoid faces (e.g., ATP, 186ff.).

The *overcoding* of the despotic machine (or imperial barbarian formation) is characterised by the mobilisation of the categories of *new* alliance and *direct* filiation. The eyes watching the hands' inscription of bodies are replaced by the Eye and the Hand of the despot, who watches everyone through the eyes of his bureaucrats, officials, and priests, and subordinates graphism to the Voice that 'no longer expresses itself except through the writing signs that it emits (revelation)'. Now, interpretation becomes all important: 'The emperor, the god – what did he mean?' (AO, 224). Having claimed a direct and transcendent filiation, the despot appropriates all the forces of production. All alliances are now organised around and oriented towards him. Instead of blocks of mobile and finite debt coded by horizontal alliances, the despot extracts taxes for a vertical tribute that feeds a constantly expanding glorious expenditure. The despotic State, Deleuze insists, is an abstraction that is realised only as an abstraction (AO, 240).

As an abstract machine, the despotic machine can be conceived as 'the common horizon' to what comes 'before' and what comes 'after', that is, as a complex of syntheses that can overcode the territorial machine's coding of break-flows and, in turn, that can become relativised and incorporated within the *capitalist* machine's axiomatisation of decoded break-flows. This *decoding* of flows that characterises the capitalist (or civilised) social machine has also always been present in human populations, even if only as that which was 'warded off' by primitive and barbarian social inscriptions (and the nomads). This social machine has a deterritorialising effect, but it is only 'relative'. It immediately reterritorialises the decoded flows on the 'full body' of capital. The surplus value of production, as well as the qualities of alliances, which had been coded through kinship or overcoded through tribute, are now decoded, rendered quantitative and relativised in relation to the surplus flux of the market, which registers value on the basis of the potential for earning wages or generating profit. The capitalist machine is fully installed when money begets money, when capital itself becomes filiative. 'It is no longer the age of cruelty or the age of terror, but the age of *cynicism*, accompanied by a strange *piety*...' (AO, 245, emphasis added).

What about the *war* (or *revolutionary*) machine? Despite its name, the primary use (and effect) of this machine is not war. Only when it is appropriated by the State apparatus of capture does war necessarily become its object. The essential aim of the war machine is 'revolutionary movement', escaping the molar organisation and conjugation of flows through a becoming-molecular that effects an *absolute* deterritorialisation (whether artistic, scientific, or philosophical). Once the capitalist machine has relativised the despotic machine's overcoding of the territorial machine and taken over the socius, every struggle involves the construction of '*revolutionary connections*' in opposition to the '*conjugations of the* [capitalist] *axiomatic*' (ATP, 522). Resisting facialisation (and Oedipalisation), the war machine creates and populates smooth space with 'probe-heads' that draw lines of flight, cutting edges of deterritorialisation that become positive and absolute, 'forming strange new becomings, new polyvocalities' (ATP, 211).

How can the conceptual framework of theogonic reproduction theory, derived from bio-cultural scientific models of the origin and evolution of religion, shed light on the repressive (and liberating) functions of the Deleuzian social machines? My intuitions about the way in which evolved credulity and conformity biases are operating 'well beneath' social-machinic ideologies are depicted in Figure 3.

It is important to keep in mind in what follows that one should distinguish carefully between the desiring-machines that compose the individual level tendencies described above and the social machines that 'fall back upon' them. In each case, the four basic Deleuzian social machines indicated in Figure 3 should not be thought of as a conglomeration of individuals characterised by the integration of the relevant tendencies, but as a third dimension (or perhaps as Minkowski planes or as shifting space-time curvatures within

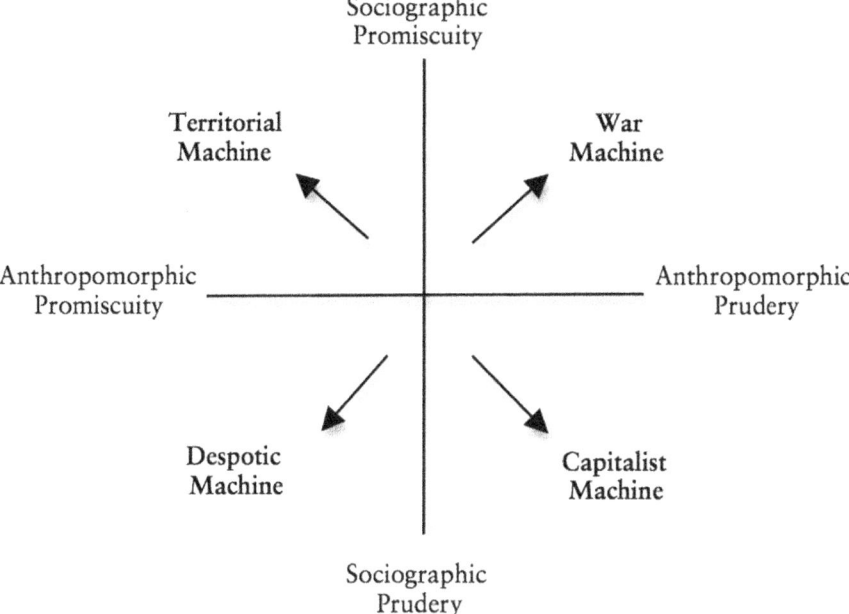

Figure 3. Social machines

a Riemannian manifold) that creatively informs and is informed by those individual level variables.

Let us begin with the 'primitive' territorial machine. Archaeological evidence and ethnographic analogy suggest that the hominids that flourished in the Upper Palaeolithic were extremely anthropomorphically promiscuous. They somewhat automatically postulated ambiguously embodied intentionality behind everything – rivers, trees, crystals, the weather, and the earth itself. Apparently early hominids were also relatively sociographically promiscuous. In the wide open spaces of Africa and the Levant, interaction with other in-groups would have been more rare. It seems that even Neanderthals and *Homo sapiens* got along surprisingly well in Europe, at least until around 35,000 BCE. The integration of these promiscuous tendencies can still be found today in some small-scale cultures as well as some relatively loose coalitions in 'Western' societies informed by New Age beliefs and practices. The difference between the typical social formations wrought by the territorial and capitalist machines is well illustrated in the first *Avatar* movie. The Na'vi, inhabitants of the planet Pandora, who are portrayed as similar to some indigenous societies on Earth, are doubly promiscuous (anthropomorphically and sociographically). They are animistic and perceive all things as filled with conscious energy and, at least early in the plot narrative, the Na'vi are also open to learning about the insights and norms of the scientists studying their culture.

The movie *Avatar* also provides us with an example of a coalition most of whose members are prudish in both in both their anthropomorphism and their sociography. The RDA mining corporation is only interested in profiting from the 'unobtainium' under the surface of the Na'vi's home planet Pandora. The invaders are tight-fisted in their refusal to acknowledge out-group members and miserly when it comes to sharing with and learning from other cultures. Formed by an extreme actualisation of the 'civilised' capitalist machine, the leaders of RDA do not detect human-like agency even in the human-like Na'vi, whom they refer to as 'blue monkeys'. It might initially seem as though capitalism promotes sociographic promiscuity since it decodes the qualitative alliances that code human affiliations and encourages the multiplication of images. In fact, however, its inscriptive prudery is absolute: the abstract capitalist machine forces *all* surplus value to fall back on the 'full body' of capital, converting all codes to abstract quantities (money). It has the potential to spread a universal anxiety in which everyone must accumulate surplus value for their own group.

The anxiety spread by the 'barbarian' despotic machine, on the other hand, is of a different sort: everyone must follow the laws of the god of a particular group. As we have seen, monotheism is infinitely sociographically prudish. The one true God has revealed the norms by which all human groups are to be regulated and judged. There is no point in arguing with or trying to trick an infinite, unchanging despot-God, whose prescriptions and proscriptions are absolute. Unlike the capitalist machine, however, the despotic machine is excessively promiscuous in its anthropomorphism. First and foremost, it promotes the detection of a supernatural agent who is allegedly determining all things everywhere at all times. However, it also promotes paranoia about his bureaucrats (whether spirit-filled embodied priests or disembodied angels or saints) who are also watching and waiting to enforce divine judgements.

The nomads who invent the 'revolutionary' war machine, on the other hand, want to 'have done' with the judgement of God (ATP, 126). Although the phrase 'war machine' does not appear in *Anti-Oedipus*, we do find references there to a 'revolutionary machine', and to hunters in nomadic space who follow the flows and escape the 'sway of the full body of the earth' (AO, 354, 163). The monotheistic machine exists only by overcoding territories and resisting the axiomatisations of the immanent capitalist field that relativise its preferred religious figure. The inscriptions of the territorial and capitalist machines inevitably throw spanners into the monotheistic machine, promoting tendencies that resist or threaten the despotic mode of theogonic reproduction.

The war machine, however, fractures the repressive 'representations' of all three of the other modes of social production. It has no time (or place) for the segmentarity of Oedipus, much less for the sedentary arborescence of the transcendent icons of monotheism. In this sense, it is always consuming, registering, and producing an atheist machine. In other words, the war machine is assembled (or at least intensified) by tendencies towards anthropomorphic prudery and sociographic promiscuity. It escapes the facialisation machine and draws positive and absolute lines of deterritorialisation, populating a smooth space with 'probe-heads ... that dismantle the strata in their wake, break through the walls of signifiance, pour out of the holes of subjectivity' (ATP, 210). The nomads refuse the segmentation of sedentary collectives whose striation of the socius finds its centre of gravity in the State. The *nomos* of the war machine is a movement and composition of people that cannot be captured in the apparatus of the 'law'. Its becoming is a celerity that constantly invents tools and weapons that can be used on the move in the encounter with and the production of new modes of social assemblage. Although the nomadic war machine can be captured by the State apparatus, of which 'religion' is a piece, the nomads' sense of the absolute is 'a singularly *atheistic* one' (ATP, 422, emphasis added).

It is important to remember that all of these abstract social machines, according to Deleuze, are operative in *every* human population – although in each concrete context they are more or less successful in their coding, capturing, axiomatising, or escaping in relation to one other. I have tried to show how they are also shaped by underlying cognitive and coalitional tendencies, which are distributed and contested in various ways across and within real human populations. In a growing number of those populations, the atheist machine is producing a wide array of naturalist and secularist assemblages.

## Becoming-atheist: Naturalism and Secularism

The tenth chapter of *A Thousand Plateaus* explores a host of becomings: becoming-intense, becoming-animal, becoming-imperceptible, becoming-molecular, etc. In every case, these becomings have to do with movements that undermine the arboreal and the molar. Here I am using the phrase 'becoming-atheist' in the same way. The atheist machine undermines monotheist molarities and the pseudo-philosophical trees (or chains of being) upon which their theologies depend. We will return to some of the other becomings in this Plateau in later chapters, but here I want to highlight two movements produced by the atheist machine that will be particularly important in the arguments that follow: naturalism and secularism.

As noted in Chapter 1, the term *naturalism* can be used in a variety of ways, but it typically indicates a resistance to appeals to supernatural agency in theoretical explanations of the natural world. This is especially true in the academy, particularly in institutions not bound to a religious in-group. Some scholars in public institutions might continue to hold religious beliefs, but most are (at least) methodologically naturalistic in the sense that they exclude god-concepts from their scientific hypotheses. The term *secularism* can also be used in a variety of ways, but it usually denotes a tendency to resist appeals to supernatural authority in practical inscriptions of social fields. This is especially true in the public sphere, particularly in pluralistic democracies. Some civil leaders in such contexts might maintain membership in religious in-groups, but a growing number are (at least) methodologically secularist in the sense that their political proposals are not dependent on divine sanctions. I'm focusing here on the academy because that is the field in which most readers of this book are likely to be labouring.

Elsewhere my colleagues and I have reported on the 'Methodological Naturalism – Methodological Secularism' (MNMS) scale, which we developed as part of the 'Values in Scholarship on Religion' research project (Shults, Wildman, et al., 2020b; Taves et al., 2022; Shults and Wildman, 2023). We defined methodological naturalism (MN) as a preference for academic arguments that optimise the use of theories, hypotheses, methods, evidence, and interpretations that do not appeal to supernatural agents. We defined methodological secularism (MS) as a preference for academic practices that optimise the use of scholarly strategies that are not tied to the idiosyncratic interests of a supernatural coalition. The scale has been utilised and validated based on surveys of academic scholars of religion across a wide variety of sub-fields and institutional backgrounds.

Somewhat unsurprisingly, scholars in disciplines related to the scientific study of religion tend to have relatively high levels of methodological naturalism and methodological secularism by comparison with scholars in disciplines such as theology, religious studies, and philosophy of religion. The tension between those two broad types of scholars is evident in professional academic associations of scholars of religion, with some arguing for a 'big tent' that can include appeals to supernatural agents and authorities, while others argue that such inclusiveness is actually a form of 'protectionism' that privileges religion in a way that compromises the scientific quality of research. I'll return to a discussion of this tension in Chapter 7. We are currently developing surveys using this scale that will be sent to scholars in a wider range of disciplines, including those outside the study of religion.

My main interest in this context, however, is with the shift beyond methodological to *metaphysical* naturalism, the explicit denial of the existence of supernatural entities independent of the human mind, and to what we might call *metaphysical* secularism, the explicit denial of supernatural authorities as resources for organising the social field in pluralistic contexts. This shift is driven, in part, by the atheist machine, which undermines the need for appeals to gods when trying to make sense of nature and to act sensibly in society and produces the conditions for positive naturalistic explanations and secularistic inscriptions.

Arguments between theists and atheists all too often circle around the same cul-de-sac, in which both sides attempt to *prove* the other wrong or demonstrate the *probability* of their own claims. In my view, this is a waste of time for reasons that will be spelled out in more detail in Chapters 5–7. The relevant point at this stage is that scientists and (non-religious) philosophers might not be able to provide deductive logical arguments that *disprove* the existence of supernatural agents or inductive evidence that *invalidates* claims about their causal relevance, but they can offer powerful abductive and retroductive arguments that render their existence *implausible* (for a fuller discussion, see Chapter 4 of Shults, 2014b). Theists argue that all other religious groups are incorrect and that their coalition's God (as interpreted by their in-group) is the real origin, condition, and goal of all things. The more reasonable hypothesis is that shared imaginative intercourse with axiologically relevant supernatural agents emerged over time as naturally evolved hypersensitive cognitive tendencies led to mistaken perceptions, which in turn slowly became entangled within erroneous collective judgements about the extent of the social field, producing and sustaining all religious – including all theist – in-groups.

In addition to this theoretical claim, I will also defend a closely related pragmatic claim throughout this book: although the theogonic biases described above were naturally selected for their survival advantage in early ancestral environments, today they are maladaptive in a growing number of contexts because of the way in which they can implicitly intensify superstitious beliefs and segregative behaviours of the sort that exacerbate contemporary challenges related to escalating cultural conflict, extreme climate change, and excessive consumer capitalism. I am not claiming that the atheist machine will solve all these problems, and history compels us to acknowledge that it will no doubt cause other problems. It is also important to emphasise that, in Deleuze's understanding of social machines, the nomadic atheist machine does not simply overcome the territorial, despotic, or capitalist social machines, but always moves along in tension with them all. In a sense, then, my claims are not that radical. I am simply arguing that in the natural and social contexts in which many of us find ourselves, the atheist machine has an important role to play in our theoretical analysis and political innovation.

We do not yet know all that naturalist-secularist bodies can do. Whatever they *can* do, hypothesises the atheist, their axiological engagement is not conditioned or regulated by human-like, coalition-favouring gods. Atheism follows out the logic and practices that flow from the integration of the theolytic forces, pressing beyond methodological versions of anthropomorphic prudery and sociographic promiscuity and insisting on *metaphysical* naturalism and secularism. The atheist machine cuts away at superstitious beliefs and segregating behaviours based on shared imaginative engagement with axiologically relevant supernatural agents, and constructs pragmatic plan(e)s within socio-ecological niches in which survival no longer depends on the detection and protection of the gods of particular in-groups.

Deleuze has helped clear the ground for revolutionary experimentation by disclosing the repressive power of despotic (monotheistic) social-machinic representations. I have tried to show how *theogonic* machines, which integrate and intensify superstitious and segregative tendencies, make this process of clearing far more complicated that it initially appears. The repressive representations they (re)produce are reinforced by naturally evolved biases that all too easily lead to the detection of gods and the protection of in-groups. This is why we also need to pay closer attention to the uses and effects of *theolytic* machines. How can we produce atheistic registrations and consumptions on the field of immanence as we clear the ground of the religious figures of transcendence that make us anxious and distract us from creating new connections? As Deleuze consistently emphasised, the criteria for answering such questions can only be discovered in the actual, immanent, problematic process of schizoanalysis (rhizomatics, micropolitics, pragmatism, etc.).

Developments in the bio-cultural sciences provide us with conceptual tools that can supplement those efforts. They help us unveil the secrets of theism, especially the cognitive incoherence and coalitional irrelevance of representations of an infinite personal God. Such prodding exerts a pressure that intensifies the secretion of atheism. But this is not enough; the forces of theogonic reproduction have led to adaptive defences that continue to hold subjects within religious coalitions. For example, theologians committed to monotheistic in-groups can insist that these 'mysteries' are part of what is adorable about the divine nature or part of what is hidden in the divine plan. Appealing to concealed secrets, secrets that are appealing in part because of their concealment, keeps the secretion in check.

It is important to keep talking about where the god-conceptions within in-groups come from in the first place, because unveiling theogonic mechanisms automatically weakens them; they function well only when they are hidden. I have argued elsewhere (2014c) that having 'the talk' about *religious* reproduction should involve more than simply explaining how 'it' works. It is equally important to work out the physical, emotional, and social consequences of 'doing it'. This is just as true for religious education as it is for sex education. We need an atheological (philosophical) version of 'the birds and the bees' that deals with the dynamics by which supernatural agents are reproduced in human minds, and the consequences of nurturing them in human coalitions. Part of the problem is that we are socialised not to ask where gods come from, and we learn early that it is not polite to ask people why they keep them around.

When it comes to having the talk about where babies come from and what it takes to care for them, we know that waiting too long can have devastating effects. Of course, it can be equally devastating if the conversation makes people feel attacked, afraid, or ashamed. As we will see in more detail in Chapter 6, the same is true when talking about where gods come from. The activities that lead to sexual and religious reproduction can feel terrific to our bodies, but baring our souls about them can feel terribly vulnerable. When discussing such intimate issues, it is important to be sensitive – but it is also important to be direct. We do not know where such conversations will lead. We cannot know ahead of time what effects the atheist machine will have; the secretion of productive atheism will not solve all our problems and will surely create some new ones. However, insofar as it clears the ground of arborescent religious icons that reinforce mythical and superstitious interpretations of nature and divide us through supernatural segregations of society, at least it gets us moving.

## 10,000 Years of Non-linear, Social-machinic History

To reiterate, for Deleuze, social machines do not emerge in a linear fashion, one replacing the other. Each operates in relation to the others in every human population, even if its primary role is negative during a particular phase (e.g., the capitalist machine being 'staved off' by the territorial machine in early human ancestral environments and many contemporary indigenous societies). The non-linear approach of *A Thousand Plateaus* is wholly consistent with the claims of more recent archaeologists and anthropologists such as Graeber and Wengrow in *The Dawn of Everything: A New History of Humanity* (2021). The latter provide significant evidence for challenging the linear thinking that has dominated so many scholarly debates about the 'origin' of agriculture or the State. Humans have been creatively playing with political forms (or social machines, to use Deleuze's phrase) from the beginning, or at least as far back as archaeology and anthropology can take us. In this sense, the atheist machine has always been with us, as have the territorial, despotic, and capitalist machines. As in every era, the question is how we humans creatively (or reactively) engage with these social machines as they 'fall back upon' our desiring-machines.

The remainder of this book focuses on the present and the future, that is, on understanding and promoting the use of the atheist machine in philosophy at it increasingly engages with some of the recent, revolutionary developments in computational modelling and simulation. Before moving on, however, I want to offer one more way of thinking about how we got to where we are today. Although the history of the development of human societies is far more complex, it is heuristically helpful to point to three major shifts in civilisational form: the so-called Neolithic, axial, and modern transitions. Elsewhere Wesley Wildman and I have reported on system-dynamics computational models (which specialise in simulating non-linear systems) of each of these transitions, and explored their implications for the future (Wildman and Shults, in press). Each of these models incorporates insights from the bio-cultural sciences of religion as well as other relevant disciplines in their computational architectures. And, in each case, the models were able to simulate the transition from a population primarily characterised by one civilisational form to another. Here my limited goal is to describe briefly how this type of social simulation can shed light on the transitional dynamics of human civilisations.

The first model simulated the shift from a population with primarily hunter-gatherer lifestyles to the sedentary-agricultural lifestyle that increasingly characterised the Neolithic. This model was calibrated and validated using empirical evidence gathered as part of a multi-year interdisciplinary project studying the results of the excavation of the Neolithic 'town' of Çatalhöyük in what is now southern Turkey (Shults and Wildman, 2018). Çatalhöyük is one of the best-known archaeological sites in the world, and Deleuze and Guattari themselves referred to this site in their discussion of the Apparatus of Capture (ATP, 473–4). The domestication of plants and animals had occurred well before the founding of this settlement, but it has a special significance because of its unusually large size (up to 5,000 people on about thirty-four acres) and its unbroken temporal extension (continuous settlement from 7,400 to 6,000 BCE). The material culture and artistic symbolism of Çatalhöyük is also more complex than earlier sites in the region such as Göbekli Tepe and Aşıklı Höyük.

Elsewhere I have discussed some of the evidence for anthropomorphic promiscuity and sociographic prudery at Çatalhöyük (Shults, 2014a). A wide variety of artefacts indicate that shared imaginative engagement with supernatural agents was pervasive within the community. Feasting deposits, wall art, pottery symbolism, the installation of wild auroch buchrania, and the hiding of other animal and human skeletal remains in the houses and under the foundations, all suggest ritual interaction with imagined disembodied agents. The cognitive tendency to detect human-like intentionality in inanimate objects is also implied by the way in which the inhabitants of Çatalhöyük buried (some of) their dead within their houses, usually immediately under the sleeping area, occasionally unearthing their bones and engaging with them in a variety of ways. Ethnographic analogy suggests that the discovery of hundreds of figurines at the site could be a sign that the young were socialised to imaginatively engage with animal spirits and ancestor ghosts (Coe et al., 2012).

There is also an apparent transition in *sociographic* strategies over the centuries at Çatalhöyük. Based on an extensive review of the archaeological evidence, Hodder and Whitehouse (2010) have argued that there was a slow shift of ritual modes during the life of the settlement. Initially, it was characterised by the dominance of the 'imagistic' mode, in which rituals tend to be highly emotionally arousing but relatively infrequent – this is typical of small-scale, non-hierarchical societies. In the later levels of the site, however, the consistency of symbolic patterns, the use of moulds, and the reduction of wild animal parts suggest the emergence of a more 'doctrinal' mode, which is characterised by more frequent, less emotionally arousing rituals. The latter are typical of larger, more hierarchical societies. This hypothesis was expanded by Whitehouse et al., who argued that religious routinisation was a major factor in the emergence of more complex social forms at Çatalhöyük. One of the primary functions of religion in hunter-gatherer societies was to hold small groups together, but 'gradually, as agriculture intensified, this ancient function faded and religion became a means of reproducing much larger (if more diffuse) group identities'. The vitality of religious life would have shifted from 'esoteric mystery cult to something more ideologically uniform, in some ways less awe-inspiring and more controlling' (Whitehouse et al., 2014: 134).

In other words, it appears that the 'doctrinal' ritual mode slowly began to replace the 'imagistic' mode, with a phase shift around the year 6500 BCE. Several factors would have played a role in this shift, but cross-cultural multiple regression analysis indicates that agricultural intensity is the most significant predictor of this sort of change in civilisational form (Atkinson and Whitehouse, 2011). This does not mean that 'despotism' or 'monotheism', in the sense they emerged millennia later in the Bronze and Iron Ages, were already present in the Neolithic. Rather, I am suggesting that what Deleuze calls the abstract machine of despotism was increasingly installed in some places during this revolutionary period in human history. At the very least, however, Çatalhöyük represents one example of an apparatus of capture in which the coding of various terrestrial machines (hunter-gatherers and perhaps even nomads) was slowly overcoded as the socius on the Neolithic Konya plain became more stratified, arboreal, and hierarchical. Anthropomorphic promiscuity continued to run wild, but as the population grew and religious routinisation intensified at the settlement, its members became increasingly sociographically prudish. Over time the default slowly shifted from the upper left to the lower left quadrant of Figure 3.

This brings us to the second computational model, which simulates the emergence of civilisational forms typical of the axial age (Shults, Wildman, et al., 2018). We can deal with this period more briefly since we have already touched on it above in our discussion of the assemblage of (a)theism. This model also integrated a variety of theories and insights from scholars of history and cultural studies, as well as from scholars in the cognitive sciences and quantitative sociology, within a single computational architecture. It was able to simulate the shift from populations with a preference for pre-axial modes of organising the social field into the civilisational forms of human society characteristic of the axial age (first millennium BCE). It was during this period that despotic monotheism became fully installed and took over the social fields of west Asia. As noted above, such an installation occurred only after the emergence of a class of intellectual and priestly elites who tried to detect the biggest God they could conceive (an infinite intentional disembodied force) and ended up protecting the cohesion of empires by inscribing the most terrifying social segmentarity imaginable (the negative disjunction between eternal pleasure and eternal pain).

The third system-dynamics model, which simulates the emergence of post-supernatural cultures during what we might call the 'modernity' transition (Wildman et al., 2020), can also be dealt with briefly here because we will return to it in Chapter 5. The construction of the causal architecture of this model required the integration of six major theories of secularisation, including some whose insights are based largely on qualitative research and hermeneutical judgements. It was able to simulate the shift from populations in which social cohesion depends largely on shared belief in supernatural agents to modern, secular populations in which the majority of individuals have naturalistic worldviews. Although we did not base that model on the conceptual frameworks outlined in the current chapter, its findings can be illuminated in light of them. Briefly, the modernity model revealed that the conditions under which post-supernatural cultures are likely to emerge include high levels of education, existential security, pluralism, and freedom of expression. To put it the other way around, supernatural cultures in which religion flourishes are more likely to be maintained if people do not have easy access to scientific and humanist education, feel anxious about their economic future, insist on the moral superiority of their own in-group, and do not feel safe exploring and expressing views that challenge the status quo.

Our modernity model did not deal with the capitalist machine explicitly, but it did include variables such as economic development and social liberalisation. As noted above, for Deleuze the axiomatic of capitalism relativises the coding of the territorial machine and the overcoding of the despotic machine. Its quantification of surplus value, which always falls back on the full body of capital, tends to dissolve the absolute, qualitative claims of monotheism. Can subjects in a modern socius really serve both God and Mammon? But why should we serve either? The (creative, nomadic, revolutionary) war machine resists the repressive representations of the other social machines, refusing to fall back on the full body of the despot or capital or even the earth. It should be obvious enough that Deleuze was not (nor am I) calling for a return to an idealised, historical period in which we all give up our actual houses and begin literally roaming around like nomads. However, I am following Deleuze in calling for a creative engagement with the nomadic atheist machine as a way of resisting the repression of the other social machines, especially the despotic monotheist machine.

The practical question is whether or not we can learn to contest the evolved defaults of anthropomorphic promiscuity and sociographic prudery, mechanisms that served (some of) our ancestors well in the Upper Palaeolithic and the Neolithic, but which do not seem to be serving us well today as we try to adapt within pluralistic, globalising socio-ecological niches. Superstitious renderings of the cosmos and segregative striations of the socius that appeal to the gods (or God) of a particular in-group are no longer contributing to our survival. Where does this leave us? How can we use the atheistic, schizoanalytic machine; what creative effects will it have? We do not yet know, which is what makes it a rhizomatic adventure. But we are coming to a better understanding of the underlying theogonic forces that can block revolutionary lines of flight as well as the theolytic forces of naturalism and secularism that can facilitate them. The next three chapters focus on the role that computational modelling and social simulation can play in promoting the philosophical (and other) uses of the atheist machine.

# 3

# The Reversal of Platonism and the Rise of Simulation

In this chapter I turn more explicitly to the second main goal of this book, highlighting some of the metaphysical implications of recent advances in the field of computer modelling and social simulation (CMS), which provide material warrant (and methodological weapons) for the Deleuzian task of articulating a flat ontology that can account for the morphogenesis of existing things (or the becoming of assemblages) through resources immanent within the world of matter and energy without any appeal to transcendence. I argue that the rise of simulation within and across scientific disciplines is accelerating the reversal of Platonism, whose emphasis on transcendence and reliance on hierarchical, static categories has dominated Western philosophy for over two millennia. A full defence of such a claim would require, among other things, tracing the historical precursors of this reversal of the Platonic obsession with transcendent essences, a reversal that was initiated in the work of some of the ancient Stoics and Epicureans and intensified by early modern philosophers such as Spinoza and Nietzsche, as well as describing the pragmatic ramifications of this shift on a wide variety of scientific disciplines that neighbour computational modelling and social simulation.

In order to make my task more manageable, I limit myself to an exposition and expansion of aspects of the work of Manuel DeLanda, a philosopher and computer programmer (as well as an artist and architect) who has done more than any other scholar to illuminate the potential of computer modelling and simulation to help resolve longstanding debates about whether philosophers need to postulate transcendent essences or types in order to makes sense of the metaphysical conditions for the existence of actual entities or events. The short answer is no: we *can* account for the morphogenesis of all existing things by describing the immanent intensive processes that generate actual forms, showing how that individuation is actualised by resources immanent to the world of matter and energy, and explaining the mechanisms of immanence by which virtual multiplicities themselves are produced in relation to the actual – all in the context of an absolutely flat ontology.

The main point of this chapter is that the success of CMS methodologies opens up new conceptual space for articulating a philosophy of pure immanence that might provide a more adequate basis for understanding and solving many of the problems facing contemporary human societies. As I suggested at the beginning of Chapter 1, the capacity of such tools to simulate the emergence of and macro-level patterns of social (and other) assemblages from the micro-level behaviours and meso-level interactions of their component parts (a process involving both the production of a 'virtual' phase space and the individuation of 'actual' events in simulation experiments) lends plausibility to Deleuze's metaphysics of immanence. Conversely, Deleuze can provide more adequate philosophical moorings for social scientists and others interested in utilising such techniques, whose popularity is growing rapidly in disciplines as diverse as biology, psychology, anthropology, sociology, and history.

CMS is a relatively new field and stands on the shoulders of a gigantic number of other scientific disciplines. Although it did not initiate the process, the emergence of computational modelling and simulation methodologies has had a powerful accelerating effect on the dissolution of Plato's hierarchical transcendence-reinforcing categories. The philosophical use of these tools is growing so rapidly that the latter may come to play a role in the twenty-first century similar to that played by logic in twentieth-century philosophy. If so, then identifying some of the ways in which Deleuze's univocal ontology, which finds unique expression in his work with Guattari, can help to ground and more adequately explain the success of such tools provides one way of fostering more interest *among philosophers* in the analytic and synthetic use of concepts created within the Deleuzian corpus. This is meant to complement my efforts elsewhere to foster more interest among *computer scientists* in the way in which their discipline has been promoting the reversal of Platonism (Shults, 2019c).

## The Reversal of Platonism

As we saw in Chapter 1, Deleuze follows Nietzsche in seeing the task of philosophy (or the philosophy of the future) as effecting a reversal or overturning of Platonism. Before turning again to Deleuze's interpretation of that task, let's back up and remind ourselves of the impact of Plato's metaphysical categories in the history of philosophy. The philosophical sub-discipline of 'metaphysics' gets its name from a (posthumously titled) book by Aristotle in which he described what he called 'first philosophy', which considers 'being *qua* being – both what it is and the attributes which belong to it *qua* being' (*Metaphysics* 1026$^a$30). However, Aristotle's analysis of (and proposals for) the study of 'being' or 'that which is' was explicitly framed within the context of a long series of debates that had recently culminated in the integrative efforts of his teacher Plato.

In the *Sophist*, Plato portrayed a dialogue between Theaetetus, a young participant in Socrates' circle of philosophical friends, and a Visitor who engages him in a dialectical discussion about types of being. What does one mean to signify when one says 'being'? In the course of the dialogue, the Visitor leads Theaetetus to affirm the appropriateness of five generic categories, that is, five ways of signifying things that are: 'being', 'rest', and 'motion', 'the same' and 'the different' (*Sophist* 254d–259d). For Plato, and indeed for the vast majority of Western philosophers over the last two millennia, the categories of *substance*, *stasis*, and *sameness* have been more strongly emphasised and valued than the categories of relation, motion, and difference. *Substance* (being or essence) comes first in the list because Plato's metaphysical theory (outlined in more detail in other places, such as the *Republic* and *Timaeus*) seems to presuppose that everything that 'is' has an essence, a transcendent Form (or Idea) in which it participates. The fact that things are *related* to other things is secondary and is relevant to their being only indirectly (in the sense that the essence of one thing is – or is not – the same as the essence of another thing). For Aristotle too 'the relative' is 'least of all things a real thing or substance' (*Metaphysics* 1088$^a$22). As the Neo-Platonist Plotinus would put it some centuries later, the term 'Relation' is 'remote from Being' (*Enneads* 6.2.16).

When it comes to the dyads *stasis/kinesis* and *sameness/difference*, Plato clearly privileges the first member of each pair over the second. Both stasis (rest) and kinesis (motion) are generic categories – that is, they can be used to signify the being of things – but static being is in some sense more valuable and even more 'real' than being-in-motion (or becoming). In the case of the last dyad too, the sameness of a thing (its identity) is typically thought of as more important than its difference (alterity) from other things, although the latter is in some sense constitutive of its being. This becomes more obvious when we think about Plato's vision of the Forms, which are eternally static and identical, in contrast to the material things that populate the world we perceive, which are susceptible to decay and alteration, because they merely 'participate' in the reality of the Forms. Plato's own view is more complex than this, and he is not always consistent across his writings, but this all too brief synopsis does capture the most common interpretation of his metaphysics, which dominated Western philosophy until the early modern period.

Even philosophers who preferred Aristotle's more extensive (and more science-friendly) list of genera in his *Categories* have usually still bought into the basic Platonic assumptions about the metaphysical priority of 'being', 'rest', and 'the same'. Aristotle went out of his way to emphasise that the relativity of a thing is not as real as its essence or substance – the latter term appearing, as with Plato, at the top of his list of categories for signifying being. Although Aristotle did indeed stress the value of particular, material things more than Plato, he still postulated an 'Unmoved Mover' as the metaphysical ground and telos of all other realities. This most valuable reality is 'thought thinking itself' – unchanging immaterial substance reflecting its own static identity. Aristotle's epistemology and ethics were also shaped by these categories: for example, like is known from like, and true friendship is based on similarity.

For most of its history, Western philosophy has laboured under the constraints of a metaphysics of substance, stasis, and sameness. During the first few centuries of Christian 'philosophy', under the influence of Neo-Platonism, doctrinal formulations were saturated in these categories. For example, the single sentence that is the Symbol of Chalcedon, which was produced in the middle of the fifth century CE as a result of decades of debate over whether the Son had the same static substance (*homo-ousios*, same-substance) as the Father, has fifteen references to sameness or identity. Western philosophy in the Middle Ages was more dominated by Aristotle's categories, but it remained within what Deleuze calls the Platonic 'Eidetic' framework, presupposing transcendent models as the basis for selecting among rival images (icons). This obsession with substances, stasis, and sameness was still dominant in early modern philosophers such as Descartes, whose *Principles of Philosophy* highlights the importance of accepting divine revelation as the basis for all motion and diversity and of distinguishing thinking substance from corporeal substance.

All of this might sound quite strange to computer modellers whose day jobs involve the simulation of *dynamic* relations in complex systems using *differential* equations in order to discover and analyse the effects that altering parameters can have on the *processes* that shape the *relations* among *variables*. Indeed, most CMS professionals will be able to live their entire lives without worrying about the long shadow cast by Platonism and go about their work in the scientific sunshine happily (and productively) using *relational*, *dynamic*, and *differentiating* categories. This is the case for the vast majority of scientists in other disciplines as well.

It is often surprising to non-humanities scholars, and especially non-philosophers, that people still spend so much energy arguing about the role that categories can play in human thought. It is important to note that essentialist categorising can have a significant psychological and political impact on human life by structuring the way we think and engage in social discourse and practice, which in itself is a sufficient reason to keep on arguing about it. My main point here, however, is that the weakening of the influence of Platonic categories in the work of practising scientists, and increasingly in the thought worlds of everyday people, has had – and continues to have – a profound impact on those of us whose day jobs involve philosophising about metaphysics.

In fact, for the last couple of centuries philosophers have been participating in (or resisting) what we might call a turn to *relationality*, *celerity*, and *alterity* – a shift in the valuation of categories that had already begun in earnest in the work of early modern philosophers such as Locke, Hume, Kant, Hegel, and Kierkegaard. Kant, for example, in his 'Table of Categories' in the *Critique of Pure Reason*, explicitly reversed the hierarchy between substance and relation, identifying the former as a sub-category of the latter (Kant, 1965: 113). The shift away from Platonic categories continued to intensify in the work of late modern philosophers such as Whitehead, Heidegger, and Levinas. Of course, some philosophers today still rely on the category of transcendence to account for the metaphysical ground of being (and becoming), assuming that the only way to account for the genesis (and duration) of actual entities or events is to posit a distinction between the field of immanence in which they exist and a transcendent dimension that somehow serves as the ground of their existence (and subsistence). The metaphysical theories that are based on this assumption may vary significantly, but insofar as they appeal to some transcendent reality to make sense of the existence of being(s) they are 'Platonic' in the broad sense in which I am using the term here.

As noted in Chapter 1, the 'reversal of Platonism', for Deleuze, involves the reconstruction of metaphysics in purely immanent terms without any appeal to transcendence. This would rather obviously have a profoundly erosive effect on theological edifices erected within the Abrahamic monotheist traditions whose coherence and cohesion rely on belief in a transcendent personal creator upon whom the existence of all creaturely beings depends. Although there is ongoing debate among scholars about what Plato himself really meant (Brumbaugh, 1991; Welton, 2002; Annas, 2009), or even whether Deleuze himself really meant to complete rather than overturn Plato (De Beistegui, 2012; Altamirano, 2015), our concern here is with Deleuze's unambiguous critique of the effects of some aspects of 'Platonism' (as mediated throughout the Western philosophical tradition), which he explicitly attempts to overthrow or reverse (*renverser*). The reversal of Platonism is a recurring theme in many of Deleuze's works but receives special attention in *Difference and Repetition* and *The Logic of Sense*; I will focus on the latter whose content (as well as its rhizomatic structure) clearly anticipates *A Thousand Plateaus*.

In an appendix to *The Logic of Sense* Deleuze interpreted Nietzsche's call for such a reversal as an invitation to track down the 'motivation' of Platonism. The latter initially seems to be distinguishing 'essence from appearance, intelligible from sensible, Idea from image, original from copy, and model from simulacrum' (LOS, 266). But Deleuze points out that these are not equivalent expressions. What is the distinction that most deeply inspires Platonism? Deleuze finds the 'totality' of the Platonic motivation in the drive to 'select' between two sorts of images: to distinguish true *copies* (icons), which resemble the Ideas that transcend them, and *simulacra* (false pretenders), which are engulfed in dissimilarity. Earlier in *The Logic of Sense*, he had identified the Stoics as 'the first to reverse Platonism, and to bring about a radical inversion'. If the characteristics of substance and cause are assumed by bodies, as in the Stoics, then Ideas are 'relegated to the other side, that is to this impassive extra-Being which is sterile, inefficacious, and on the surface of things: *the ideational or the incorporeal can no longer be anything other than an* "effect"' (LOS, 6). This somewhat obviously undoes the Platonic privileging of the intelligible over the sensible.

But it also unravels the deeper dualism identified above. It is no longer necessary, desirable, or even possible to 'select' the true copies of an Ideal model. For the Stoics, the simulacra 'cease to be subterranean rebels and make the most of their effects', which include all possible ideality (LOS, 8). Deleuze argues that the donation of sense occurs at the frontier between propositions and things, as the 'paradoxical element' (or aleatory point) runs 'through the two series at the surface ... tracing between the two series the straight line of the Aion...' (LOS, 83). This frontier that is established between bodies and propositions is the 'metaphysical surface', which 'is not a separation, but rather the element of an articulation, so that sense is presented both as that which happens to bodies and that which insists in propositions' (LOS, 129). The paradoxical element that traverses the heterogeneous series is a 'two-sided entity' that 'circulates without end in both series' (LOS, 43), and that coordinates the series, making them resonate and ramify with disjunctive syntheses (LOS, 69). We'll return to some of the practical and ethical implications of this approach in later chapters.

Deleuze acknowledges the importance of the discontinuity between the intelligible and the sensible, and the 'manifest duality of Idea and image' in Platonism, but insists that these are subservient to the goal of 'assuring the triumph of the copies over simulacra' (LOS, 266). He exposes this 'more profound and secret dualism', which judges beings based on their supposed resemblance to transcendent originals, and instead affirms the unlimited as pure becoming, which 'is the matter of the simulacrum insofar as it eludes the action of the Idea and insofar as it contests *both* model *and* copy at once' (LOS, 2). To overthrow Platonism, then, means 'to make the simulacra rise' and to affirm their 'positive power which denies *the original and the copy, the model and the reproduction*'. Such a 'reversal' leaves the same and the similar (which Plato had privileged over the different and the dissimilar) with no essence 'except as *simulated*, that is as expressing the function of the simulacrum'. And what is that function? 'Simulation designates the power of producing an *effect*' (LOS, 300). Among these effects are the same and the similar, which 'become simple illusions when they cease to be simulated' (LOS, 302).

## The Rise of Simulation

But how is *computer* simulation related to the reversal of Platonism? I will now explore the extent to which the overturning of Platonism (with its metaphysical reliance on transcendent Ideas as the basis for selecting true copies and judging simulacra) can be accelerated by engaging with developments in the *computer sciences*, especially some of the mathematical and meta-mathematical developments that facilitated the *rise of simulation*. Although CMS techniques have been a staple in the physical sciences for over half a century, their use in the social sciences only began to pick up in the 1990s, where they have grown in popularity ever since (Gilbert and Conte, 1995; Alvarez, 2016). More recently, these tools for thinking have been making their way into the humanities (Dignum and Dignum, 2014; Wildman et al., 2017; Fishwick, 2018). In the remainder of this chapter, I explore ways in which a classical issue in philosophy (a discipline with traditionally deep roots in the humanities) – namely, the tension between transcendence and immanence in metaphysics – might be illuminated by developments in CMS.

No scholar has explored this topic as deeply as Manuel DeLanda, whose books *Philosophy and Simulation: The Emergence of Synthetic Reason* (2011) and *Intensive Science and Virtual Philosophy* (2002) will inform much of my discussion in what follows. Prior to these publications DeLanda was already well known for his work on the relevance of cybernetics, intelligent machines, and non-linear dynamics for understanding and explaining emergent social phenomena in human history such as warfare (DeLanda and Crary, 1997; DeLanda, 1991). His more recent work has had an impact on the field of artificial intelligence in general (e.g., van der Zant, Kouw, and Schomaker, 2013), which is now shaping conversations among scholars interested in multi-agent artificial intelligence and other forms of social simulation. DeLanda's interpretation of Deleuze is not without its critics, and I'll return to some of these below. At this stage, however, I want to highlight some of the ways in which DeLanda's approach is helpful for my current purposes, namely, making a connection between the rise of CMS technologies and the construction of a metaphysics of pure immanence.

My goal here is to introduce philosophers to the creative way in which DeLanda teases out the implications of the scientific efforts of CMS practitioners for metaphysics. One important implication has to do with the way in which the rise of simulation has impacted philosophical debates over the concept of emergence. Ever since Plato, the most common philosophical ways of explaining the *emergence* or formation of new material beings have involved appeals to static transcendental *essences* or types (genera and species). Today, after centuries of scientific analysis of actually emergent phenomena, most philosophers would accept the idea that interactions among a population of entities can lead to the emergence of new complex wholes (or assemblages) with new properties, capacities, and tendencies irreducible to their parts (although they might want to continue arguing about whether this involves 'weak' or 'strong' emergence; see Wildman and Shults, 2018). But what does this have to do with CMS? As DeLanda explains:

> Simulations are partly responsible for the restoration of the legitimacy of the concept of *emergence* because they can stage interactions between *virtual* entities from which properties, tendencies, and capacities *actually* emerge. Since this emergence is reproducible in many computers it can be probed and studied by different scientists as if it were a laboratory phenomenon. In other words, *simulations* can play the role of laboratory experiments in the study of emergence complementing the role of mathematics in deciphering the *structure of possibility spaces*. And *philosophy* can be the mechanism through which these insights can be synthesized into an emergent *materialist* world view that finally does justice to the creative powers of matter and energy. (2011: 6, emphases added)

Let's briefly unpack these claims. First, why was the legitimacy of the concept of emergence under scrutiny in the first place? The short answer is that philosophers who promoted the term in the late nineteenth and early twentieth centuries loaded it with baggage about transcendent essences (Life, Soul, Deity) that they inherited from Plato and the vast majority of the Western tradition, baggage that most practising scientists have increasingly found unnecessary, embarrassing, or even detrimental to their work.

Second, how, precisely, did computer simulations help restore the legitimacy of the concept? As DeLanda notes, successful simulations are able to produce the actual emergence of new assemblages from the staged interaction of virtual entities. To use the terminology of Josh Epstein, simulations can enable a modeller to 'grow' the macro-level phenomena in which she is interested from behaviours and interactions at the micro-level; this is the sense in which such methodologies foster a 'generative' social science (Epstein, 2006; 2014). By offering a new way of computationally reproducing and 'experimenting' with the conditions under which – and mechanisms by which – emergence occurs, simulations provide 'laboratories' for testing claims about such phenomena.

Insofar as CMS provides scientific techniques for actually generating wholes with emergent properties, tendencies, and capacities that are irreducible to their parts, it not only strengthens the case for 'weak emergence' but also weakens the case for what we might call 'strong essentialism' (which relies on the postulation of empirically intractable transcendent forces), thereby lending credibility to philosophies of immanence. The ongoing success of computer engineers in constructing virtual complex systems that can explain emergent properties makes it increasingly unlikely that strong-emergence hypotheses of the sort that rely on appeals to mystical entelechies or supernatural beings will make a comeback in philosophy. In another context, my colleague Wesley Wildman and I invited computer scientists to take some time, at least occasionally, 'to chat with us philosopher types to learn more about the havoc you are wreaking in our disciplines' (Wildman and Shults, 2018: 33).

In this context, I make a similar invitation to my philosophy colleagues: come and chat with us social simulation types to hear how work in our field is not only fostering conceptual analysis and the creative synthesis of ideas but also facilitating a revolution in metaphysics. This is particularly relevant for philosophers of religion. In recent years, we have seen the emergence of what we might call a computational social science of religion. Given the characteristics and capacities of CMS identified at the end of Chapter 1, it is not surprising that scholars interested in religion (and non-religion) have also increasingly engaged with these methodologies in recent years (Nielbo et al., 2012). Pioneers in the computational science of (non-)religion used such methods to model the behaviour of agents in artificial societies, addressing classical issues such as the mechanisms of religious cognition (Bainbridge, 2006) and the emergence of new religious movements (Upal, 2005). Many early computational models of religion had relatively simple agents, often presupposing 'rational choice' theory, and lacked sophisticated social network structures and structurally realistic simulated environments.

Increasingly, however, modellers have been developing more complex cognitive architectures for heterogeneous networked agents with 'bounded rationality' and whose interactions are guided by algorithms more deeply informed by scientific research on bio-cultural systems. As the computational and explanatory power of CMS techniques expanded, other scholars applied them to explore a wide variety of hypotheses about topics such as the persistence of religious regionalism (Iannaccone and Makowsky, 2007), the function of costly beliefs and practices in the stability of religious groups (Wildman and Sosis, 2011), the emergence of extremism within religious clubs (Makowsky, 2012), the relationship between group size and religious identification (Hoverd, Atkinson, and Sibley 2012), the divergent modes of religiosity theory (Whitehouse et al., 2012), the transmission of religious violence in the Radical Reformation (Matthews et al., 2013a), the rise of a priestly class in complex societies (Dávid-Barrett and Carney, 2015), and the role of cooperation style and contagious altruism in proselytising religious groups (Roitto, 2015).

As we will see in more detail below, an approach called multi-agent artificial intelligence (MAAI) modelling (Lane, 2013) has proven particularly fruitful in the analysis of causal mechanisms within a variety of cybernetic cultural systems with (non-)religious variables, such as increased ritual engagement in response to environmental threats (Shults, Lane, et al., 2018), the escalation of intergroup religious conflict (Shults, Gore, et al., 2018b), and the role of education and existential security in the expansion of secularism (Gore et al., 2018). In fact, the *Journal of Cognition and Culture* hosted a special issue on computer models of religion (Lane and Shults, 2018) and social simulation was included in a special issue on methodology in the *Journal for the Cognitive Science of Religion* (Lane and Shults, 2020). We will look at several other examples below.

Throughout the middle chapters of *Philosophy and Simulation*, DeLanda illustrates the power of computer simulation methodologies (e.g., cellular automata, artificial chemistries, genetic algorithms, neural nets, and multi-agent simulations) to help explain key mechanisms and processes in the emergence of complex systems (e.g., ancient organisms, insect intelligence, mammalian memory, primate strategies, and Stone Age economics). Each of these is 'discussed in terms of the mechanisms of emergence involved, drawing ideas and insights from the relevant fields of science, as well as in terms of the structure of their possibility spaces, using the results of both mathematical analysis and the outcomes of computer simulations' (DeLanda, 2011: 6). All of this will be relatively familiar to CMS scholars. In the next two sections, I describe some of the insights that DeLanda takes from these scientific developments as he engages in what may for some be a less familiar philosophical task: articulating a flat ontology in the context of a transcendence-free, naturalistic metaphysics in which morphogenesis is explained purely with mechanisms of immanence.

## DeLanda on Multiplicities and Mechanism-independence

So, how exactly does the rise of CMS contribute to the reversal of Platonism in Deleuze's sense? In *Philosophy and Simulation*, to which we will return in more detail below, DeLanda focused primarily on the techniques of computer modelling and secondarily on their implications for philosophy (especially epistemology and ontology). The latter are in the forefront of his earlier book on *Intensive Science and Virtual Philosophy*, which he described as an attempt 'to present the work of philosopher Gilles Deleuze to an audience of analytic philosophers of science, and of scientists interested in philosophical questions' (DeLanda, 2002: 3). Deleuze is sometimes all too quickly lumped into the same category as 'postmodernists' such as Derrida, Marion, and Baudrillard, who are not taken very seriously (to put it mildly) by either analytic philosophers or working scientists. This is unfortunate because, as DeLanda demonstrates, Deleuze 'has nothing to do with that tradition', and his work is deeply influenced by his engagement with the history of mathematics and developments in modern science.

In fact, Deleuze is probably the first scholar to have recognised the radical philosophical consequences of the efforts of mathematicians such as Lagrange, Abel, and Galois whose work transformed the problem–solution relation embedded within traditional differential calculus and led to what we today call group theory – a transformation that was, in Deleuze's words, 'a more considerable revolution than the Copernican' (DR, 180). A discussion of all of the philosophical implications of such mathematical and computational developments is beyond the scope of this book, and so I limit myself here to the same strategy followed in the previous section. I begin with a lengthy citation from DeLanda, and then explore some of its key ideas, showing how they can contribute to the reversal of Platonism.

> From a Deleuzian point of view, it is this *universality* (or mechanism-independence) of multiplicities which is highly significant. Unlike essences which are always abstract and general entities, multiplicities are *concrete universals*. That is, concrete sets of attractors (realized as tendencies in physical processes) linked together by bifurcations (realized as abrupt transitions in the tendencies of physical processes). Unlike the generality of essences, and the resemblance with which this generality endows instantiations of an essence, the universality of a multiplicity is typically *divergent* ... unlike essences, which as abstract general entities coexist side by side sharply distinguished from one another, concrete universals must be thought as *meshed together into a continuum* ... a continuous immanent space very different from a reservoir of eternal archetypes ... Unlike a transcendent heaven which exists as a *separate dimension* from reality, Deleuze asks us to imagine a continuum of multiplicities which *differenciates itself* into our familiar three-dimensional space as well as its spatially structured contents. (DeLanda, 2002: 21)

As we will see below, DeLanda follows Deleuze in referring to this continuous immanent space as *the virtual*, a novel ontological category meant to replace the transcendent realm of Forms (or Ideas, or Archetypes). This concept of 'virtual' reality has nothing to do with digitally simulated environments of the sort popular in some video games; it refers to a *real virtuality* that is an objective ontological component of the world (or Nature).

But first let's unpack the idea of *multiplicities*, which are said to populate this real continuous immanent space(time). Deleuze introduced the concept of *multiplicity* to replace the philosophical concept of *essence*. For Plato, a thing's essence is supposed to be that which explains its identity, those key characteristics without which it would not be what it is. The fact that some entities resemble one another is a result of their participating in a common essence. Aristotle's metaphysics was less obviously essentialist but it was still typological; that is, he still explained the resemblance of members of a species as a result of their belonging to the same type of being, the same 'natural kind' of thing.

For Deleuze, however, 'a species (or any other natural kind) is not defined by its essential traits but rather by the *morphogenetic process* that gave rise to it'. Species are not timeless categories but historically constituted entities, and the fact that they resemble one another is explained by the common processes of natural selection that produced their shared phylogenetic inheritance.

> In short, while an essentialist account of species is basically static, a morphogenetic account is inherently dynamic. And while an essentialist account may rely on factors that transcend the realm of matter and energy (eternal archetypes, for instance), a morphogenetic account gets rid of all *transcendent* factors using exclusively form-generating resources which are *immanent* to the material world. (DeLanda, 2002: 9–10)

But what does this have to do with multiplicities? DeLanda defines a multiplicity as 'a nested set of vector fields related to each other by symmetry-breaking bifurcations, together with the distributions of attractors which define each of its embedded levels' (2002: 30). Insofar as they are defined in terms of differential relations and singularities, multiplicities can be understood as concrete sets of attractors that are linked through cascades of symmetry-breaking bifurcations which, as we will see below, can be actualised as tendencies and transitions in material processes. As DeLanda emphasises, this definition 'separates out the part of the model which carries information about the actual world (trajectories as series of possible states) from that part which is, in principle, never actualized' (2002: 30).

The concept of the *mechanism-independent* structure of possibility spaces is crucial here. Multiplicities have a mechanism-independent structure that allows for divergent actualisations (e.g., topological spaces with a particular number of degrees of freedom may be actualised through different gradients). Regardless of the mechanisms involved, actualisations bear no resemblance to the multiplicities (unlike essences, which bear an image–copy relation to their instantiations). Some aspects of a multiplicity are never actualised in principle because of their mechanism-independent nature. Moreover, there are a host of tendencies and capacities that are never actualised because they are not manifested or exercised by the actual assemblages that emerge as a result of the intensive processes and mechanisms through which they are unfolded. *Essences* are eternally identical and static substances, while *multiplicities* are relational, dynamic, and differentiated. Plato describes the former as transcendent forms in relation to which matter serves as a passive receptacle. Deleuze describes the latter as immanent to material processes, as differential manifolds with an intimate relation to the morphogenesis of actually emergent entities.

But replacing the role played by essences in metaphysics with multiplicities requires more than a description of their formal differences; it also requires an alternative account of morphogenetic processes. DeLanda provides this account in great detail in *Intensive Science and Virtual Philosophy*, reviewing the relevant mathematical and scientific developments that informed this part of Deleuze's philosophy, outlining a theory of virtual space and virtual time, and explaining how the idea of general laws of physics can be replaced by universal multiplicities while maintaining a robust commitment to philosophical realism. He also articulates the role of 'the intensive' in relating 'the actual' and 'the virtual' (the three ontological 'dimensions' of Deleuze's world). Just as 'virtual multiplicities are meant to replace eternal essences, the intensive individuations that embody them, as well as the individuals that are their final product, are meant to replace general classes, a natural replacement given that general classes are often defined in terms of essences' (DeLanda, 2002: 61).

As we noted above, DeLanda spells this out in terms of the mechanism-independence of structured possibility spaces. As he puts it in *Philosophy and Simulation*, this way of explaining the success of computational models in simulating the behaviours and interactions of complex material systems 'imposes an ontological commitment to the *autonomous existence* of topological singularities, or more generally, to the *structure* of possibility spaces' (2011: 19, emphasis added). It might be tempting to think of such topological spaces as transcendent and immutable in contrast to the immanent and dynamic material processes that mathematical and computational models attempt to simulate. However, such a move would uphold rather than overthrow Platonism. In order for singularities of the sort we have been discussing to be considered immanent to the world of matter and energy, DeLanda argues that they 'must be both *irreducible* to any particular material process while at the same time requiring that *some* process or another actually exists' (2011: 20, emphasis added). In fact, these conditions seem to be met when we look at the way topologists approach their subject.

For example, when studying models with different numbers of dimensions or degrees of freedom, topologists focus not on specific mechanisms or material gradients but on the structure of the singularities that exist in all models of that sort (e.g., models with two degrees of freedom). In other words, 'topological facts about possibility spaces can be discovered without reference to the *nature* of the degrees of freedom, only to their number, and without reference to the nature of the gradient (thermal, gravitational, mechanical, chemical) only to its *existence*'. DeLanda spells out the implication of this approach: 'the fact that the *existence* of a gradient, any gradient, is *necessary* confirms the *immanent* status of singularities. Singularities are, therefore, perfectly acceptable entities in a materialist philosophy' (2011: 20, emphases added).

Singularities are mechanism-independent in the sense that they can be divergently actualised in various material mechanisms and in the formal mechanisms of differential equations. But the existence of singularities requires the existence of *some* material-energetic gradient. If there were no such gradients, there would be no singularities. To use terms from Deleuze's *Logic of Sense* and *Difference and Repetition*, the 'existence and distribution' of a singularity within a 'problematic' field of vectors (the virtual) is distinct from the 'nature' of a singularity as defined by the integral curves of a particular 'solution' (the actual), but neither of the 'two sides' of the singularity can exist without the other.

An ontological commitment to the reality and causality of 'singularities', DeLanda suggests, opens up a properly philosophical question. 'Do they exist, for example, as *transcendent* entities in a world beyond that of matter and energy? Or are they *immanent* to the material world?' If all matter and energy in the universe disappeared, would singularities continue to exist (implying their transcendence) or would they also disappear (implying their immanence)? For DeLanda, understanding singularities in the sense outlined above (in light of Deleuzian philosophy and topological possibility spaces) fulfills the two main conditions for plausibly postulating their immanence: singularities require that some material process actually exists but they are irreducible to any particular material process.

## Virtual Phase Space and Actual Simulations

In his earlier book on Deleuze, *Intensive Science and Virtual Philosophy*, DeLanda describes the way in which singularities can undergo transitions or bifurcations at particular thresholds of intensity (when parameters such as temperature or density reach a critical value). A state space that is structured by a single point attractor, for example, may 'bifurcate into another with two such attractors, or a point attractor may bifurcate into a periodic one, losing some of its original symmetry ... this symmetry-breaking cascade of bifurcations can, in turn, be related to actual recurring sequences in physical processes [e.g., steady-state, cyclic, and turbulent flow]' (2002: 19). However, when these cascades of bifurcations are actualised (or effectuated) within a physical system, this actualisation involves specific mechanisms but it does not resemble the (virtual, mechanism-independent) mathematical or topological cascade, nor does the latter transcend the former.

Moreover, the singularities that structure possibility spaces are not immutable. Here we are dealing not with eternal and unchanging natural laws, but with 'an *immanent real virtuality* that changes and grows as new tendencies and capacities arise' (DeLanda, 2012b: 15). In other words, not only assemblages, but also abstract machines, diagrams, the plane of consistency and every other entity described in the ontology of *A Thousand Plateaus* is mutable, changing, pure becoming. We are not dealing here with 'possibilities' in the abstract modal sense typically used in possible world semantics and other philosophical approaches in which 'the possible' is treated as that which may or may not (ever) be 'real'. On the contrary, for DeLanda, both mechanism-independent (virtual) structured possibility spaces and the mechanisms that actualise their singularities in material processes are *real*.

As Deleuze insisted in *Difference and Repetition*,

> the virtual is opposed not to the real but to the actual. *The virtual is fully real in so far as it is virtual* ... the reality of the virtual consists of the differential elements and relations along with the singular points which correspond to them. The reality of the virtual is structural. We must avoid giving the elements and relations which form a structure an actuality which they do not have, and withdrawing from them a reality which they have. (DR, 208–9)

The virtual does not 'transcend' the actual, nor does the latter 'resemble' the former, and neither are 'immutable'. In other words, the plane of consistency upon which diagrammatic abstract machines are developed is *changing* along with the assemblages that effectuate abstract machines as the latter are enveloped in the strata. No transcendence. No resemblance. No immutability. Only pure becoming.

It is important to emphasise that the mechanism-independent singularities that structure possibility (or phase) spaces are not only immanent to the world of matter and energy, but also that they do not *resemble* the material-energetic processes that actualise them. There are no 'icons' here: the whole model–copy ensemble of the Platonic domain of representation is overturned. In group theory, *neither the system first contemplated nor any other model* need be imagined as the *original*, of which each model is a *copy*. The theory of groups is about anything that is a group but does *not require the existence of an original* or prototype group to serve as the *ultimate* ontological target of the theory. (Holdsworth, 2006: 145; emphases added)

Computer models usually have a 'target' material system that they aim to simulate, but the physical process being studied and the phase space of the computational architecture do not resemble one another, and neither has a Platonic (original) ideal that transcends them. Moreover, the phase space of a model is itself produced by the existential distribution of (actualisable) singularities explorable by simulation experiments.

What, then, is the ontological status of capacities and tendencies in the (virtual) phase space of a computer model when they are not actualised in a simulation? To say that they are 'possible' is too vague. DeLanda suggests that we think of these unexercised capacities and unmanifested tendencies as defining 'a concrete *space of possibilities with a definite structure*' (2011: 17). 'Possibilities' only exist when entertained by a mind, but structured possibility spaces have an objective existence, and their singularities (e.g., critical points, attractors, bifurcations) can be mapped and analysed mathematically. The tendencies of a system can be studied by the mathematical analysis of its state space, but capacities are more complex and varied because they can be exercised 'in interaction with a potentially innumerable variety of other entities'. This is where CMS techniques are particularly valuable insofar as they 'can supply the means to explore these other possibility spaces in a rigorous way because the interactions in which the capacities are exercised can be staged in a simulation and varied in multiple ways until the singular features of the possibility space are made visible' (DeLanda, 2011: 21).

Elsewhere DeLanda discusses the sense in which the ontological status of assemblages is 'two-sided'. Every assemblage is an *individual* singularity, 'but the possibilities open to them at any given time are constrained by a distribution of *universal* singularities, the *diagram* of the assemblage, which is not actual but *virtual*' (DeLanda, 2006: 40, emphases added). Computer models can help scientists discover the *actual causal mechanisms* at work in assemblages but, as we noted above, the mechanism-independence of the topological structures that define the diagram of an assemblage is particularly relevant for understanding DeLanda's (and Deleuze's) proposals for a machinic (or materialist) metaphysics of pure immanence.

In this context, however, I want to stay focused on the unique ontological status that Deleuze (and DeLanda) grant to multiplicities (their real virtuality), and the role they play in the articulation of a metaphysics of pure immanence. Multiplicities are concrete universals that are part of 'a real dimension of the world, a nonmetric continuous space which progressively specifies itself giving rise to our familiar metric spaces as well as the discontinuous spatial structures that inhabit it' (DeLanda, 2002: 26). The concept of a singularity (borrowed from mathematical discussions of state space) is particularly important here. As indicated above, singularities can undergo transitions or bifurcations at particular thresholds of intensity when control parameters display critical values.

The multiplicities that populate the virtual are differentiated through processes of intensification into what we experience as a spatio-temporal field. Intensive processes and mechanisms are material and energetic, while the mechanism-independent structures of multiplicities are not, 'but even the latter remain *immanent* to the world of matter and energy' (DeLanda, 2002: 5). The ontological visions inspired by Plato and Aristotle, which are based on general types and particular instances, are '*hierarchical*, each level representing a different ontological category (organism, species, genera)', but 'an approach in terms of interacting parts and emergent wholes leads to a *flat ontology*, one made exclusively of unique, singular individuals, differing in spatio-temporal scale but not in ontological status' (DeLanda, 2002: 58).

The precision with which mathematical equations can model the patterns and behaviours of 'real world' material processes has appeared almost miraculous to many philosophers, leading some to interpret this as evidence for the independent existence of mathematical objects within a 'Platonic' realm of unchanging essences, or even for a divine creator, as the transcendent ground for this astonishing correspondence. Computational models might seem even more miraculous, since they can not only simulate and track the actual mechanisms driving a dynamic process but also help identify the conditions under which new properties, tendencies, and capacities can emerge. In the next chapter, we will return to the importance that the concept of emergence plays in DeLanda's articulation of assemblage theory and explore several concrete computational models that illustrate their 'generative' and explanatory power.

The main point here is that, for DeLanda, the 'miracle' of mathematical (and computer) models can be explained by considering both the formal relations in the equations of the latter and the causal mechanisms in the material processes whose behaviour they capture as *co-actualisations* of the singularities that structure the same diagram (or overlapping diagrams). These virtual diagrams – or universal singularities – are independent of any particular material mechanism and any particular mathematical solution, but they are not *transcendent*, nor do they *resemble* the material processes they model. DeLanda insists that we must always treat diagrams 'as immanent to matter, energy, and information'. Following Deleuze, he tries to accomplish this by philosophically synthesising insights from meta-mathematical developments in differential calculus, topology, and group theory. If successful, the payoff will be a powerful argument for 'breaking with the ontology we inherited from the classical Greek philosophers, and an incentive to develop a new one based on the individual singular and the universal singular' (2011: 203).

## The Achievement of Deleuze's Metaphysics

Philosophers define the terms 'metaphysics' and 'ontology' in different ways, but here I have been implicitly thinking of the latter as a philosopher's list of existential inventory items (and sorts of existing things), and of the former as the way in which she explains the conditions for the existence of things (if she does). For the most part, we have been exploring DeLanda's exposition of Deleuze's ontology, but he also tackles his metaphysics (in the sense of the term just mentioned). It involves not only the actualisation of material entities and intensive processes, but also an account of the production of the virtual continuum itself which is immanent to both the actual and the intensive. Throughout his work, Deleuze articulated a metaphysics (and ontology) of pure immanence utilising a diverse (and sometimes divergent) vocabulary, referring, for example, to 'machinic phylum', 'the body without organs', 'the aleatory or paradoxical point', 'lines of flight', 'desiring-machines', and 'the quasi-causal operator'. It is hardly surprising that this is sometimes all too quickly dismissed as 'postmodern' nonsense.

In my view, DeLanda has done philosophers (and scientists) a great favour by reconstructing Deleuze's view of the world using more straightforward and tractable terminology. Deleuze's philosophical engagement with the mathematical revolutions that made computer modelling and simulation possible produced a way of accounting for the becoming of beings without any appeals to transcendent realities or realms (DeLanda, 2012b). Deleuze himself was ambivalent about the use of the term metaphysics. At times, he seems to reject it: 'There is no metaphysics, but rather a politics of being' (Deleuze, 2005a: 717). At other times, however, he clearly embraces it, as when he equates desiring-production or desiring-machines with the metaphysical (e.g., AO, 392). For our purposes, it is less important that we call it metaphysics than that we recognise the radical achievement of Deleuze's philosophical atheist machine, the overturning or 'reversal' of Platonism.

As DeLanda points out, Deleuze appears to have been the first thinker in history to articulate mechanisms of immanence that could do the job. All of this might be unfamiliar to us, but 'he must at least be given credit for working out in detail (however speculatively) the requirements for the elimination of an immutable world of transcendent archetypes' (DeLanda, 2002: 88). In his own distinctive way, Deleuze worked out the radical philosophical consequences of the transformation of the problem–solution relation that resulted from the efforts of mathematicians such as Lagrange, Abel, and Galois, whose debates around differential calculus contributed to what today is called group theory. As we noted above, Deleuze called this transformation 'a more considerable revolution than the Copernican' (1995a: 180). Instead of allowing the 'solvability' of an equation to determine the well-posedness of a problem, the revolution to which Deleuze refers inverted the priority: 'It is not the solution which lends its generality to the problem, but the problem which lends its universality to the solution.' The problematic field does not simply 'condition' mathematical or conceptual solutions, but provides the '*differential* elements in thought, the *genetic* elements in the true' (DR, 162; emphases added).

Even (or especially) readers who are keen on accelerating the reversal of Platonism might object to the use of the term 'modelling' in the previous pages. However, it is important to note that Deleuze himself sometimes used the concept of model (like the concept of 'Idea') in ways that were quite different from Plato's. In *Difference and Repetition*, for example, he called for replacing the model of the Same (icons) with simulacra as a 'model of the Other, an other model, the model of difference in itself from which flows ... interiorized dissimilitude' (DR, 128). It should be clear from the preceding that the term 'modelling' in computer science, with all of its emphasis on dynamic relations in differential equations, should not be understood as reinforcing the classical Platonic privileging of substance, stasis, and sameness.

Others might object that the language of computer simulations (and the meta-mathematical developments that fuelled its rise) is only 'metaphorical' and cannot have the metaphysical force DeLanda intends. We might well be able to construct 'artificial societies' and test our hypotheses about social assemblages *in silico*, but does this really have anything to do with our experience of the 'natural world' *in situ*? However, as Deleuze points out in *A Thousand Plateaus*, the diagrammatic abstract machine '*knows nothing of the distinction between the artificial and the natural* ... [it is] pure Matter-Function – a diagram independent of the forms and substances, expressions and contents it will distribute' (ATP, 156; emphasis added). There is obviously a difference between the dynamics of a simulation run exploring the state space of a computer model and the dynamics of a bio-cultural organism exploring the physical space in which it lives and moves and (de)territorialises. However, both may be taken as (mathematical or material) *effectuations* of abstract machines that are developing on the plane of consistency and being enveloped in various strata (digital or geographical).

For Deleuze, as we noted above, to reverse Platonism 'is first and foremost to remove essences and to substitute events in their place, as jets of *singularities*' (LOS, 56; emphasis added). The 'essences' of the Platonic tradition are eternally identical and static substances, but Deleuzian 'singularities' are relational, dynamic, and differentiated. The former are transcendent Ideas in relation to which matter serves as a passive receptacle, while the latter are immanent to material processes – 'virtual' differential manifolds with a morphogenetic relation to 'actual' emergent events.

In this chapter, I have attempted to show how Deleuze's metaphysics can clarify what is going on in the practice of computational modelling and social simulation – and how the latter can reinforce the plausibility of the former, thereby accelerating the reversal of Platonism. Instead of relying on the abstract categories of substance, stasis, and sameness, modern computational advances have demonstrated the concrete explanatory power of relational, dynamic, and differentiating categories. Most of the Western philosophical tradition has followed Plato in attempting to make sense of being(s) by appealing to a transcendent ground or ultimate reality. The development and relatively successful deployment of CMS methodologies have provided conceptual resources for scholars who want to renew and extend the efforts of a long line of philosophers (albeit a 'minority report' in the tradition) who have tried to invert Platonism and argue that the becoming of beings can be accounted for by mechanisms of pure immanence.

My primary intended audience here has been philosophers and other scholars who are already interested in the Deleuzian literary machine, but who may not have thought through the philosophical implications of recent developments in computer science. However, modelling and simulation techniques in the latter are growing rapidly in popularity as a tool for thinking among philosophers in general, and so I also hope to have provided a point of entry and piqued the interest of scholars not familiar with the univocal ontology developed throughout Deleuze's works.

But does this have any practical relevance in the 'real world'? Will this revolutionary metaphysical reversal of Platonism (if it continues to unfold) affect the way we think and live together as human beings? As DeLanda has argued in other contexts, the philosophical replacement of essences with multiplicities also enables a completely new way of understanding and explaining the emergent dynamics of social assemblages (DeLanda, 2006; 2016). At the end of the last chapter, we pointed to examples of computational models that have explicitly attempted to simulate major shifts in the civilisational form of human societies, and in the chapters that follow we will provide examples of models that illuminate the conditions under which – and the mechanisms by which – interactions between human groups can engender conflict or promote wider cooperation.

We humans are just beginning to utilise computational models and other simulation technologies to figure out how to adapt to our contemporary environment, with all of its social and ecological challenges. Taking advantage of these tools in order to actualise desirable human futures will not be easy; it will require a great deal of epistemic humility and ethical dialogue among a wide variety of stakeholders. Computer engineers, philosophers, and social scientists can help by working together to articulate and explore the *virtual* structures of the possibility (or phase) space of *actual* human assemblages, facilitating both a better understanding of such assemblages and a higher capacity for enhancing their sustainability.

# 4

# Assemblage Theory and Multi-agent Artificial Intelligence Modelling

Over the last few years there has been an explosion of interest among social scientists, especially those with a disposition towards philosophical reflection on the conditions for knowledge about the causal forces at work in social systems, in 'assemblage theory' as originally developed by Deleuze and Guattari in *A Thousand Plateaus* and further articulated by DeLanda (2016; 2006). It is not hard to understand why. Assemblage thinking has provided scholars with a set of heuristic frameworks and conceptual tools that have helped to dissolve the hegemony of static and essentialist notions in the social sciences and to replace them with a renewed ontological emphasis on relationality, dynamism, and differentiation (i.e., categories involved in the reversal of Platonism). Assemblage theory has been utilised among social scientists to study a diversity of topics in disciplines such as economics (Roffe, 2015), archaeology (Jervis, 2018), social planning (Van Wezemael, 2008), educational management (Bacevic, 2019), health geography (Duff, 2022), and international relations (Acuto and Curtis, 2014).

In this chapter, I focus on the discipline of human geography as my primary example. A growing number of human geographers have turned to assemblage theory as a framework for understanding and explaining the socio-material systems they study. Surprisingly, however, like most other social scientists interested in assemblage theory, they seem not to have noticed that DeLanda's own philosophical framing of the theory is informed by and linked to the use of computer modelling and simulation (CMS). This is most explicit in his book *Philosophy and Simulation: The Emergence of Synthetic Reason* (2011), which is occasionally cited but seldom examined in detail by human geographers. Those who do cite the book rarely comment on his arguments there about the key role of CMS in articulating and applying assemblage theory or about the potential of CMS methodologies for the social sciences in general. This is all the more surprising since DeLanda also alludes to CMS in his earlier *A New Philosophy of Society: Assemblage Theory and Complexity* (2006) and his later *Assemblage Theory* (2016), both of which have been rigorously engaged with by human geographers interested in assemblage theory.

It is also surprising that most scholars interested in using computational tools to address research questions in human geography seem not to have noticed that the successful development and deployment of these techniques lend plausibility to the ontological and causal claims embedded within assemblage theory. Computer simulation techniques, especially agent-based modelling (ABM), have been extensively utilised by human geographers to analyse the causal dynamics and emergent patterns within complex adaptive socio-material systems (e.g., Heppenstall et al., 2011; Manson et al., 2012). Calls for a more intensive use of ABM have been recommended for research in human geography in particular because of the way in which it provides 'a good venue for even more broadly integrative science' (O'Sullivan, 2008: 547), allows 'for experimentation in virtual worlds' (Miller, 2018: 606), offers 'an unparalleled tool for modelling human decisions' (Liu et al., 2021: 14), and can be 'used for explaining social structures and relations and *how they might change in the future*' (Millington and Wainwright, 2017: 78). This modelling literature occasionally cites DeLanda but does not spell out the relevance of CMS for *theorising assemblages* in human-geographic systems.

## Theorising Assemblages in Human Geography

In this chapter I draw attention to this conspicuous – and yet, oddly enough, rarely noticed – lack of engagement with DeLanda's *Philosophy and Simulation* by human geographers, both among those interested in the philosophical implications of assemblage theory and among those regularly utilising CMS methods in their research. I argue that highlighting the connections between assemblage theory and CMS can facilitate a more robust philosophical understanding and practical application of both. Several human geographers interested in assemblage theory have called for more attention to the processes whereby these complex socio-material wholes stabilise and change (Anderson and McFarlane, 2011; Dittmer, 2014; Turker and Murphy, 2019). Here I respond to this call by showing how the integration of CMS into this discourse can promote progress in simulating the *conditions* under which – and the *mechanisms* by which – social assemblages form and transform.

How can CMS inform the way in which assemblages are theorised in human geography? In this context I focus primarily on the ability of ABM methodologies, especially multi-agent artificial intelligence (MAAI) modelling, to simulate the *emergence* of macro-level wholes (social assemblages) with properties, capacities, and tendencies that are irreducible to their micro-level parts, and on the implications of the successful use of CMS for human geographers and scholars in related fields interested in assemblage theory.

The genealogy and use of the term 'assemblage' (the most common translation of the French word *agencement* in the work of Deleuze and Guattari) is contentious and contested among social scientists, and many scholars prefer formulations developed by or derived from Latour, Foucault, or others (e.g., Braun, 2006; Shaw, 2012; Legg, 2011; Allen, 2011; Greenhough, 2011). Here, however, I will focus primarily on some of the ways in which the field has engaged with and appropriated aspects of the work of Deleuze as modified and formalised in DeLanda's version of assemblage theory.

Following Deleuze, DeLanda conceptualises assemblages as wholes characterised by 'relations of exteriority', which implies that the component parts of an assemblage can be 'detached' from the assemblage and 'plugged into' other assemblages, and that the 'properties' of the component parts cannot explain the properties of the whole because the latter 'are the result not of an aggregation of the components' own properties but of the actual exercise of their capacities' (DeLanda, 2006: 10–11). We will return to the importance of this distinction between properties and capacities (as well as tendencies) below. DeLanda also follows the authors of *A Thousand Plateaus* in defining the concept of assemblage as operating along two concomitant axes: one that describes the intermingling of machinic assemblages of bodies and collective assemblages of enunciation, and one that describes the simultaneous movements of territorialisation and deterritorialisation.

One of the main differences in DeLanda's articulation, however, is his emphasis on assemblages as *emergent* wholes. Deleuze did not use this concept often (it was not very popular in the 1970s), but he did use a variety of other closely related terms (e.g., morphogenesis, becoming, production, individuation). In *Philosophy and Simulation*, DeLanda asks: in what kinds of concrete emergent wholes can we believe? His answer: 'Wholes the identity of which is determined historically by the processes that *initiated and sustain* the interactions between their parts. The *historically contingent* identity of these wholes is defined by their emergent properties, capacities, and tendencies' (DeLanda, 2011: 3, emphases added). As we saw in Chapter 3, DeLanda finds the concept of emergence in general (and CMS in particular) helpful not only for linking assemblage theory to contemporary debates in science and philosophy, but also for explaining how social wholes are not transcendent to their parts but exist alongside them on the same (immanent) ontological plane (DeLanda, 2016: 12).

Human geographers regularly discuss the ontological assumptions of assemblage theory (e.g., Rogers, 2018; Bridge, 2020), but the metaphysical ramifications of the success of CMS methodologies for what Deleuze called the 'reversal of Platonism', the philosophical move that undergirds assemblage thinking, have not been as deeply explored. The following sections further spell out some of the implications of CMS for understanding and explaining the *emergence* of new social assemblages within a materialist metaphysics of *immanence*. In the remainder of this section, I describe some of the ways in which assemblage theory has been appropriated and applied by human geographers. Scholars have discussed the potential (as well as the limitations) of assemblage thinking for engaging with a wide variety of topics such as the instability of 'oil landscapes' (Haarstad and Wanvik, 2017), the need for 'critical data studies' in a world increasingly dominated by computation and big data (Pickren, 2018), and the importance of taking more seriously feminist analyses of social difference, power, and inequality (Kinkaid, 2020b). Here I focus on examples of human geographers who have explicitly engaged with DeLanda's work in ways that highlight the relevance of the concept of emergence.

In their article 'On Assemblage and Human Geography', which includes a rigorous engagement with DeLanda as well as Deleuze and Guattari, Anderson et al. identified four things that assemblage thinking offers to human geography:

> an experimental realism orientated to processes of composition; a theorization of a world of relations *and* that which exceeds a present set of relations; a rethinking of agency in distributed terms and causality in non-linear, immanent terms; and an orientation to the expressive capacity of assembled orders as they are stabilized and change. (2012a: 171)

Each of these topics is more or less related to the issue of emergence, a link that the authors make explicit: 'An assemblage is finite: an emergent effect of processes of gathering and dispersion' (2012a: 177). They spell this out in the context of a discussion of agency and causality: 'Assemblage operates not just as a concept aimed at understanding how a set of relations emerge and hold together across differences, but as an ethos for thinking the relations between durability and transformation' (2012a: 180).

The authors do discuss DeLanda's *Philosophy and Simulation* and highlight the value of his use of the distinction in that book between properties, capacities, and tendencies in his solution to the 'problematic of the stability in form' (2012a: 185), but they do not examine the central role of CMS in the solution that he exposits in that book. Elsewhere two of these authors point out that the term assemblage 'is often used to emphasize emergence, multiplicity and indeterminacy, and connects to a wider redefinition of the socio-spatial in terms of the composition of diverse elements into some form of provisional socio-spatial formation' (Anderson and McFarlane, 2011: 124; see also McFarlane and Anderson, 2011; Anderson et al., 2012b). One of the goals of the current chapter is to show how more detailed attention to DeLanda's reliance on CMS in his articulation of assemblage theory can render the latter even more useful for human geographers and other social scientists.

Some other human geographers have misinterpreted DeLanda's version of assemblage theory as utilising 'essentialised' concepts, leading to 'fixed' rather than dynamic boundaries, and failing to adequately conceptualise the 'manifold mechanisms' of social change (Müller and Schurr, 2016; Turker and Murphy, 2019). These misreadings ignore DeLanda's explicit claims to the contrary in his philosophical and computational writings (e.g., 2002; 2011), which are not cited by these authors. As DeLanda makes clear throughout *Philosophy and Simulation*, CMS provides distinctive tools that can identify the *mechanisms* at work in the *dynamic* and *historical* processes by which the new properties, capacities, and tendencies of emergent social assemblages are produced. The heterogeneity of the parts and the intricacies of their interactions in the histories of such assemblages renders the process of modelling them quite complex. It is precisely here, however, that one finds the greatest opportunities for making progress in simulating human geography. Incorporating DeLanda's treatment of CMS into this discourse will not only protect against such misreadings, but also facilitate the outcome for which his critics are calling: the wider use of assemblage theory as an 'adaptable template' for studying phenomena such as the emergence, resilience, and sustainability of community economies in a way that emphasises '*relations* between heterogeneous actors constituting an assemblage, *resources and constraints* which flow from an assemblage to its constituent actors, and *processes of (de)stabilization*' (Turker and Murphy, 2019: 17).

One notable exception to the relative lack of attention to DeLanda's focus on CMS in *Philosophy and Simulation* in the assemblage theory literature is an article on 'Geopolitical Assemblages and Complexity' (Dittmer, 2014). In that context, Dittmer mentions several of the unique benefits of CMS technologies highlighted by DeLanda in his 2011 book, including their ability to identify the 'tipping points' or thresholds for non-linear change in complex social systems. In his concluding methodological section, however, Dittmer leaves CMS aside and calls for more applications of assemblage theory in 'historical analysis' in a way that complements other methods such as 'ethnography, interviews and performative research' (2014: 396). I agree that the latter methods ought to be embraced and renewed in human geography, but hope that scholars in the field will pause a little longer to explore the value of CMS as a way of promoting assemblage thinking and fostering policy-oriented research that can incorporate insights gained from all of these other methods.

First, however, it is important to note a potential objection. Ian Buchanan has criticised some human geographers for detaching the concept of *agencement* from its philosophical roots and replacing it with 'a synthetic accumulation of readings of Deleuze and Guattari' (Buchanan, 2017: 459), and confusing it with concepts proposed by Latour, Foucault, and others (Buchanan, 2015). As Buchanan makes clear in his recent book on *Assemblage Theory and Method*, which is quite critical of DeLanda, his interest in returning to the original authors of the concept is not simply a matter of scholarly precision but also, and even primarily, the potential role that Deleuze and Guattari's emphasis on what assemblages *do* (how they work, what they produce, etc.) could play in the critical analysis and evaluation of policies and politics (Buchanan, 2020). While I share many of Buchanan's concerns about these issues, as well as his passion for utilising assemblage theory for policy analysis and evaluation, in my view the adaptation or bricolage of elements from various conceptualisations of 'assemblage' is not inherently problematic, as long as theorists are clear about the genealogy of their claims and the operationalisation of their terms. And it is to this task of clarification that we now turn.

## A Thousand Abstract Machines

Deleuze and Guattari first set out the concept of assemblage in detail in *A Thousand Plateaus*. As we saw in Chapter 1, assemblages and abstract machines can only be understood together. In an interview given soon after it was published, Deleuze indicated that he thought of *A Thousand Plateaus* as 'just plain old philosophy' (Deleuze, 2007: 176). My interest here is also in plain old philosophy, indeed in what Aristotle called 'first philosophy' (metaphysics). This chapter continues to explore the potential benefits of bringing the conceptual apparatus of *A Thousand Plateaus* (and the broader Deleuzian corpus) and the computational apparatus of 'simulating machines' into more explicit philosophical dialogue, sketching some of the ways in which the former can help to explain the methodological success of the latter – and indicating the extent to which that success can itself bolster the articulation of a metaphysics of immanence.

Building on the argument set out in Chapter 3, here I aim to show how incorporating insights from the theory and practice of computer modelling and simulation can inform the machinic metaphysics articulated in *A Thousand Plateaus* – and vice versa. On the one hand, the conceptual apparatus of *A Thousand Plateaus*, and especially its machinic metaphysics, can be connected to recent developments in computer modelling and social simulation, which provide new tools for thinking that are becoming increasingly popular among philosophers and social scientists. On the other hand, the successful deployment of these tools provides warrant for the flat ontology articulated in *A Thousand Plateaus* and therefore contributes to the 'reversal of Platonism' for which Deleuze had called in his earlier works, such as *Difference and Repetition* and *The Logic of Sense*.

As noted above, Deleuze had argued in *The Logic of Sense* that '[t]o reverse Platonism is *first and foremost* to remove essences and to substitute events in their place, as jets of *singularities*' (LOS, 56; emphasis added). In that context he used the idea of singularities as a 'hypothesis' for explaining the determination of the 'transcendental field' (or 'metaphysical surface') as well as its 'genetic power' (LOS, 101). As discussed in Chapter 3, the concept of *singularities* is particularly important for our purposes here, both because of the mathematical role it plays in modelling possibility (or phase) spaces for computer simulation experiments and because of the philosophical role it plays in overturning Platonism through the experimental affirmation of the simulacra. This concept provides a way of answering the question about the *effectuation* of abstract machines by assemblages (or, to use the terms of *Difference and Repetition*, the actualisation of the virtual) without appealing to the causal power of transcendent Ideals (or a divine Creator).

Deleuze explicitly based his proposal in *The Logic of Sense* on Lautmann's interpretation of the theory of differential equations, which distinguishes between the (topological) *existence and distribution* of singularities within a field of vectors and the *nature* of the singularities as defined by the integral curves in the vicinity of singularities inside the field of vectors. For Deleuze, the former are related to the *problem* that is defined by the equation as such, while the latter bear on the *solutions* of the equation over whose genesis the singularities preside. We saw in the previous chapter the crucial role that this distinction, drawn from developments in mathematics related to differential calculus, group theory, and topology, played in his speculative argument for a metaphysics of pure immanence. (For a discussion of Deleuze's philosophical engagement with the relevant historical developments in mathematics, especially Poincaré's concept of singularities, see Duffy, 2013. For a discussion of the implications of Deleuze's use of the concept of the diagrammatic, derived from developments in what is now often called category theory, for a philosophy of immanence, see Gangle, 2015.)

From the point of view of what Deleuze calls the 'static ontological genesis' in *The Logic of Sense*, it is the 'nature' of a singularity, 'in conformity with which it extends and spreads itself out in a determined direction over a line of ordinary points' (rather than its 'existence and directionless distribution') that marks 'a beginning of the *effectuation* of the singularities'. Deleuze argues that this 'first level of *effectuation* produces correlatively individuated worlds and individual selves which populate each of these worlds. Individuals are constituted in the vicinity of singularities which they *envelop*' (LOS, 113, 115; translation emended and emphases added).

Deleuze's interest in overturning Platonism is maintained and sustained in the 'machinic' metaphysics of *A Thousand Plateaus*, which makes significant use of some of the same mathematical concepts (such as *singularities* and *multiplicities*) whose development has fuelled advances in computer modelling and simulation. In his description of the ideally continuous 'machinic phylum' in *A Thousand Plateaus*, Deleuze defines an assemblage as any *'constellation of singularities* and traits deducted from the flow – selected, organized, stratified – in such a way as to converge (consistency) artificially and naturally; an assemblage, in this sense, is a veritable invention' (ATP, 448–9; emphasis added). Each concrete assemblage is a 'multiplicity' of 'the abstract Machine' (ATP, 278) which *simultaneously* stratifies the plane of consistency and deterritorialises assemblages.

The concept of multiplicities, which is explicitly tied to singularities in both *Difference and Repetition* and *The Logic of Sense*, also plays a key role in the discussion of a 'mathematical model' for depicting the relation between smooth and striated space (ATP, 532–8). The language of differential calculus is also used in the description of the war machine and nomad sciences: '*There are itinerant, ambulant sciences that consist in following a flow in a vectorial field across which singularities are scattered like so many "accidents"* (problems)' (ATP, 411). Just as the 'problematic field', as an ideal event defined by the equation, is distinguished, without being separated, from the spatio-temporal effectuation of the event in *The Logic of Sense* (see, e.g., LOS, 56–7, 105–11; cf. *Difference and Repetition*, chapters 3 and 4), in *A Thousand Plateaus* Deleuze distinguishes, without separating, the plane of consistency (as diagrammed by abstract machines) from machinic assemblages (as effectuations of abstract machines).

Innumerable abstract machines developed on the plane of consistency that they draw and enveloped within the strata that they organise. This is Deleuze's attempt to explain the ontogenesis of assemblages without reference to any transcendent models that they are supposed to resemble. But what does any of this have to do with computer 'modelling' and 'simulation', which I have suggested can accelerate the reversal of Platonism? In this chapter my claim is that the fabrication of a metaphysics of immanence can be facilitated by connecting ideas developed by Deleuze in *A Thousand Plateaus* (and elsewhere) more explicitly to insights derived from philosophical analyses of CMS and the social scientific use of DeLanda's version of assemblage theory. Moreover, engaging with developments in CMS can help clarify the concepts at work in assemblage thinking and provide new practical tools for cautious (or prudent) experimentation in the formation and extension of rhizomes, the relaying of lines of flight, the conjugation of deterritorialised flows, the construction of a Body without Organs etc.

As I noted in Chapter 3, DeLanda has done more than any other scholar to highlight and explicate the potential value of CMS for facilitating these philosophical and pragmatic tasks. Among Deleuze scholars, DeLanda is best-known for his reconstruction of Deleuze's philosophy in *Intensive Science and Virtual Philosophy* (DeLanda, 2002), which has been widely engaged with in the secondary literature. Among social scientists, DeLanda is best-known for his unique formulation of assemblage theory, which itself relies heavily on the conceptual apparatus of *A Thousand Plateaus*. This is another reason for selecting him as a guide in this context. What seems to be least well-known about DeLanda, however, is the extent to which both his version of assemblage theory and his reading of Deleuze are shaped by his practical experience and scholarly expertise in CMS. He does allude to mathematical state spaces and computational methods in both *A New Philosophy of Society: Assemblage Theory and Social Complexity* (DeLanda, 2006) and his more recent *Assemblage Theory* (DeLanda, 2016), but the central role that CMS has played in shaping his approach may not be immediately obvious there.

The centrality of CMS as a motivational and regulative force in DeLanda's reading of Deleuze and his formulation of assemblage theory becomes exceptionally clear in *Philosophy and Simulation: The Emergence of Synthetic Reason* (DeLanda, 2011a), which has been almost completely ignored by Deleuze scholars and assemblage thinkers alike. Fans of DeLanda have used his version of assemblage theory to illuminate a wide range of social dynamics including urban planning, human geography, and culture-led policymaking (Baker and McGuirk, 2017; Blok and Farías, 2016; Dovey and Ristic, 2017; Lysgård, 2019), and have called for its application in disciplines such as psychology (Price-Robertson and Duff, 2016) and international relations (Acuto and Curtis, 2014). Some critics have worried that DeLanda's use of the term 'assemblage' in his new philosophy of society fails to carry over the richness of Deleuze and Guattari's original concept of *agencement* (Acselrad and Bezerra, 2010; Buchanan, 2015; 2017; Clough et al., 2007).

My interest here, however, is not in defending DeLanda's appropriation of Deleuze (the former explicitly acknowledges several points at which his approach moves beyond and even disagrees with the latter), but in encouraging both fans and critics of assemblage theory to pay closer attention to the role played by CMS in DeLanda's metaphysical and social scientific proposals. For that reason, I will focus primarily on his formulation of assemblage theory in the context of *Philosophy and Simulation*. Most of that book is an overview of developments in computational technologies (e.g., cellular automata, neural nets, multi-agent modelling) that have enabled scientists to account for the emergence and behaviour of complex wholes or 'assemblages' by simulating the (fully immanent) intensive differential processes that actually generate them in the real world. Thunderstorms, chemical flows, prebiotic soup, ancient organisms, insect intelligence, mammalian memory, Stone Age economics, and archaic states: all of these assemblages (and more) can be studied in virtual environments through simulation experiments that can help scientists discover the conditions under which – and the *mechanisms* by which – new properties, tendencies, and capacities emerge. In other words, CMS provides us with the ability to 'simulate' *agencement*.

## DeLanda's Assemblage Theory and the Simulation of Emergence

DeLanda's distinctive conceptualisation and articulation of assemblage theory can only be fully understood by taking into account the extent to which he has drawn from both the generative philosophy of Gilles Deleuze *and* the generative science of CMS. The former has received far more attention (e.g., Bell, 2006; Bryant, 2003; De Beistegui, 2004; 2010; Hughes, 2008a; 2012; Kerslake, 2019; Lundy and Voss, 2015; Rolli, 2016; Smith, 2012; Voss, 2013), and so in this context I focus more on the role of the latter in DeLanda's work. His first book, *War in the Age of Intelligent Machines* (DeLanda, 1991), which explicitly adopted and adapted language from *A Thousand Plateaus*, also explicitly explored the relevance of developments in CMS for social science. Over the years that followed, DeLanda has often returned to the potential epistemological implications of the capacity of computational techniques to create 'virtual environments' that could be experimentally explored and analysed in ways that shed light on the mechanisms by which new synergistic properties of social systems can emerge from the bottom-up interactions of their agents.

In his earlier book on Deleuze, *Virtual Philosophy and Intensive Science*, DeLanda outlined the metaphysical naturalism or 'materialism' more or less explicitly articulated in the former's theory of assemblages (DeLanda, 2002). But how is this related to emergence and what exactly does CMS contribute to this discussion? To frame our answers to these questions, it may be helpful to point again to the debates between proponents of 'weak' and 'strong' emergence. Advocates of the former typically interpret higher-level emergent properties in a complex system as the result of the organisation of causes among (or, equivalently, the form of) their lower-level components. Advocates of the latter who reject supervenience (the claim that there are no differences in emergent properties without matching differences in the organisation of lower-level components) make metaphysical room for entities and causal forces that are qualitatively different from and transcendent to the natural world studied in the sciences (Wildman and Shults, 2018).

The popularity of this quasi-theological 'strong' view of emergence in the twentieth century led many social scientists to resist the concept itself and focus instead on reductive explanations.

As we saw in Chapter 3, DeLanda emphasises the role of simulation in restoring the legitimacy of the concept of emergence as well as clarifying the mechanisms and interactions by which properties, tendencies, and capacities of new dynamic complex wholes (assemblages) actually emerge. Emergence is now reproducible through simulations that function as laboratory experiments for studying the structure of the phase (or state) space of a computational model. Because 'virtual' structured possibility spaces are mechanism-independent, topological facts about them (such as attractor spaces that constitute and constrain their tendencies and capacities) can be discovered by studying the nature and number of their degrees of freedom without reference to any 'actual' material-energetic gradient – as long as *some* gradient exists. To cite the key conclusion again: 'The fact that the *existence* of a gradient, any gradient, is *necessary* confirms the *immanent* status of singularities. Singularities are, therefore, perfectly acceptable entities in a *materialist* philosophy' (DeLanda, 2011: 20, emphases added).

How is this related to Deleuze's project of reversing (or inverting) 'Platonism'? As we saw above, the latter is commonly understood as promoting a view that explains the apparent *emergence* of new forms of matter by postulating static and eternally identical 'essences' that function as transcendent Ideas in relation to which matter serves as a passive receptacle. Deleuze replaces essences with relational, dynamic, and differentiated singularities or 'multiplicities' that are immanent to material processes; that is, differential manifolds with an intimate relation to the morphogenesis of *actually emergent* entities. As noted in the previous chapter, DeLanda credits Deleuze as being the first thinker in history to articulate mechanisms of immanence that could account for the becoming of beings without any appeal to transcendence, a feat made possible only though his rigorous engagement with developments in meta-mathematics that paved the way for CMS (DeLanda, 2002: 88).

DeLanda's *Philosophy and Simulation* focuses in almost every chapter on the way in which CMS sheds light on the philosophical problem of emergence. He provides many examples of computational tools – such as cellular automata, neural nets, and multi-agent modelling – that enable the simulation of the emergence of a wide range of 'assemblages' (such as thunderstorms, mammalian memory, and archaic states) in 'virtual worlds'. Below I will discuss some examples of computational models that are particularly relevant for making progress in simulating human geography. At this stage, however, I want to briefly illustrate the intimate link between DeLanda's fascination with CMS and the three main tenets of his version of assemblage theory. The latter can be reconstructed in the following way:

- Every assemblage is an *individual* singularity whose *properties* are the product of a *historical* process.
- Every assemblage is actualised in relation to a *universal* singularity whose real, mechanism-independent, *structured possibility space* defines the *capacities* and *tendencies* of the assemblage.
- Every assemblage is part of a *population* with distributed *variables* whose alteration is conditioned by *parameters* such as (de)territorialisation and (de)coding.

What does it mean to say that an assemblage is an *individual* singularity? This is DeLanda's way of insisting that an assemblage is 'always contingent and not guaranteed by the existence of a necessary set of properties constituting an unchanging essence'. On the contrary, assemblages must be understood as the emergent outcomes of historical processes that produce 'unique and singular individuals' (2011: 185). For example, the temperature or density of any assemblage of water molecules is an emergent property of that particular, historically formed individual singularity. The same holds for properties such as the solidarity or legitimacy of an assemblage of persons. We do not need 'essences' (such as human nature or a discrete political state) to make sense of either the properties of a social assemblage nor the social assemblage itself. All individual singularities are 'irreducible and nondecomposable wholes' and can be explained by 'elucidating the mechanisms that produce them at one scale and by showing that emergent entities at that scale can become the component parts of a whole at a larger scale' (2011: 12).

DeLanda is eager, like Deleuze, to replace the traditional philosophical reliance on essentialist and hierarchical notions of entities as particular instances of a general category with a 'flat' ontology that 'contains nothing but differently scaled *individual singularities* (or *hacceities*)' (DeLanda, 2006: 28, emphasis in original). In this approach, an assemblage's properties, whether 'physical' (such as the temperature or density of water molecules) or 'social' (such as the solidarity or legitimacy of an assemblage of persons), are considered to be emergent. But how do they emerge? This is where computer simulations come in. As DeLanda points out, they are able to identify the *mechanisms* at work in the dynamic historical processes by which the new properties of emergent wholes are produced. No other tool can link micro- and macro-level factors in this way, which helps to explain why such computational methodologies are rapidly gaining in popularity among social scientists.

The concept of a *universal* singularity might initially sound more difficult, but DeLanda is actually referring to a reality that is well understood in the field of CMS: a mechanism-independent, structured possibility space in relation to which every individual singularity is actualised. One can think here of the 'phase space' of a computational model within which individual simulation runs are (dynamically, historically, and uniquely) executed. While the first tenet above focuses on the properties of an emergent assemblage, the second introduces the concepts of capacities and tendencies. Let's stick with DeLanda's own example: a kitchen knife. The triangular shaped blade of a knife may have the emergent *property* of sharpness, a property not shared by the molecules of which it is composed. The knife will have this property as long as the metallic atoms of its blade are so arranged. But the knife also has the *capacity* to cut, a capacity that will only be exercised if its blade interacts in a particular way with some cuttable assemblage. The knife also has the *tendency* to liquefy at a particular temperature, a tendency that will only be manifested if its temperature reaches that critical point. The properties of a sharpened knife are always actual, but its capacities and tendencies may never be actualised.

What is the ontological status of these latter two qualities? DeLanda argues that we should think of unexercised capacities and unmanifested tendencies as defining 'a concrete space of possibilities with a definite structure' (2011: 17). The possibilities that are opened up to an individual singularity at any given time 'are constrained by a distribution of universal singularities, the diagram of the assemblage, which is not actual but virtual' (DeLanda, 2006: 40). In other words, capacities and tendencies are ontologically real (as virtual). This second aspect of DeLanda's definition of an assemblage is of even more relevance for understanding the way in which CMS can play a role in accelerating the reversal of Platonism. Every assemblage is actualised (or effectuated) in relation to a *universal* singularity. Although he does not explicitly refer to 'abstract machines' in this context, DeLanda is engaging with the 'most important' problem posed by Deleuze and Guattari in *A Thousand Plateaus* which, as we saw in Chapter 1, explores the effectuation (or actualisation) of assemblages.

The third main tenet of assemblage theory identified above helps to make the value of CMS methodologies for disciplines such as human geography even more explicit. DeLanda argues that 'population thinking' enables us to account for the similarities between some assemblages (e.g., the resemblance of members of a species or the isomorphism of political systems) in a way that avoids the need for appeals to transcendent essences or generic categories. Every assemblage is a unique *individual* singularity but still belongs to a *population* of assemblages that are more or less similar. This is because processes that lead to assemblages tend to be recurrent, and this 'recurrence itself is explained by the fact that the assembly process is governed by *universal* singularities', the actualisation of which 'is always subject to contingent events so what is generated is a population in which *variants* are distributed in a certain way' (2011: 186, emphases added). As we will see below, social simulation may include 'variables' such as individual psychological tendencies or institutional political capacities.

How can we make sense both of the way in which the members of any population change and of the status of their identity at any given stage of their productive historical process? DeLanda's answer to this question is to *parametrise* the concept of assemblage. In the context of CMS methodologies, a 'parameter' can specify environmental factors (e.g., demographic density, resource scarcity) that impact the interactions of agents within a complex adaptive socio-ecological system. Simulation experiments can then explore the behaviour of that system as the relevant parameters are varied (or held stable). 'Variables', of course, designate the relevant ways in which the system or its components can change (such as an agent's tolerance towards outgroups). As DeLanda argues throughout *Philosophy and Simulation*, computer modelling provides a unique way of discovering the actual mechanisms that generate the emergent properties of assemblages as well as the parametric conditions under which the various tendencies and capacities defined by virtual mechanism-independent structures are most likely to be manifested or exercised.

The value of this philosophically informed use of computational modelling for social scientists interested in applying assemblage theory to analyses of real-world societal challenges should be increasingly clear. In the next section, I introduce and illustrate a particular approach to modelling and simulation that I believe shows particularly strong promise for studying human-geographical systems and other phenomena studied by social scientists.

## Emergent Social Assemblages in Multi-agent Artificial Intelligence Modelling

As noted above, several human geographers have already taken advantage of CMS methodologies, especially ABM, in order to analyse the interactions among the heterogeneous parts of the complex human-geographical systems they study. However, the potential fecundity of the link between such approaches and assemblage theory has not yet received significant attention. In the final chapter of *Philosophy and Simulation*, DeLanda discusses ways in which multi-agent modelling can provide a distinctive way of illuminating the actual mechanisms that generate the emergent properties of social assemblages, such as status and legitimacy. He also explains how they can illuminate the parametric conditions under which the manifestation of their tendencies and the exercise of their capacities (as defined by their structured possibility spaces) are most likely to occur. For example, 'rigid social stratification' emerges from the interaction of increased *material* and *status* gradients in complex chiefdoms (DeLanda, 2011: 172). Along with this new property comes new capacities and tendencies, such as those related to supernatural beliefs and incest taboos. In 2011, when *Philosophy and Simulation* was published, agent architectures that incorporated beliefs, desires, and intentions were in relatively early stages of development, as were techniques for exploring the structured possibility spaces of artificial societies.

A lot has happened in CMS since DeLanda's book was published. Of particular relevance for human geography and related disciplines is the development of a method sometimes referred to as multi-agent artificial intelligence (MAAI) modelling, which strives to develop simulated agents and virtual worlds that are more cognitively and culturally realistic than traditional ABMs (Lane, 2013; Gore et al., 2018; Diallo et al., 2019; Shults, Wildman, et al., 2020a; Lane and Shults, 2020). The implications of this approach for the scientific study of religion has been discussed in most detail in Justin Lane's *Understanding Religion Through Artificial Intelligence* (2021). It is important to note that the use of the term 'artificial' in this context has nothing to do with a dualism between the natural and the artificial of the sort that Deleuze explicitly rejected (e.g., ATP, 156). 'Artificial intelligence' is as natural as human intelligence, and the algorithms driving the latter are as artificial as those in computational programs.

Unlike most traditional AI technologies such as machine learning, multi-agent artificial intelligence simulates artificial *societies* populated by heterogeneous agents in realistic social networks and parametrised *environments*. Unlike most game theoretic approaches such as prisoner's dilemma models, the computational architectures in MAAI typically involve adaptive agents characterised by bounded reasoning whose behaviours and interactions occur within differentiated social networks (informed by disciplines such as evolutionary biology, social psychology, and political sociology). When appropriately calibrated, verified, and validated such models can shed light on the *conditions* under which – and the *mechanisms* by which – the variables that compose complex adaptive socio-material systems can be altered. This approach moves beyond correlational observations, providing plausibility to claims about *causality* in human-geographical systems by 'growing' the macro-level structural patterns of interest from the micro-level behaviours and meso-level interactions of simulated agents.

In the remainder of this section, I provide a couple of brief case studies meant to illustrate some of the ways in which MAAI can be especially useful for human geographers interested in assemblage theory. To exemplify the potential of CMS, we might have selected one of the models cited above, which were developed explicitly to address topics of relevance in human geography. Or we might have highlighted the use of other computational techniques that have been used to simulate change in a wide variety of complex socio-material systems, addressing topics such as migration in the wake of climate change (Robinson et al., 2020), sustainability practices in concrete geographical areas (Pedercini et al., 2018), and policy scenarios in spatially distributed systems (Polhill et al., 2019). However, none of these incorporate cognitively realistic and socially networked agents within a spatio-temporal environment in the same way that MAAI modelling does. The two closely related models described below were selected because of the way in which they illustrate the explanatory power of MAAI approaches and lend themselves to explicating the three tenets of DeLanda's version of assemblage theory (identified in the previous section).

The first case study is a model of a human-geographical system that simulates the socio-material dynamics and effects of various environmental threats on the behaviours and interactions of agents in the spatio-temporal dimensions of a pluralistic artificial society (Shults, Lane, et al., 2018). This model simulated assemblages (or *individual* singularities) at a variety of scales, including 'agents' with psychological, demographic, and religious variables, 'ritual clusters' of ideologically similar agents, social 'in-groups' tied to religious identity, and each of the distinctive virtual 'societies' produced by 150,000 simulation experiments. Each of these assemblages is produced by a historical process (a simulation run) and is part of a *population* (of agents, clusters, groups, or societies) with distributed *variables* whose alteration is conditioned by *parameters*. In this case, parameters included initial levels of religiosity, levels of mortality salience toleration or 'terror management', and levels of contagion, social, predation, or natural hazards in the environment. The purpose of this model was to simulate the impact of mortality salience on the social interaction of religiously heterogeneous individuals in a population under a wide variety of parametric conditions.

The way in which the first and third tenets of assemblage theory (see bullet points above) can be implemented within an artificial society is relatively easy to understand. The second tenet is a bit trickier, but it is precisely DeLanda's concept of *universal* singularities (in relation to which every assemblage is actualised) that holds the greatest potential for facilitating philosophical and empirical progress in simulating human geography. The key here is the way in which the real, structured possibility space of a universal singularity defines the capacities and tendencies of an assemblage (or individual singularity). Several scholars in the field have commented on DeLanda's distinction between properties and *capacities* in the context of theorising assemblages (Baker and McGuirk, 2017; Dovey and Ristic, 2017; Haarstad and Wanvik, 2017), but most seem to have missed his discussion of *tendencies* and failed to see the extent to which all of these are wrapped up in his enthusiasm for computer modelling. As noted above, Dittmer (2014) is an important exception, but even he does not explicitly spell out the way in which DeLanda's version of assemblage theory is significantly shaped by his engagement with CMS methodologies.

As DeLanda points out, the mathematical analysis of possibility spaces is typically sufficient to study the tendencies of a system, but capacities are more complicated because they involve a much larger set of possibilities. Assemblages can exercise their capacities in interaction with a potentially innumerable variety of other assemblages, which makes it more difficult to study the nature of the universal singularities that structure possibility spaces associated with capacities. However, 'computers can supply the means to explore these other possibility spaces in a rigorous way because the interactions in which capacities are exercised can be staged in a simulation and varied in multiple ways until the singular features of the possibility space are made visible' (DeLanda, 2011: 21).

Because the component parts of the computational architecture are characterised by 'relations of exteriority', the programmed rules of interaction at a *micro*-level (e.g., agent attitudes and behaviours) can under the right conditions lead to the emergence of new *macro*-level wholes with qualities irreducible to the component parts. As DeLanda points out elsewhere, assemblage theory provides a way of detailing the 'mechanisms of emergence' that link the micro and the macro without associating the latter with 'two fixed levels of scale', but rather using these terms 'to denote the concrete parts and the resulting emergent whole *at any given spatial scale*' (DeLanda, 2006: 32).

Let's illustrate this by focusing on the emergence of the 'ritual cluster' assemblages in the terror management model briefly introduced above. In the majority of simulation runs in that model, temporarily stable clusters emerged as anxious agents reacted over time to the hazards in their spatial environment and sought out religious in-group members with whom they could engage in anxiolytic ritual behaviours. These socio-material clusters had *emergent* properties, tendencies, and capacities not shared by the agents that composed them. For example, they had properties such as the average level of anxiety among ritually clustered agents, the tendency to dissolve when the average anxiety of its members reached a critical point, and the capacity to be affected by demographic distributions of agents representing majority and minority religious groups.

The simulation experiments revealed several features of the structured possibility space of the universal singularities that defined the relevant capacities and tendencies of the ritual clusters. For example, smaller ritual clusters were more likely to form when the population had relatively high heterogeneity, and when there were lower probabilities of natural hazards and higher average tolerance levels for out-group members (Shults, Lane, et al., 2018: 93). It is important to note that this model was constructed with subject matter experts in the relevant disciplines, who argued about (and specified) the assumptions underlying the cognitive architectures, the social dynamics, and the environmental threats within the simulated social geographical system, all of which are implemented within the code available in the supplemental materials published with the original paper. The model was also face-validated by comparing the simulation results to real-world dynamics, including the emergence (and eventual decline) of religious ritual engagement in the wake of the 2011 Christchurch earthquake in New Zealand, and the emergence of macro-level demographic patterns that characterise religious minorities and religious conservative groups in the US from the micro-level behaviours and meso-level interactions of the agents in the model. The theoretical and empirical literature informing the operationalisation of key concepts in this model are described elsewhere (Shults, 2018b).

To reiterate, socio-material assemblages such as the 'ritual clusters' in the terror management model are *individual* singularities with new emergent properties, tendencies, and capacities that interact within simulated space and time. Each simulation run produces 'historically' contingent *populations* of agents (or assemblages with agents as component parts) with distributed *variables* whose alteration leads to increased (or decreased) anxiety and religiosity spread in the artificial society under different *parametric* conditions. Each simulation run explores the *universal* singularities within the model's possibility (or phase) space. The construction of such models enables human geographers, as well as policy professionals and other stakeholders, to perform simulation experiments to test their hypotheses about the causes and consequences of stabilisation and change in social assemblages.

Let's briefly look at another example. The model just described was adapted and expanded in order to simulate the conditions under which – and the mechanisms by which – mutually escalating religious violence (MERV) can emerge in a pluralistic society (Shults, Gore, et al., 2018b). In both models, 'religiosity' was operationalised as 'shared imaginative engagement with axiologically relevant supernatural agents', and fractionated into 'anthropomorphic promiscuity' (religious belief in disembodied intentional forces) and 'sociographic prudery' (religious behaviour related to in-group ritual norms). These concepts were outlined in Chapter 2. The validation of this second multi-agent artificial intelligence model involved comparing the results of simulation experiments with empirical data about real-world intergroup conflicts (e.g., the Gujarat riots in India and 'The Troubles' in Northern Ireland).

The MERV model also includes several 'assemblages' or *individual* singularities at different scales, including 'agents' with religious, psychological, and demographic *variables*, emergent 'ritual clusters' of agents with shared ideologies, religious 'in-groups', and the artificial 'society' itself produced within each simulation run. Each of these exists as part of a *population*, including the 'societies' themselves – the experimenters produced 20,000 artificial societies in order to compare the emergent behaviours within them under different parametric settings. The *parameters* of the model included the percentage of the population that was part of the 'minority' religious group, the average levels of religiosity in the simulated agents at initialisation, and the average tolerance levels for perceived (mortality-salient) threats such as contagion, cultural otherness, predation, and natural hazards.

The artificial societies in which mutually escalating religious anxiety (taken as a proxy for conflict) was most likely to occur were those in which the majority group was less than or equal to 70% of the total population, and the average tolerance levels for contagion and cultural otherness threats were greater than or equal to the actual threats in the simulated environment. While this might seem obvious in hindsight, it is important to keep in mind that MERV was able to 'grow' the macro-level *emergent* phenomena in the social assemblages from the micro-level behaviours and interactions of personal assemblages (based on the formalisation of relevant social psychological theories in the cognitive architectures of the simulated agents), which enables us to move beyond mere statistical correlations between variables and make claims about some of the key *causal mechanisms* involved in such complex social systems.

But what about *universal* singularities? First, remember that DeLanda describes these as mechanism-independent structured possibility spaces that can help us make sense not only of the *actual properties* that characterise an individual singularity (assemblage) but also of the *real virtuality* of its unmanifested *tendencies* and unexercised *capacities*. Here too we can take the 'ritual cluster' assemblage as our example of an individual singularity. In most of the simulation runs of the MERV model, such clusters emerged as a result of anxious agents responding to threats and scanning their social networks for in-group members with whom to engage in anxiolytic ritual behaviours. As in the terror management theory model, these clusters have emergent properties, such as the average level of religiosity or anxiety among ritually clustering agents, that the agents themselves do not have. But these ritual assemblages (which we might think of as solidarity gradients) might also have emergent tendencies, such as dissolving when the averaged anxiety of its members reaches a critical point, and emergent capacities, such as influencing the averaged anxiety of individual agents. In the simulated historical production of any actual assemblage, only some of its tendencies will be manifested and only some of its capacities will be exercised (depending on environmental parameters and interactions with other assemblages).

We can think of the structured phase space produced by a computational model as containing *universal* singularities – critical tipping points and attractors that define the tendencies and capacities of the *individual* singularities (assemblages such as those simulated in the two models just discussed) that are actualised in the vicinity of those singularities. Notice that the singularities that structure this possibility space are mechanism-independent in the sense that their reality does not depend on the existence of any particular mechanism (agent, cluster, threat, etc.) or the actualisation of any particular tendency or capacity. However, they do depend on the existence of *some* actual mechanism and are therefore *immanent* in the sense DeLanda intends. In other words, if there were no agents with variables related to religiosity and anxiety, etc., there would be no state space and so no singularities. This applies to (non-simulated) actual societies as well. The universal singularities that structure the possibility space of the human species today, such as the tendencies and capacities of xenophobic religious assemblages, would not exist if biological and cultural evolutionary mechanisms had not historically produced (some) actual *Homo sapiens* with cognitive and coalitional biases that engender superstitious beliefs and segregative behaviours related to putative supernatural agents and authorities.

## Simulating Sustainable Social Assemblages

Both of the examples just described, and several others to be discussed in Chapter 5, are models that explicitly engage with variables related to religiosity. Given the overarching theme of the current book, it made sense to select such models to illustrate how MAAI techniques can simulate the actual emergence of social assemblages in relation to virtual, mechanism-independent phase spaces. In Chapter 6 we will explore some of the practical implications of such modelling endeavours, returning to the themes outlined in Chapter 2 related to anthropomorphic promiscuity and sociographic prudery. Humans need sects (belonging in groups) to live, or at least to live well. But can we learn to have 'safe sects', that is, to live together without bearing gods in our minds and cultures? The next two chapters will address these and other issues in the context of my continued attempt to show the explanatory power of plugging the Deleuzian atheist machine into ongoing debates about the role of computational simulation in promoting sustainable societies.

First, however, let me round off the discussion of theorising about assemblages and computer modelling in the field of human geography. Like most social scientists, human geographers regularly analyse the moral assumptions and implications of the application of assemblage theory in the field (e.g., Rankin, 2008; Pow, 2014; Burrai et al., 2017; Kinkaid, 2019). While some highlight the promise of assemblage thinking for 'analyzing and intervening in the emergent politics of socio-material-affective assemblages' (Ghoddousi and Page, 2020: 22), others worry that overly simplistic investment in 'assemblage-as-ethos' can all too easily have politically regressive effects (Kinkaid, 2020b: 481). Given the relevance of the theoretical and empirical efforts of human geographers and the practical concerns of politicians and public policy professionals, it is no surprise that the appropriation of assemblage theory in the former has fuelled debates about its potential impact on the latter. Many scholars in the field have addressed ways in which assemblage theory can illuminate the ethical issues – and inform inclusive conversations – around such debates (Gorur, 2011; Palmer and Owens, 2015; Briassoulis, 2017; Dalton, 2019). Others have explicitly explored the ethics and politics of assemblage thinking in a variety of domains (Ruddick, 2012; Greenhough, 2012).

The use of CMS tools could also contribute to debates within critical geography about the political exclusion of feminist and other relational approaches to (and within) digital-social-spatial assemblages (Elwood, 2021) or about hegemonic forces within epistemic geographies of climate change (Mahony and Hulme, 2018). How? Participatory and collaborative methods in the simulation of human-geographical assemblages help to surface ethical presuppositions driving the construction of models and the design of simulation experiments (Shults and Wildman, 2020b). The co-production of MAAI models in transdisciplinary teams of social scientists, computer modellers, and policy stakeholders provides conceptual scaffolding and experimental tools that make it easier for everyone involved to see and critique one another's ethical assumptions and to explore the political implications of alternative proposals.

These methodologies also have implications for ongoing discussions about 'digital geographies' or 'virtual geographies'. One popular way of categorising ways of relating geography and the digital distinguishes between 'geographies produced *through*, produced *by*, and *of* the digital' (Ash et al.,

2018: 27). To this threefold schema, we can add geographies produced *in* the digital. Computational models of the sort described above produce human-geographical assemblages *in* artificial societies. These virtual worlds are susceptible to experimentation in ways that would be impossible or unethical in the real world. Such techniques open up new possibilities for fostering wider discussions about the ethical (and ontological) assumptions at work in theorising assemblages in human geography and other social sciences.

The development of new models of the sort described above is one way of facilitating progress in human geography and other social sciences. Like all methodologies, CMS has its limitations, and its use in the simulation of human-geographical systems faces real challenges, including the difficulty of forming the sort of transdisciplinary teams that are usually required to produce such models and finding data for calibrating and validating them (Diallo et al., 2019). Moreover, despite advances in computational power and techniques, we should not expect these models to predict events with high levels of specificity (Cederman and Weidmann, 2017; Conte et al., 2012; Edmonds, 2017). However, they can help us get a clearer view of the conditions under which – and the mechanisms by which – particular events are likely to occur. Insofar as they can also help us get a grip on the mechanisms underlying these processes, computer simulations can inform the discussions and decisions of policymakers (Gilbert et al., 2018). Because it forces us to make all of our assumptions explicit (so that they can be rendered in computer code), the construction of such models might also militate against the problem of 'policy-based evidence making', the process by which a particular political ideology surreptitiously shapes policy in a way that fulfils its prophecies (Mythen, Walklate, and Peatfield, 2017).

However, this approach also offers unique opportunities. It provides human geographers with tools for synthesising insights across disciplines and analysing socio-material assemblages in ways that render their efforts even more relevant for public discourse and policy evaluation. It also creates new opportunities for interdisciplinary exploration of the methodological implications of assemblage theory across a wide variety of social sciences (Shults, 2020a). I have argued that more explicitly integrating assemblage theory and computer modelling can provide a better philosophical understanding of both, and facilitate progress in scientific research on the ways in which complex socio-material systems form and transform. I have also highlighted connections between Manuel DeLanda's version of assemblage theory and recent advances in CMS, especially in the practice of MAAI modelling. More careful attention to these connections will facilitate progress in simulating human-geographical systems in ways that can enhance the philosophical grounding of the relevant fields as well as their capacity to produce policy-oriented scientific insights.

But doesn't this great power come with great responsibility? Will the CMS 'revolution' in the philosophy of science reinforce the divide between the STEM disciplines on the one (dominant) side and the social sciences and humanities on the other (often marginalised) side? Even scholars in the latter fields who decide not to adopt or engage with CMS in their own work may still have a vested interest in exploring the ethical and epistemological implications of the rapidly growing deployment of such tools in their own and neighbouring disciplines. It is important to acknowledge some of the ethical concerns that inevitably arise when discussing the use of social simulation to analyse and predict changes in social systems. As with artificial intelligence in general, so with multi-agent artificial intelligence, many worry that the development and use of such technologies will have a deleterious effect on human well-being. This is a valid concern that applies to all new technologies. Whose moral assumptions are built into the model and whose goals are reflected in the simulation experiments?

I have argued elsewhere that it is worthwhile tackling these ethical concerns head on, surfacing the normative assumptions at work in the construction of model architectures as well as in the purposes for which simulation experiments are designed (Shults, 2023). Moreover, in the case of CMS technologies, we have the opportunity to scientifically *test* our hypotheses about the *social* effects of changing norms in human populations under varying conditions (Shults, Wildman, and Dignum, 2018; Shults and Wildman, 2020a; Diallo et al., 2021). This has the potential to alter the way in which public ethical debates occur, as well as to increase the diversity of individuals who are able to participate in them.

The unique capacities of CMS tools, briefly outlined above, provide exciting new opportunities for social scientists, philosophers, and other scholars in the humanities. As programming and participatory techniques for incorporating insights derived from qualitative research and hermeneutical analysis, and insights derived from quantitative research and evolutionary anthropological analysis, into computer modelling and simulation continue to improve, it will become increasingly easy for computationally challenged scholars to take advantage of these methodologies. The use of such tools, especially multi-agent artificial intelligence models, will also enable researchers in these fields to have a more direct impact on public policy discussions and decision-making in relation to the major societal problems such as those reflected in the United Nations Sustainability Development Goals (Shults and Wildman, 2020b).

To take full advantage of this approach, policymakers, computer scientists, and subject-matter experts working in the field will have to work together closely (Mehryar et al., 2017; Moallemi and Malekpour, 2018; Ramanath and Gilbert, 2004). Given the relative lack of interaction among academics and practitioners in the relevant areas, one of the most significant challenges as we move forward in the construction of computational models that study the sustainability of social machines may be finding the right people to work together in collaborative teams. But it seems worth the effort. If we can build empirically validated computer models that can simulate artificial societies (*in silico*) that replicate emergent patterns of sustainable social behaviour in the real world (*in situ*), then we could shed light on the plausibility of hypotheses about the causes – as well as the feasibility of policies aimed at the promotion – of sustainable socio-ecological systems.

The use of social simulation tools such as MAAI to address societal challenges is still relatively new. Nevertheless, their initial deployment has been successful enough to warrant further research to extend and improve their capacity for understanding, explaining, and forecasting changes in the complex human-geographical systems in which we find ourselves striving to adapt. This chapter has also attempted to introduce philosophers to some of the major opportunities and challenges associated with the growing application of computational methods to the phenomena they study. I conclude with an invitation to consider adding these techniques to their methodological toolkits, and to join in with the fascinating and important conversations about simulating sustainable societies that these models engender (Shults, 2021b).

Where to start? A good place to begin would be with the edited volumes *Complexity and the Human Experience* (Youngman and Hadzikadic, 2014) and *Human Simulation: Perspectives, Insights, and Applications* (Diallo et al., 2019). Both of these books provide a rationale for and examples of the process of building models and running simulations with subject-matter experts from the humanities and social sciences. For those preferring an article-length introduction, any of the following provide a good introduction: Grim, 2002; Conte et al., 2012; Squazzoni et al., 2014; Wildman et al., 2017; Shults, 2023. It is important to keep in mind that one can participate in model construction and simulation design without programming experience or mathematical expertise (as long as other team members bring these to the table). However, based on my experience (and the experience of other colleagues whose initial training, like mine, was in fields outside the computer sciences), the best place to start is with a conversation about CMS with someone you trust who is familiar with the methodology. Engaging with any new approach, but especially computational approaches that involve robust transdisciplinary cooperation, can be challenging. On the other hand, such engagement also opens up new opportunities, not only for expanding one's toolkit with novel collaborative methods but also for refining and sharpening one's use of long-established and time-honoured tools of the academic trade.

Insofar as computer modelling and simulation can aid in the exploration (and alteration) of the singularities that structure the phase space of contemporary human life, it too might play an important role in the ongoing discussions about the ethical and political challenges facing humanity today (Shults and Wildman, 2019). As DeLanda has observed, '[p]erhaps one day virtual environments will become the tools we need to track the machinic phylum in search of a better destiny for humanity' (2005: 100). Indeed, perhaps the philosophical and pragmatic use of such tools could also open up new lines of flight for *us* to become *simulating machines* in a quite different sense; that is, to become machinic and collective assemblages of enunciation who make the simulacra rise in order to overturn the Platonic metaphysics of transcendence (and ethics of judgement) that has all too often led us humans to desire our own repression and justify the oppression of others wrought by (mono)theist social machines.

# 5

# Simulating (Non-)Religion

This chapter highlights some of the challenges and opportunities associated with constructing philosophically precise and policy-relevant computational models of 'religion'. It is important to begin by remembering how we are operationalising this contentious and contested term. As outlined in Chapter 2, and briefly summarised below, we are utilising a definition that incorporates insights from a variety of disciplines that converge in the bio-cultural science of *religion*: shared imaginative engagement with axiologically relevant supernatural agents. Most of the models described below simulate the causes and consequences of 'theism', or 'theistic machines', which are religious assemblages of the sort that Deleuze links to the despotic social machine (especially monotheisms such as Christianity). *Theistic* machines are social assemblages whose cohesion relies primarily on shared ritual engagement with axiologically relevant, coalition-favouring supernatural agents *and* an infinite supernatural agent whose representation is sacerdotally authorised and policed.

As I argued in Chapter 1, this is what Deleuze has in mind when he identifies 'the infinity of religion' as the target of the speculative and practical tasks of philosophy, and atheism as the achievement of philosophy. The three central sections of this chapter illustrate the explanatory power of computational social simulation techniques, especially multi-agent artificial intelligence modelling, when studying religion in general and theism in particular. This will involve, first, reviewing our earlier discussions of the bio-cultural causes of these social assemblages and describing one of the most problematic consequences of these phenomena, namely, religious radicalisation and polarisation as they emerge in contexts shaped by monotheism. The second step is to dive more deeply into the importance – both conceptually and computationally – of distinguishing micro-, meso-, and macro-level mechanisms and the relations among them when attempting to understand these sorts of phenomena. Third, several examples are provided of computational models whose simulation experiments illuminate the conditions under which religion (and theism) can be 'predicted' and 'prevented'.

The successful development and deployment of such techniques with high levels of explanatory and even predictive power are clearly relevant for stakeholders interested in discovering and promoting policies that can reduce religious radicalisation and violent extremism. However, all of this also raises epistemological issues that will be of interest to philosophers, social scientists, and other scholars of (non-)religion. The last section of this chapter addresses some of these in the context of a discussion of the achievement of Deleuze's (atheist) meta-epistemology.

First, however, it is time for another confession. Although I spent most of my educational and professional career in the humanities (theology and philosophy), over the decades I explored as many of the social sciences and physical sciences as I could. These interdisciplinary explorations, which increasingly undermined the plausibility of the supernaturalist doctrines of Christianity (and other religions), contributed powerfully to my atheist turn. Then, about ten years ago, I was introduced to computer modelling and simulation (CMS). For all the reasons outlined so far in this book, it felt as though I had met the scientific methodology from which I had been separated at birth.

## The Modelling Religion Project(s)

My first encounter with CMS was during the interdisciplinary project in Çatalhöyük, Turkey, described briefly in Chapter 2. My colleague Wesley Wildman suggested that we attempt to develop a computational model that would be able to simulate the shift towards agriculture and sedentarism at this Neolithic site. This process was so successful and energising that we decided to apply for funding for additional research projects that would utilise these computational tools in other areas. The first of these was the Modeling Religion Project (MRP), which was led by Wildman through the Center for Mind and Culture (CMAC) in Boston where he is executive director. MRP was funded by the John Templeton Foundation (JTF), and CMAC's main partners for this grant were the Virginia Modeling, Analysis and Simulation Center (VMASC) and the Social Simulation Research Group at the University of Agder in Kristiansand, Norway.

MRP ran from the summer of 2015 to the summer of 2018 and produced several computational models of religion. For example, this was the team that constructed the model of the role of religiosity in terror management, described in Chapter 4, which was able to simulate the emergence of increased population-level anxiolytic ritual behaviours in the wake of threats related to contagion, natural hazards, predation, and cultural others (Shults, Lane, et al., 2018). The architecture of that model was expanded to include behaviours and interactions informed by social identity theory and identity fusion theory, enabling the simulation of the mutual escalation of xenophobic anxiety between religious groups that is observed in the real world. This was the other model (MERV) that I described in some detail in Chapter 4 above (Shults, Gore, et al., 2018b). MRP also sponsored the development of a radically transdisciplinary and policy-oriented participatory modelling approach in the process of constructing several other models, some of which are described in *Human Simulation: Perspectives, Insights, and Applications* (Diallo et al., 2019).

Once MRP was off the ground and running, we applied for and received a grant from the Research Council of Norway, which led to the Modeling Religion in Norway (MODRN) project. This project was based at the University of Agder (UiA), where I served as the principal investigator, and ran from the summer of 2016 to the summer of 2019. In addition to strengthening the collaboration between UiA, CMAC, and VMASC, the MODRN project also laid the groundwork for the founding of the NORCE Center for Modeling Social Systems (CMSS) in Kristiansand, Norway, in January 2018. Some of the MODRN models were explicitly oriented towards understanding and responding to the 2015 Syrian refugee crisis, whose causes and consequences involved variables related to religiosity, humanitarian aid, and peacebuilding (Padilla et al., 2018; Paloutzian et al., 2021). MRP and MODRN overlapped both conceptually and temporally, and included many of the same team members, who collaborated in the development of a variety of computational models for studying (non-)religion. One of the most interesting and complex was a model of minority integration in a Western city (Puga-Gonzalez et al., 2019), which was based on a more generic platform for simulating societal changes such as secularisation (Shults, Wildman, et al., 2020a).

For the purposes of the current book, some of the most relevant MODRN computer models were those that emerged out of a 2018 seminar at UiA's Metochi Centre in Lesbos, Greece. This seminar brought together three teams of computer scientists and subject-matter experts for a week to work on three different models designed to explore cognitive variables and mechanisms involved in the increase of religious disbelief (analytic atheism), the growth of prosocial attitudes and behaviours among the non-religious (altruistic atheism), and the role of social networks in exiting religion (affiliated atheism). Another relevant model is one we called NoRM (the Non-Religiosity Model), which simulated the role of education and existential security in promoting secularisation. I will return to some of these models below in the context of explaining what it means to 'predict' and 'prevent' religion (and theism).

The third major funded project in this series of collaborations was the Modeling Religious Change (MRC) project, which began in early 2020 and ended in 2023. MRC was also made possible by a grant from JTF and was led by Wildman at CMAC, with several collaborating institutions including VMASC and CMSS. One of the main goals of the MRC project was to develop and execute a new approach to the demography of religion and non-religion that built on and expanded agent-based modelling and social simulation techniques developed in the team's prior work (Wildman, Shults, and Diallo, 2021). Traditional approaches in the demography of religion tend to focus on self-reports of religious identity or affiliation, in part because these are variables on which longitudinal data is most readily available. Such approaches often employ cohort-component methodologies to make projections. MRC aims to enhance demographic projections of religion (and secularisation) by using multi-agent artificial intelligence modelling of the sort described above. This will allow us to take account of other dimensions of religiosity such as supernatural belief and private religious practice. Moreover, linking cohort-component methods to simulations in artificial societies could also help demographers to take account of non-linear feedback loops and interaction among variables, produce narrower error estimates, and integrate a rich array of disciplinary insights relevant to religious and non-religious change in demographic projections.

In 2020 we began collaborating with Konrad Talmont-Kaminski and his team at the Cognition and Society Unit at the University of Bialystok in Poland on the 'Religion, Ideology, and Prosociality' (RIP) project. Funded by an EEA-Norway grant, this project will run through early 2024. RIP is led by Talmont-Kaminksi and involves a collaboration with CMSS in Norway and a host of subject-matter experts including Wesley Wildman and David Voas. The latter's work is the basis for one of the major models being developed by the team, which aims to simulate the role of the growth and decline of 'fuzzy fidelity' in a secularising population (Voas, 2009). The other models in that grant aim to implement causal architectures based on leading theories in the cognitive and evolutionary sciences of religion that have played a central role in Talmont-Kaminski's earlier work (Talmont-Kaminski, 2014). These include epistemic vigilance theory, error management theory, and theories about the role of religion in prosocial attitudes and behaviours. Several papers on these models have already been completed (Laskowski et al., in press; Puga-Gonzalez et al., 2022; in press; Rybnik et al., in press), and many others are currently in progress.

The Research Council of Norway also awarded CMSS a research grant in 2020 to run a project called 'Emotional Contagion: Predicting and Preventing the Spread of Misinformation, Stigma, and Fear during a Pandemic' (EmotiCon). The main goal of the EmotiCon project, for which I also served as principal investigator, was to develop user-friendly multi-agent artificial intelligence tools that could enable Norwegian municipalities and other governmental agencies to 1) analyse and forecast the societal effects of their public health responses and social countermeasures to pandemics and 2) experiment with alternative intervention strategies for 'flattening the curve' of psychologically and politically debilitating social contagion before trying them out in the real world. EmotiCon collected and analysed Twitter content (using new natural language processing techniques) and attitude data (via a representative Norwegian panel survey) that could be used to specify, calibrate, and validate an ABM or artificial society ('digital twin') of Norway. Simulation experiments on the ABM have been designed to explore the religious variables, psychological mechanisms, and cultural factors that have shaped reactions to COVID-19 and to forecast the way in which individuals and communities are likely to understand and react to future pandemics under various conditions (Antosz et al., 2022; Shults, 2023).

Each of the institutions that are part of this international collaboration have other grant proposals under review or in process and are working on models that are not linked to specific funded projects. And, of course, there are other research groups pursuing similar projects and developing other models. Our experience has been that simulating (non-)religion with cognitively realistic agents in culturally realistic 'artificial societies' requires teams of competent and open-minded subject-matter experts and computer scientists who are willing to devote a significant amount of time and energy to the collaborative process of participatory modelling. As noted at the end of Chapter 4, we call this process 'Human Simulation' (Diallo et al., 2019; Shults and Wildman, 2020b).

Finally, I have also been involved in modelling (non-)religion in my role as chief research officer at CulturePulse, a company that utilises both computational modelling and artificial intelligence algorithms to study the cognitive and cultural dynamics shaping conversations on social media as well as offline. Most of our work at CulturePulse deals with issues that are not directly related to religion, but some of our projects do address such concerns. In our work with the Woolf Institute at the University of Cambridge, for example, we have recently developed a computational model designed to illuminate the conditions under which – and the mechanisms by which – forgiveness and reconciliation are likely to emerge in post-conflict societies such as Northern Ireland, the Balkans, and South Sudan (Lane, 2023). Religion is not the only, or perhaps even the major, factor at work in these and similar contexts, but there is a general consensus in the literature on intergroup conflict and extremism that religion – and theism in particular – can have an amplifying effect on polarisation and radicalisation.

## The Causes and Consequences of 'Religion'

First, let's back up and remind ourselves of the *causes* of religion as hypothesised by theogonic reproduction theory. As explained in Chapter 1, for the purposes of computer modelling (as for most scientific approaches to the study of religion), we do not need a universally valid definition of 'religion' upon which everyone agrees. Good luck with that! What we need is to identify a set of statistically measurable traits that consistently engender recurrent sorts of beliefs and behaviours that mutate culturally in relatively predictive ways. The traits we are interested in are those that engender beliefs in gods and foster ritual behaviours oriented towards engaging with them. As operationalised above, in accordance with the hypotheses of theogonic reproduction theory, 'religiosity' has to do with individual and situational factors that contribute to the emergence and maintenance of shared imaginative engagement with axiologically relevant supernatural agents in a population.

To reiterate, there are many biologically evolved and socially entrained mechanisms that contribute to this set of phenomena, but we can compile most of them into two categories: the tendency to *detect* supernatural agents (human-like, coalition-favouring, disembodied intentional forces) and the tendency to *protect* supernatural coalitions (in-groups whose coherence depends in part on ritual interaction with such agents). The reciprocal reinforcement of evolved credulity and conformity biases that were naturally selected as a result of error-management and risk-management strategies in early ancestral environments helps to explain why gods are so easily born in human minds and borne in human cultures. *Reliance* on supernatural concepts to explain confusing phenomena amplifies *compliance* with supernaturally authorised in-group norms and vice versa. Religiosity involves the intensification and integration of a hyperactive propensity towards *inferring* hidden supernatural agents and a hyperactive tendency towards *preferring* the supernaturally authorised norms of an in-group. In other words, religion is caused by the integration of cognitive and coalitional tendencies aggregated within the cluster of traits I have called anthropomorphic promiscuity and sociographic prudery.

The coordinate grid in Figure 1 (Chapter 2) portrays the integration of these two sorts of tendencies in the lower left quadrant. As explained above, the horizontal line represents a continuum on which we can mark the tendency of persons to guess 'supernatural agent' when confronted with ambiguous or frightening phenomena. The anthropomorphically promiscuous are always on the lookout, jumping at any opportunity to postulate such agents as causal explanations. The anthropomorphically prudish, on the other hand, are suspicious about such appeals. They tend to reflect more carefully before giving in to their intuitive desire to grab at agential explanations. The continuum represented by the vertical line registers the extent to which a person holds on to supernaturally authorised in-group norms and modes of inscribing the social field. Sociographic prudes are firmly committed to the authorised social standards of their own religious coalition, following them (and punishing others for not following them) even at significant cost to themselves. They are more likely to be suspicious of out-groups and to accept claims or demands that appeal to authorities within their in-group. The sociographic promiscuity of those at the other end of the continuum, on the other hand, leads them to be more open to intercourse with out-groups about different normativities and to the pursuit of new modes of a creative social inscription. Such persons are also less likely to accept restrictions or assertions that are based on appeals to ritually engaged disembodied intentional forces.

Let's approach this from a different direction, beginning with the prevalence of these traits in contemporary human populations. Why are humans today so prone to religious *superstition*, that is, to proposing and accepting interpretations of ambiguous (and especially frightening) natural phenomena that are based on faulty conceptions of causation? Such interpretations are due, in part, to evolved *cognitive* defaults that pull us towards the left side of the horizontal line in Figure 1. When we encounter some pattern or movement that we do not understand, our first guess is likely to involve the attribution of characteristics such as mentality and animacy. This over-active predilection helps to explain why we so easily see 'faces in the clouds' and worry about hidden forces that might intend us harm. Moreover, we quite often double down on such guesses and keep scanning for human-like agents even when there is no clear evidence of their presence. This tendency to assume that hard-to-detect agents are the cause of hard-to-understand events served our Upper Palaeolithic ancestors well; otherwise, we would not be here to talk about them.

Early hominids who developed hyper-sensitive cognitive devices that scanned for agency were more likely to survive than those who did not. What made that noise in the tall grass? Was it a human enemy or some other animal? Or was it just the wind? Those who quickly guessed 'intentional force' and acted accordingly were more likely to avoid being eaten or to find food (if the noise was in fact caused by a predator or a prey, respectively). Despite almost constant false positives in the short run, this over-active perceptual strategy would have granted survival advantage in the long run. It would have paid off to keep searching for and believing in such hidden agents. Anxiety about the failure to find an actual agent generates other hypotheses; just because we are paranoid does not mean that an animal spirit or angry ancestor ghost was not really lurking in the grass before it mysteriously disappeared.

Most contemporary humans have inherited this anthropomorphic *promiscuity*. We jump at any opportunity to postulate human-like entities as causal explanations even – or especially – when these interpretations must appeal to counter-intuitive disembodied intentional forces, that is, to 'supernatural agents'. Of course, it is also possible to contest this sort of evolved default. Scientists and philosophers, for example, are trained to become anthropomorphically *prudish*. Far more cautious about such appeals, and typically critical of superstition in general, they are more likely to resist ascribing intentionality to unknown causes. If something strange happens in a test tube during an experiment, the scientifically trained chemist will not guess that it was a 'ghost'. If something seems to be missing in a causal (or logical) chain, the (non-religious) philosopher will not insert a 'god'.

Why are humans also so readily prone to *segregation*, that is, to making and reinforcing inscriptions of the social field that protect their own in-groups from contamination or domination by out-groups? Our evolved *coalitional* defaults pull us towards the bottom of the vertical line in Figure 1. This (often vehement and sometimes violent) fortification of boundaries is engendered, in part, by an evolved over-active tendency to embrace and defend conventional modes of segmenting and regulating society. This naturally generated prejudice towards one's own collective makes it tempting just to stay at home, where the proscriptive and prescriptive norms feel most comfortable. This default tendency is so powerful that we will often engage in costly and painful behaviours in order to follow the rules – and willingly inflict pain on those who do not. It makes sense that such a hyper-sensitive propensity towards protecting one's own coalition would also have served our early *Homo sapiens* ancestors well.

When it comes to competition among small-scale societies, especially when resources are scarce or under other stressful conditions, the groups that are most likely to survive are those in which the individual members are able to cooperate and remain committed to the group. Natural selection reinforces the tendency of an individual organism to watch out for itself, but if there are too many cheaters, freeloaders, or defectors in a society it will quickly fall apart. Research in the bio-cultural sciences of religion suggests that this problem was solved in some hominid coalitions during the Upper Palaeolithic by an intensification of shared belief in and ritual engagement with potentially *punitive* supernatural agents (such as animal spirits or ancestor ghosts). Such coalition-favouring 'gods' could catch misbehaviour that regular natural agents might miss and could punish not only the miscreants, but their offspring or even the entire group. Belief in invisible or ambiguously apparitional 'watchers' helped to enhance the motivation to follow the rules and stay within the coalition.

Contemporary humans have also inherited this sociographic *prudery*. Most people somewhat automatically follow the authorised social norms of their in-group, or at least put great effort into building up a reputation for doing so. Here too, however, the evolved default can be contested. Those who are *promiscuous* in their sociography are less likely to accept claims about (or demands for the segregation of) human groups that are based on appeals to supernatural authorities within a religious in-group. They are more likely to be open to dialogue with out-groups about alternative normativities and to the pursuit of novel modes of cooperative social engagement. In-group bias helped (some of) our ancestors survive in small-scale societies in difficult socio-ecological niches. Today, however, this evolved default does not always serve us well – especially those of us who live in large-scale, urban societies characterised by the pressures of globalisation and radical pluralism. A growing number of policymakers and legislators in such contexts refuse to appeal to 'ghosts' or 'gods' in their attempts to inscribe the public sphere.

What are the *consequences* of religion? It is important to acknowledge that shared imaginative engagement with axiologically relevant supernatural agents can promote cooperation, commitment, and cohesion in the face of out-group threats and environmental challenges. However, it is equally important to acknowledge that religious beliefs about person-like, coalition-favouring supernatural agents, and religious behaviours within emotionally arousing, in-group rituals, are part of a complex of evolutionary mechanisms that all too easily lead to anxiety about and violence towards out-group members under stressful conditions (Alcorta and Sosis, 2013; Avalos, 2013; Brubaker, 2015; Clarke et al., 2013; Garcia, 2015; Sela et al., 2015; Sosis et al., 2012; Teehan, 2010). There is little doubt among religion scholars that religiosity is related to mechanisms that can trigger or exacerbate intergroup violence in general, and radicalisation in particular. But how 'religious' is religious violence? Empirical findings and theoretical developments in the cognitive and evolutionary sciences of religion suggest that

> violence *is* attributable to religion because it rests on evolved human organ-isational and behavioral patterns. While religion need not cause violence and can, in fact, foster beneficent behavior, religion is prone to violence given its set of dangerous dynamics (both coalitional and ideological) that stimulate underlying biological tendencies toward violence. (Tremlin, 2010: 38)

What about *theism*? We have already discussed some of the *causal* factors that played a role in the assemblage of the despotic monotheist machine during the axial age. But what about the *consequences* of theism? Given violent extremism and religious radicalisation, what machine can produce it? Small-scale, relatively homogeneous societies (territorial social machines) certainly often involved violence between group members and towards out-group members. However, the level of ideological polarisation and intergroup conflict that promotes religious radicalisation and violent extremism only exists in large-scale, heterogeneous societies of the sort that emerged in the wake of the axial age. Moreover, most cases of religious extremism in the modern world occur in contexts deeply shaped by the monotheisms of the west Asian axial age. As I hinted in Chapter 2, and have discussed elsewhere in more detail (Shults, 2014c), this is partly because those traditions (unlike the dominant traditions of south and east Asia) pressed anthropomorphic promiscuity to infinity and sociographic prudery to eternity, ratcheting up what is at stake in intergroup conflict. Although there are a wide variety of material and broadly social factors, there is little doubt that the theist machine has played a role in the production of such religious radicalisation and violent extremism.

Given the theist machine, what can it be used for? As we have seen, this social machine can help hold together complex, large-scale, literate societies by encouraging (or enforcing) the cultivation of virtues that promote cohesion. However, the theist machine can also be used to create ideologies that evoke political polarisation and spread anxiety that, under certain conditions, boils over into radicalisation and violent extremism. Although violence inspired by religion is nothing new, it does increasingly seem to dominate the news, with all too regular reports of terrorist attacks by religiously radicalised individuals and escalating conflicts between religious in-groups throughout the world. Violence has historically been an important part of religion, from ritual mutilation and human sacrifice to the justification of wars allegedly commanded or sanctioned by the god or gods of an in-group. However, the forms it takes today in contexts traditionally nurtured by monotheism are particularly problematic (Juergensmeyer et al., 2013; 2016; Lewis, 2017; Nelson-Pallmeyer, 2005; Wellman, Jr, 2007).

In recent years, research in cognitive psychology, anthropology, sociology, and other fields has shed light on some of the causal dynamics at work in the emergence of extremist behaviours related to religion. At the level of cultural variance, for example, structural equation models based on global measurements of religious freedom suggest that state restrictions on the latter may lead to an increase in religiously sanctioned violence (Grim and Finke, 2011). At the level of individual variance, for example, statistical path analyses of psychological surveys indicate that personality factors such as social dominance orientation and religious fundamentalism mediate prejudice towards religious out-groups (Banyasz et al., 2014). Moreover, both individual and cultural variance can play a significant role in shaping the levels of religiosity and violence in any given context (Shaver et al., 2016).

To reiterate, of course violence is not the only feature of religion, and religion is not a necessary or a sufficient condition for violent radicalisation. Some religious people are not radicals, and there are radicalised people who are not religious. Multiple *motivational* factors can be at work that drive individuals into, through, and out of the radicalisation process, including social, cultural, political, psychological, and religious factors. Moreover, multiple *situational* factors also need to be taken into account. For example, radicalisation may be more likely to occur in contexts where some members of the population experience economic distress or prejudice against their in-group. In the next section, we parse some of these causes and consequences in order to clarify how and why computational modelling is a valuable tool for teasing out the causal mechanisms and conditions under which religious – and particularly theist – social machines can help to produce violent extremism.

## Micro-, Meso-, and Macro-level Mechanisms in Religious Radicalisation

Developing the capacity to predict and prevent religious radicalisation and violent extremism is a high priority for a variety of stakeholders, including local and state governments, law enforcement institutions, NGOs, national and international security organisations, and concerned citizens everywhere (Atran, 2010; Callimachi, 2016; Ekblom, 2012; Ekblom et al., 2016; McCauley and Moskalenko, 2008; Sirseloudi, 2005). Policymakers wonder: what policies (if any) can help mitigate the causes and effects of forms of extremism that appear to be motivated – or at least justified – by religion? Policy analysts wonder: what scientific tools (if any) can determine the conditions under which – and the mechanisms by which – radicalisation processes are likely to occur? Subject-matter experts wonder: what role (if any) does religion play in processes of radicalisation? This section explores these questions and highlights the way in which the answers – or at least the processes involved in seeking those answers – are closely intertwined.

Are the primary causal drivers of radicalisation to be found at the micro-, meso-, or macro-level? Scholars disagree. Some emphasise the importance of *micro*-level variables. A study of the determinants of religious radicalisation in Kenya, for example, found 'no evidence that macro-level political or economic grievances predict radicalization'. On the contrary, the authors argued, radicalisation is 'strongly associated with individual-level psychological trauma' (Rink and Sharma, 2017). Some studies have found that support for violence is strongly predicted by individual factors such as religious conspiracy beliefs and religious fundamentalism (Beller, 2017; Beller and

Kröger, 2017). Additional psychological factors known to be correlated to radicalisation include identity conflicts, relative deprivation, identity fusion, and various personality characteristics (King and Taylor, 2011; Swann et al., 2010; 2014).

Other scholars focus more on the *macro*-level factors that shape religious radicalisation. A study of Islamic radicalisation in Ghana, for example, explored a variety of variables, including socio-economic and political dynamics, different doctrinal and interpretational approaches to the concept of jihad, external financial support, and the presence of a youth bulge. The authors concluded that the intensity and frequency of radicalisation and violence are promoted, first and foremost, by intergroup struggles for doctrinal pre-eminence (Aning and Abdallah, 2013). Another study that explored the multiple pathways to violence, and analysed mechanisms of political radicalisation at the individual, group, and mass-public levels, concluded that the trajectory of action and reaction at the level of intergroup competition was the key. Radicalisation should be understood 'as emerging more from the dynamics of intergroup conflict than from the vicissitudes of individual psychology' (McCauley and Moskalenko, 2008: 415).

This tension between theorists who emphasise micro- or macro-level variables is not unique to scholars of religious radicalisation and violent extremism. It is the reflection of a longstanding debate within and across a variety of disciplines between those who tend to explain behaviour by appealing primarily to individual factors, those who refer mainly to contextual factors, and those who try to balance or integrate both.

One approach to the latter strategy is to look for mechanisms at the *meso*-level. For example, a study of the behaviour of Jewish settlers in the West Bank identified organisational membership, or 'networks of mobilization', as a key mechanism that served as a bridge between religious identity and radical action. The authors found that 'settler populations in non-religious settlements were significantly less likely to engage in radical action than those in religious communities' (Hirsch-Hoefler et al., 2016: 512). Another study of the evolution of the Hamburg Cell, which played a role in the 9/11 attacks, explored the interplay of social networks and religious violence. The study found that coercion and social tension increased the likelihood that groups would distance themselves from broader society, which in turn increased the probability that group members would adopt more extreme beliefs. This process is facilitated by religious beliefs and practices that heighten the tension between the group and society (Everton, 2016).

Another approach is to develop theoretical models that explicitly incorporate both micro- and macro-level factors. For example, one study of the role of religion and identity in the Turkish diaspora in Germany emphasised the influence of three factors that contributed to violent radicalisation. These were the status of Islamist movements in the home country of immigrants, the extent to which religion fulfilled the material (rather than only spiritual) needs of immigrants in the host country, and personal crises that rendered individuals more susceptible to extremist ideology (Sirseloudi, 2012). Another example is the 'personality × threat × affordance' hypothesis about the motivation for aggressive religious radicalisation, which is grounded in goal-regulation theory (McGregor et al., 2015). In this model, three sorts of variables combine to produce extreme behaviour: personality factors (such as oppositional and identity-weak traits), threat factors (such as external control threats and life circumstances that promote hopelessness), and affordance factors (such as situational opportunities for engagement, religious narratives that justify aggression, and religious arguments that cannot be disproved).

The development of conceptual models of religious radicalisation based on research on 'new religious movements' (NRMs) or 'conversion theory' provide another way of bridging the gap between micro- and macro-level factors. We know a great deal about the processes involved in the emergence of NRMs, as well as the conditions under which their separation from conventional religions can lead to violence. It makes sense to apply these insights when trying to understand the paths to violence taken by some emergent religious groups (Shterin and Yarlykapov, 2011). Conversion theory also has decades of research behind it and offers insights into the role of (and relationship between) both predisposing conditions and situational factors. Taking advantage of this research can help radicalisation scholars 'get beyond a dualistic view and begin the much-needed journey to understand how features of the person and the situation/context recursively influence one another throughout the radicalization and engagement process' (Borum, 2011a: 25). Another example of a multi-factor approach is Hafez and Mullins' use of a 'puzzle' metaphor. To understand how ordinary individuals transform into violent extremists, they argue, one has to fit together at least four sorts of factors: personal and collective grievances, networks and interpersonal ties, political and religious ideologies, and enabling environments and support structures (Hafez and Mullins, 2015: 958).

The complex interplay of both individual *and* contextual factors in religious radicalisation has implications not only for the prediction but also for the prevention of this phenomenon. Often policymakers and counter-terrorist teams focus on the long-range causes (e.g., historical, social, or political grievances) or the short-range precipitants of terrorist campaigns (e.g. acquisition of weapons, the hiring of external experts). Such a focus leaves out medium-range 'proximate' causes, such as specific actor (or audience) constellations, and intra-group dynamics in a concrete conflict situation.

Appropriate prevention, as well as qualified prediction, requires attention to all of these levels and their reciprocal interactions.

Scholars of religious radicalisation are well aware that this level of complexity poses severe challenges for researchers in the field, and helps to explain why, despite the apparent practical significance of the topic, the amount of empirically rigorous research on it is surprisingly low (Neumann and Kleinmann, 2013). A systematic review of the research evidence in the field observed that despite the prolific output of research, very few studies contained *empirical* data or systematic data analysis or developed *causal* models of the relevant dynamics. Instead, most of the literature 'listed several probable factors, usually social-psychological models, but failed to specify the interactions between the listed factors in any detail' (Christmann, 2012: 42). Another survey of the leading conceptual models and empirical research in the field described radicalisation as 'multiply-determined'. Radicalisation may be driven and sustained by multiple causes, including 'push' and 'pull' factors, and pathways that are characterised by 'equifinality', that is, different pathways can lead to the same outcome, as well as by 'multifinality', that is, different persons on the same pathway may have different outcomes (Borum, 2011b: 57).

What do scholars in this field think is needed to tackle so complex a phenomenon? Some have noted that although particular theories are valuable, 'a *comprehensive* effort to verify our understanding of radicalization, using empirical verification as a standard, might be more beneficial to the current state of knowledge concerning the transformative processes that precede acts of terrorism' (King and Taylor, 2011: 618, emphasis added). Others call for research designs that do not simply select the dependent variable but select 'cases where the presumed causal variables are present, even if radicalization is not. In other words, researchers should seek evidence that disconfirms the putative causes of radicalization to nuance their analysis of what's necessary, sufficient, or inconsequential in the radicalization phenomenon' (Hafez and Mullins, 2015: 971). Still others express the need for 'empirically testing leading hypotheses on radicalization in multiple conflict settings … [and] research designs that attempt to examine the correlates of extremist behavior in different contexts' (Rink and Sharma, 2017: 25).

On top of all this, radicalisation researchers face severe ethical and experimental challenges. As Bjørgo and Gjelsvik point out in their summary of Norwegian research on the prevention of radicalisation and violent extremism, scholars in this field have to face several ethical challenges at the boundaries of the usual standards for ethical research. Such complicating factors include transparency requirements, informed consent, and the limits of confidentiality and anonymity when dealing with individuals who may be dangerous to the broader society (Bjørgo and Gjelsvik, 2015: 21). Another ethical problem, not mentioned by these authors, is that experimental research on religiously radicalised individuals and their effect on the environment is neither feasible nor ethically appropriate. No internal ethics review board would approve a research design in which one *experimented* with different policies for preventing – or predicting – religious violence in the real world. For example, we cannot merely insert more or less radicalised individuals into different sorts of social networks to see what happens.

Despite the theoretical advances described above, researchers and policymakers interested in these phenomena still face the challenge of integrating relevant empirical findings from so many diverse disciplines. They are also faced with the pragmatic challenge of discerning the relevant policy implications of the multiple (and often reciprocal) causal connections within complex adaptive systems such as those in which radicalisation processes are embedded. We need some powerful new methodological tool to help us tackle the job of determining the conditions under which – and the mechanisms by which – some individuals in some contexts move through the radicalisation process and commit acts of violence.

These are just the sorts of challenges that computer modelling and simulation methodologies are designed to tackle. Given the advantages of CMS enumerated in previous chapters, it is not surprising that these methodologies have already been used to illuminate a variety of issues related to social conflict in general. For example, computational models have been used to predict patterns of violence and segregation (Weidmann and Salehyan, 2013), the escalation of ethnonationalist radicalisation (Neumann, 2014), and the decline of ethnic civil war (Cederman et al., 2017). In fact, several scholars have brought computational methodologies to bear on issues related to radicalisation, such as counter-terrorism, political ideology, ethnic violence, and terrorist recruitment (Fellman et al., 2015; Ko and Berry, 2004; Subrahmanian, 2013; Voinea, 2016). Increasingly, one finds studies that even focus explicitly on radicalisation processes. For example, one scholar has constructed an agent-based model based on the Individual Vulnerability, Exposure and Emergence (IVEE) framework for understanding radicalisation (Pepys, 2016).

We have reviewed a few of the many (more or less complementary) theories of radicalisation in the literature and alluded to some of the currently available datasets. How do we decide which approaches and which data to use? How do we choose to operationalise 'radicalisation'? Should we go with a definition that focuses on the individual: 'Radicalization is a personal process in which individuals adopt extreme political, social or religious ideas and inspirations, and where the attainment of particular goals justifies the use of indiscriminate violence' (Wilner and Dubouloz, 2011: 38). Or do we need a definition that involves groups: 'Radicalization refers to an increase in or reinforcing of extremism in the thinking, sentiments or behavior of individuals or groups' (Mandel, 2010: 111). Or is there some other definition that would serve us better for this task? There is no way to find the 'right' answer to this question ahead of time. In my experience, the best approach is to bring together a team of subject-matter experts and computer programmers for a few days to discuss the options and develop a strategy (Wildman, Fishwick, and Shults, 2017).

Given the cognitive and psychological, as well as sociological and ecological, factors that contribute to religious radicalisation, multi-agent artificial intelligence modelling is more up to the task than traditional modelling strategies. We have already noted some such models above and will return to several others below. My colleague Ross Gore and I have taken the first steps in developing a causal architecture, informed by our work on these other models, that is specifically designed to simulate the mechanisms of radicalisation (Shults and Gore, 2020). What are the next steps? As with the construction of any new model, we would need to identify a particular theory (or integrate a set of theories) and operationalise the relevant variables in a way that could be implemented in a computational architecture. We would also need to decide which parameters the model needs to facilitate the sort of simulation experiments that could provide insights into the causal dynamics of those aspects of the radicalisation process in which we are most interested. Moreover, we would need to identify empirical datasets that could be used to calibrate and validate the model. These steps do not necessarily have to be in any particular order; the process is iterative, moving back and forth between theory, data, and experimental design until everything falls together (Wildman, Diallo, et al., 2021). This sort of approach might also contribute to the growing theoretical literature on *de*-radicalisation and provide concrete insights for policies oriented towards countering violent extremism (Doosje et al., 2016; Koehler, 2016; Kruglanski et al., 2017; 2019; Webber et al., 2017).

The process of radicalisation is not merely a cognitive transformation: it also involves collective actions, rituals, and physically embodied 'aesthetic' practices that link the individual to a group (Crone, 2014). In other words, models of religious radicalisation and extremism should pay attention to both radical religious ideas and extreme religious actions. As Borum concluded at the end of his review of social science theories on radicalisation into violent extremism: 'Radicalization – the process of developing extremist ideologies and beliefs – needs to be distinguished from action pathways – the process of engaging in terrorism or violent extremist actions' (Borum, 2011b: 30).

One popular image for understanding radicalisation has been a pyramid; the majority of a population at the base of the pyramid has conventional views, and a few at the top have extremist views. More recently, however, some scholars have argued that we need to visualise two pyramids, one that measures radicalisation of opinion and another that measures radicalisation of action (McCauley and Moskalenko, 2017). Of course, ideas and action, belief and behaviour, and thought and practice are reciprocally reinforcing.

The fractionation of religiosity into mechanisms related to belief in supernatural agents (anthropomorphic promiscuity) and mechanisms related to behaviour within groups with supernaturally authorised ritual engagements (sociographic prudery) offers a fruitful way to respond to the concern often expressed in the radicalisation literature about the inordinate focus on ideology at the expense of attending to the significant material challenges affecting the daily practice of individuals who are at risk of becoming radicalised (Mythen et al., 2017). Some of the models described below explicitly include these variables, while others utilise different ways of distinguishing between supernatural beliefs and behaviours while simultaneously attending to the causal dynamics between them.

### Computational Models that Predict (and Prevent) Theism

In this section, I briefly outline some more computer models that our team has already developed that integrate leading theories in the bio-cultural sciences and shed light on the conditions under which – and the mechanisms by which – religiosity increases or decreases among individuals in contemporary populations. In this sense, they 'predict' when religiosity is likely to grow or decline. They also disclose some of the policy-relevant levers that could 'prevent' (or promote) a rise in the sort of supernatural beliefs and behaviours that exacerbate intergroup tensions. The title of this sub-section indicates that the target is theism, rather than religion generally. This is because the models about to be discussed simulate the emergence, maintenance, or decline of supernatural beliefs and behaviours of the sort that occur in large-scale, secularising societies shaped by west Asian monotheisms.

Theogonic reproduction theory hypothesises that theism (and religiosity in general) is 'predicted' by a host of individual and contextual factors that contribute to anthropomorphic promiscuity and sociographic prudery. In other words, gods are born(e) as a result of a variety of evolved cognitive and coalitional mechanisms. As noted in Chapter 2, such mechanisms include individual-level factors such as poor analytical reasoning skills, ontological confusion, and high schizotypy (Gervais and Norenzayan, 2012;

Lindeman et al., 2015; van Der Tempel and Alcock, 2015), as well as contextual factors such as ecological duress, socio-economic dysfunction, and existential insecurity (Norris and Inglehart, 2011; 2015; Paul, 2009; Pazhoohi et al., 2017).

On the other hand, theism is 'prevented' by high levels of anthropomorphic prudery, which can be the result of science education based on naturalistic principles, and by high levels of sociographic promiscuity, which can be fostered by strong, relatively transparent secular institutions that provide existential security to a population. For example, individuals who are more highly educated and have analytic thinking styles are less likely to be religious (Ganzach and Gotlibovski, 2013; Lewis, 2015). And democratic countries in which the state invests significantly in social welfare, thereby providing existential security for its citizens, will tend to have lower levels of church attendance and religious affiliation in the population (Habel and Grant, 2013; Scheve et al., 2006; Zuckerman, 2010).

Some readers might object that these studies, and some of the others I have cited in earlier chapters and analysed and integrated in detail elsewhere (e.g., Shults, 2018b), only show that these variables are correlated and – wait for it – correlation is not causation. Exactly so. Methodologies such as survey questionnaires and even most psychometric experiments only get us to correlation. However suggestive such research might be, one cannot infer from it that low analytic skills (for example) cause religiosity. Indeed, we all know religious people with high analytic skills and atheists with low analytic skills, which undermines the idea of a linear causal link between analytic skills (for example) and religiosity. So taking a statistical 'snapshot' of the relationship among some variables at a particular time only gives us correlation. This is why we need a methodology that provides us with a 'video' of the non-linear changes within a complex adaptive system and that is capable of *growing* the macro-level phenomenon in which we are interested from micro-level individual behaviours and meso-level networked social interactions.

This, of course, is precisely what is provided by computational social simulation in general and multi-agent artificial intelligence modelling in particular. The two models we discussed in Chapter 4 already illustrated the capacity to *predict* theism in the artificial societies being simulated. The terror management model (Shults, Lane, et al., 2018) was informed by psychological experiments and other research based on terror management theory (TMT) that indicate that anxiety related to death awareness tends to ratchet up religiosity both in terms of scanning for supernatural causes and scrambling to protect in-groups (Greenberg et al., 1990; McGregor et al., 1998; McGregor et al., 2015; Norenzayan et al., 2008; 2009; Rosenblatt et al., 1989; Vail and Soenke, 2018). When human cognitive systems encounter hazards that produce anxiety about death as an 'input', they quite often have two sorts of 'output': increased belief in hidden intentional forces (especially supernatural agents) and decreased openness to out-group members. In other words, the intensification of mortality salience can amplify belief in supernatural agents (anthropomorphic promiscuity) as well as behavioural dispositions towards participating in local ritual practices (sociographic prudery). Our simulation experiments were able to replicate many of the findings in the TMT literature. They also led to new insights into the micro-level mechanisms that can lead to macro-level phenomena.

The other model discussed in Chapter 4 (Shults, Gore, et al., 2018b) began with the same agent architecture as the TMT model but incorporated and adapted critical aspects of Josh Epstein's *Agent_Zero* (Epstein, 2014), which was based on neurological and psychological research on affect, deliberation, and social contagion dynamics. Agent interactions in that model were configured in such a way that the intensification of affect in an individual agent could reach a tipping point such that its disposition would pass a threshold that could be taken as a proxy for initiating violence. This model of mutually escalating religious violence (MERV) was able to simulate some of the conditions under which mutually increasing religious violence could emerge within a population composed of two different religious groups. MERV's architecture was also designed to incorporate insights from two other well-known theories that shed light on psycho-social mechanisms that play a role in generating violence between groups: social identity theory (SIT) and identity fusion theory (IFT).

The literature on SIT supports the hypothesis that the human need to evaluate one's group positively (in the context of comparison with an out-group) can lead to stronger differentiation between groups. The interaction between groups can be powerfully determined by 'value-laden social differentiation' that increases tensions between the groups and can lead to conflict and violence (Tajfel and Turner, 1979; Tajfel, 2010). Empirical research guided by IFT has identified ways in which personal and situational factors work together to influence extreme behaviours. When personal and social identities are blurred, an individual can come to regard his or her group as functionally equivalent to his or her sense of self (identity fusion). People with less identity fusion may have strong beliefs about what 'ought' to be done for their group. People with high identity fusion, however, are far more willing to act on these beliefs even, or especially, when that involves dying or killing for the group (Swann et al., 2010; 2014). MERV's computational architecture was able to clarify some of the conditions under which the behaviour of – and interaction among – individual agents can lead to mutually escalating religious violence, drawing on insights from these theories.

All of the theories selected in these models are relevant for understanding the challenges discussed above related to religious radicalisation. Because sacred values have 'privileged links to emotions, such as anger and disgust at their violation, leading to moral outrage and increased support for violence', people who are pressured to defend such a value 'will resist trading it off for any number of material benefits, or even for peace' (Sheikh et al., 2013: 21). All of this has rather obvious implications for public policy and peace-making attempts (Atran and Ginges, 2008; Ginges et al., 2011; Ginges and Atran, 2011; Leidner et al., 2013; Sheikh et al., 2014). A sacred value can be operationally defined as 'anything that people refuse to treat as fungible with material or economic goods, for example, when people refuse to compromise over an issue regardless of the costs or benefits' (Sheikh et al., 2013: 12). When policymakers or conflict mediators ignore the function of sacred values in intensifying parochial (in-group) altruism, they pursue strategies that can make people less likely to compromise. Experimental studies have shown that 'devoted actors', that is, those primarily driven by sacred values, become more defensive and less open to conflict resolution when they are offered material incentives to compromise (Atran and Axelrod, 2008). Such offers are considered insulting and reinforce their commitment to the in-group's sacred values. Decision-making shaped by sacred values is different from the sort of cost–benefit analysis common in decision-making shaped by instrumental values, because the former incorporates moral (and sometimes religious) beliefs that can drive action independently of its prospect of success (Ginges et al., 2007).

The TMT and MERV models, which as we noted in Chapter 4 were validated in light of empirical data in the real world, provided us with tools for demonstrating some of the conditions and mechanisms involved in causing an increase in theism in simulated populations. Agents in MERV, for example, meet hazards of different sorts (social threats, disease contagion, predation, and natural disasters), which heighten their mortality salience. These encounters can increase an agent's disposition to seek explanations or help from his or her group's supernatural agents, and comfort and protection by being surrounded by fellow group members, thereby increasing his or her desire to engage in shared rituals (as predicted by TMT). As these ritual engagements intensify, some agents become more fused to their in-groups, which increases their propensity towards violence against out-group members (as predicted by SIT and IFT). MERV simulations were able to 'grow' macro-level religious inter-group violence from the micro-level behavioural rules guiding dispositional contagion within and among agents in the model. Optimisation experiments explored the parameter space to discover the conditions (combinations of parameter settings) under which mutually escalating violence was most likely to occur between theistic groups.

One of the limitations shared by these two models was that the religiosity of the (heterogeneous) agents could not go below the levels set at the initiation of each simulation run. This was adequate for the task of those models, which was to explore the way in which anxiety and violence can *increase* religiosity (and vice versa). However, when we turned to the work of simulating and analysing the mechanisms that decrease religiosity – or *prevent* theism – we needed a new sort of agent architecture.

The first of these was the Non-Religiosity Model (NoRM), whose computational architecture was based on an integration of several empirically grounded theories that show how non-religious worldviews emerge and expand in a population as critically thinking individuals learn about natural causes and human capacities within a broader social field in which they feel safe and secure (Gore et al., 2018). In other words, theism is 'prevented' (or lowered) in a population as education and existential security are increased. These are not the only relevant mechanisms, but their effects in reducing religiosity are among the most well documented (Ellis et al., 2017; Hungerman, 2014; Inglehart and Welzel, 2005; McLaughlin and McGill, 2017; Norris and Inglehart, 2011; Strulik, 2016; Zuckerman et al., 2013). The goal of the model was to understand and explain factors that influence changes in average religiosity and existential security in a population (dependent variable). The artificial society was populated with networked heterogeneous agents with cognitive architectures and distributed levels of the relevant variables such as supernatural beliefs, religious formation, and practice, as well as education and existential security (independent variable). Data for initialising the model were derived from factor analysis and structural equation modelling based on respondents from the International Social Survey Programme and from the Human Development Index for multiple countries. The simulation experiments (intervening variables) explored the conditions under which – and the mechanisms by which – the dependent variable was affected.

Validating NoRM required us to determine whether the model could simulate the emergence of *macro*-level shifts in religious practices and existential security in its artificial population (in a way that matched their change over time in the real-world datasets) from *micro*-level agent behaviours and interactions. We calibrated the model by comparing its capacity to predict the (real-world) shifts in the relevant variables that occurred during a ten-year period (1990–2000) in 11 countries. Using the calibrated model, we then predicted shifts in the relevant variables for 22 countries (including 11 for which the model was not initially calibrated) during a different ten-year period (2000–2010). NoRM's predictions were up to three times more accurate than its closest competitor, which used linear regression analysis, lending plausibility to its theoretical synthesis and causal architecture. It is important to emphasise that this macro-level shift was not programmed into the algorithms guiding micro-level agent interactions but emerged within the complex adaptive system based on the parameterised data from each country. The results of these simulation experiments strengthen the plausibility of arguments that education and existential security are mechanisms that decrement or 'prevent' theism within a population.

This brings us to a model that I mentioned briefly at the end of Chapter 2, a systems-dynamics model designed to simulate the emergence and possible decline of 'post-supernatural' cultures, that is, cultures in which the majority of the population have worldviews and lifeways that do not involve belief in coalition-favouring disembodied intentional forces (Wildman et al., 2020). This model, whose computational architecture synthesised six major theories of secularisation, included not only education and existential security (as did NoRM) but also pluralism and freedom of expression. Computational experiments were able to simulate the shift from supernatural to post-supernatural cultures – and back again. One of the key takeaways was that *all four* of the conditions mentioned above had to be relatively high, or else religious worldviews and lifeways would grow again in the population. Theism flourishes when norms or policies are in place that keep people from learning about the explanatory power of naturalistic explanations, fill them with anxiety about the future, punish expressions of opinion that question the norms of the dominant religion, or discourage appreciation of the values of out-group members. On the other hand, if one wishes to 'prevent' theism (which is the form of religion dominant in the cultures from which the data validating the model derived), one needs policies that simultaneously provide individuals with education, make them feel existentially secure, guarantee them freedom of expression, and encourage pluralistic values.

Another agent-based model developed by our teams that simulated the conditions and mechanisms involved in the prevention of theism focused on the role of worldview pluralism and family social networks (Cragun et al., 2021). This model built on other models that we had developed previously to study the role of credibility-enhancing displays (CREDs) in secularisation processes (Puga-Gonzalez et al., 2019; 2021). We wondered what caused people to leave religious groups? Under what conditions is theism prevented from growing in contemporary populations? To answer this sort of question, we began by setting up three different types of 'artificial societies', one predominantly religious, one predominantly secular, and one in between. Agents in the model had variables such as motivation to join a group, tolerance for staying in a group, personality factors, level of religiosity in worldview, and standard demographic variables. Many of these affected agents' reactions to CREDs, as well as CRUDs or credibility-*undermining* displays, such as hypocritical behaviours (Turpin et al., 2019). Simulation results suggested that worldview pluralism in an agent's neighbourhood and family social networks is among the strongest predictors of religious (dis)affiliation, especially in less pluralistic societies. Moreover, we found that there tend to be two phases in religious disaffiliation. First, early adopters who are existentially secure disaffiliate, and then, later, disaffiliation spreads as support for it in local social networks widens and it is more widely accepted in the population.

One final example. Our team also developed a computational model that could simulate the effects of (non-)religious belief and affiliation on prosociality (Galen et al., 2021). Here we focused on questions such as: Why does tolerance tend to be characteristic of the non-religious rather than the religious? How are qualities of tolerance and trust related to the process of changing beliefs and affiliation? To what extent do supernatural beliefs, group affiliation, and social interaction produce values and behaviours that benefit others, that is, prosociality? Addressing these sorts of questions requires attention to multiple variables interacting in complex social networks that shape and constrain the beliefs and behaviours of individuals. In this case, we statistically analysed the relationships among some of the relevant variables from the World Values Survey in order to inform the construction of an agent-based model that could explore the conditions and causal mechanisms at work in the promotion (or demotion) of prosocial attitudes and behaviours. The results from both the statistical analysis and the simulation experiments indicated that prosociality was more related to agents' group affiliation and social networks than to their worldview beliefs.

Confirming previous empirical studies (e.g., Welch et al., 2007; Loveland et al., 2017) our analysis of the WVS data and the computational model also indicated that individuals with a naturalistic worldview are more trusting and tolerant of others than individuals with a supernatural worldview (especially when the latter are religiously affiliated). The agent-based model was able to tease out some of the dynamics driving this process. Religious individuals tend to be less tolerant and so, insofar as those who affiliate with a particular religious in-group tend to hang out a lot with other religious individuals, their network 'alters' will tend to be intolerant, which increases their own suspicion, prejudice, and willingness to remove ideological others from their social networks. This is why religious prosociality is usually 'parochial', that is, only targeted at other religious in-group members. Non-affiliated individuals, on the other hand, were less likely to have negative (intolerant, non-trusting) interactions with their alters (by virtue of their not being affiliated to a religious group), and so less likely to remove ideological others from their networks. As with some of the others just described, this model suggests that one way to prevent theism is to encourage diverse networks of interaction. All of this has rather obvious epistemological implications.

## The Achievement of Deleuze's Meta-epistemology

Readers might understandably be wondering what any of this has to do with Deleuze. Below I will highlight a couple of ways in which this discussion of the capacity of computational modelling to simulate atheism (or non-religion) is relevant for Deleuzian philosophy (and vice versa), but first a word about the last term in the section heading. Meta-epistemology? Deleuze is not a big fan of the term epistemology itself and, to my knowledge, never discusses 'meta-epistemology'. Nevertheless, he clearly engages in the practice of this philosophical sub-field, at least if we understand it broadly as reflecting on the underlying assumptions made in debates about epistemological issues, including those about the existence and authority of epistemic facts and reasons and the psychological capacities and responsibilities of epistemic agents.

In fact, Deleuze's efforts in *Difference and Repetition* and *The Logic of Sense* in particular can be understood as effecting, or at least offering, a revolution that challenges the 'dogmatic' image of thought which, under the influence of Platonism and Christianity, had been (and still is) meta-epistemologically assumed by the majority of Western philosophers. Instead of operating in the Platonic domain of representation, with its quadripartite fetters of the identical, the similar, the analogous, and the opposed, Deleuze conceives of difference in itself and repetition for itself as that which forces us to think (the insensible, or non-sense). This Deleuzian 'epistemological' revolution has been exposited, celebrated, and critically engaged with thoroughly in the secondary literature (e.g. Hughes, 2008a; Smith, 2012; Voss, 2013; Lundy and Voss, 2015). I have discussed it in some detail in chapters 2 and 3 of *Iconoclastic Theology: Gilles Deleuze and the Secretion of Atheism* (Shults, 2014b).

My more limited goal in the concluding section of this chapter is to point briefly to two ways in which Deleuzian meta-epistemology is relevant for our discussion of models of non-religion (and vice versa). The first has to do with the epistemic implications of *simulating* atheism. In our discussion of the reversal of Platonism in Chapter 3 we pointed to Deleuze's celebration of the rising of the simulacra, rather than the resemblance of icons, as the basis for knowledge or, to be more precise, for learning. But here I want to focus on how *computational simulation* might be linked to the achievement of Deleuze's meta-epistemology. Deleuze did not live to see the successful development and deployment of the computational modelling and simulation methodologies discussed above and in Chapter 4, and so did not engage with the revolutionary epistemological implications that scholars in these disciplines have identified and exploited (Squazzoni, 2009; Winsberg, 2010; Tolk, 2013; Wolfram, 2002; Develaki, 2019; Alvarado, 2022; Parker, 2022). DeLanda, on the other hand, has lived through (and contributed to) this revolution in the philosophy of science and has explicitly shown how it can be linked to Deleuze's philosophy. We already touched on this in Chapter 3 in discussing the achievement of Deleuze's metaphysics, but now after reviewing the link between assemblage theory and methods such as multi-agent artificial intelligence modelling in the last two chapters, we can highlight some of the epistemological implications. Here too Deleuze's engagement with developments in mathematics, especially topology and group theory, are crucial for understanding these implications. However, DeLanda points out that Deleuze's use of the terms 'multiplicities' and 'Ideas' can be misleading. 'The latter suggests something Platonic, while the former is the term used by mathematicians to refer to the differential or topological manifolds themselves, that is, to non-metric spaces' (DeLanda, 2016: 121).

DeLanda points out that Deleuze does not really seem to be thinking of non-metric spaces when he uses these terms, but rather about what scientists in these fields typically call state spaces or spaces of possibilities. For example, when describing multiplicities in *A Thousand Plateaus*, Deleuze writes that 'The multiple *must be made*, not by always adding a higher dimension, but rather in the simplest of ways, by dint of sobriety, with the number of dimensions one already has available – always $n$-1 ... Subtract the unique from the multiplicity to be constituted; write at $n$-1 dimensions' (ATP, 6). And in *Difference and Repetition* Deleuze describes an Idea as 'an $n$-dimensional, continuous, defined multiplicity' (DR, 182). In that context, he also sets out the three conditions under which one can speak of a multiplicity, that is, the conditions under which an Idea *emerges*. First, its elements are not 'actually existent' but inseparable from a 'virtuality'. Second, the elements are determined by reciprocal relations that are intrinsically defined, 'non-localisable' ideal connections. Third,

> a multiple ideal connection, a differential *relation*, must be actualized in diverse spatio-temporal *relationships*, at the same time as its *elements* are actually incarnated in a variety of *terms* and forms. The Idea is thus defined as a structure. A structure or an idea is a 'complex theme', an internal multiplicity – in other words, a system of multiple, non-localisable connections between differential elements which is incarnated in real relations and actual terms. (DR, 183)

In light of our discussion of virtual phase spaces and actual simulations in Chapter 4, we might say that computational models present the structure of what Deleuze here calls Ideas or multiplicities and that computer simulations display the elements that are actualised in diverse spatial-temporal-material relationships.

DeLanda explicitly links these Deleuzian concepts (multiplicity and Idea, as well as diagram, which is spelled out in more detail in ATP) to one of the components of an assemblage: 'all three can be defined as *the structure of a possibility space*, a structure given by topological invariants like dimensionality, connectivity, and distribution of singularities' (DeLanda, 2016: 122). In other words, they are 'universal singularities' or mechanism-independent, structured possibility spaces, in the sense discussed in Chapter 4. The properties of emergent 'individual singularities' (assemblages) are the product of historical processes (simulated or otherwise), but their capacities and tendencies are defined (and so can only be known) in relation to the universal singularities in relation to which they are actualised. We do not 'know' assemblages by comparing their resemblance to transcendent (Platonic) Ideas but by empirically exploring or 'learning' about the parameters under which population-level distributed variables are altered within the structured virtual phase space of immanent (Deleuzian) Ideas or multiplicities.

Deleuze's assertion that the Idea is defined as a 'structure' also provides an entry point for bringing his approach into contemporary philosophical debates surrounding epistemological (and ontological) structural realism (French, 2017; Ladyman and Ross, 2007). For example, take Floridi's broad definition of structural realism as the view that it is possible to get the structural properties of reality right because they are in some sense knowable in themselves (Floridi, 2013: 340). Well, Deleuze would probably not want to say we get them 'right' or that they are 'knowable in themselves', but if DeLanda's reading of him as a realist is correct (and I think it is), he might say that learning about the real virtual structures (Ideas, multiplicities, diagrams) in relation to which assemblages are actualised, and the real actualisation of assemblages whose possible properties, capacities, and tendencies constitute real virtual structures, is indeed possible. At any rate, Deleuze's purely immanent epistemology (if we can call it that) can be a resource for computer modellers and social simulation scholars interested in philosophical reflection on the conditions for knowledge in their various disciplines.

For our purposes here, the key point is that CMS enables us to 'make' multiplicities and even Ideas or diagrams (in Deleuze's sense) when we create the virtual state space of a computational model, which can then be explored in order to learn about the emergent properties, tendencies, and capacities of its actualised simulated assemblages. Following Nietzsche, Deleuze rejected the traditional philosophical way of privileging 'truth' and the obsession with 'knowing'. In *What is Philosophy?* he argued that 'philosophy does not consist in knowing and is not inspired by truth. Rather, it is categories like Interesting,

Remarkable, or Important that determine success or failure' (WIP, 82). And this is precisely what tools such as multi-agent artificial intelligence modelling and social simulation can provide philosophers, regardless of the academic discipline within which they operate: insight into the interesting, remarkable, and important attractors in a state space in relation to which singularities are condensed or assemblages are actualised.

Some social scientists, humanists, and even philosophers might understandably feel an epistemological reticence to embrace (or even tolerate) the rapidly expanding application of computational techniques within the academy. CMS provides scaffolding for radical interdisciplinarity and powerful tools for analysing and forecasting changes in human minds and societies. But will the social sciences and the humanities – including philosophy – be left behind? As noted above, the teams represented in our modelling (non-)religion project(s) described earlier have been committed to the inclusion of subject-matter experts from those disciplines, including several philosophers, in a process we call *Human Simulation* (Diallo et al., 2019). While this is not always easy, our experience so far is that once humanists and social scientists, even those trained in hermeneutical and qualitative methods, begin to engage in the process they usually become enthusiastic about it as they see their own theories come to life in a computational model and are able to test their own hypotheses through simulation experiments on the artificial societies that they have helped to create.

Moreover, the use of CMS can provide scholars in these disciplines with the capacity to *explain* the emergence of the phenomena they study by growing them in artificial societies. As noted above, this approach, which is sometimes called *generative* social science (Epstein, 2006) because of the way it gets at *causality* (rather than mere correlation), has in recent years increasingly been applied in humanities disciplines such as history, literature, and culture studies. Some scholars in these and related fields may experience an allergy to language about explanation and causality, preferring to stick with the more familiar language of understanding and interpretation. However, we are not dealing here with an either/or but with a both/and. A computational architecture can be informed by and include insights from classical theories in the humanities and social sciences, while also providing techniques for experimenting and testing such theories in a way that has never been possible before.

This is likely to sound more interesting to scholars who are already comfortable with quantitative approaches, which typically or at least often include mathematical analysis and empirical experimentation. However, the use of CMS tools can also serve to highlight and even confirm the importance of claims by researchers in the social sciences and humanities disciplines.

Take, for example, a definitional issue latent in the title of this chapter: simulating (non-)religion. Just as there is no such thing as 'religion' in the abstract sense, we should avoid collapsing all processes related to the diminishing role of supernatural beliefs and religious institutions in some societies into rigid categories such as 'secularism'. Several non-religion scholars have pointed out the importance of acknowledging that there are 'multiple secularities' beyond the West (e.g., Wohlrab-Sahr and Burchardt, 2012). CMS provides a way for such scholars to *clarify* the interactions among different mechanisms at work in divergent pathways followed by various 'secularising' social assemblages, and to *demonstrate* how and why they operate differently in varying cultural and ecological environments.

But there is a second way in which our exploration of multi-agent artificial intelligence modelling of (non-)religion in the last two chapters is relevant for engaging with Deleuze's philosophy (and vice versa). It is not an accident that I have been focusing on the process of simulating *atheism*. As I have argued throughout this book so far, Deleuze's celebration of the rising of the simulacra as that which in some sense forces us to think cannot be separated from his atheism. I began Chapter 1 with his claim that atheism is 'philosophy's achievement and the philosopher's serenity' (WIP, 92). In Chapters 7 and 8, I will discuss the 'tranquillity' of Deleuze's atheism in more detail.

The main point here is that we cannot appreciate the full force of the achievement of Deleuze's meta-epistemological reflections without acknowledging the atheist machine that drives them. Where the speculative and practical purposes of philosophy coincide, it is 'always a matter of denouncing the false infinite, the infinity of religion and all of the theologico-erotic-oneiric myths in which it is expressed' (LOS, 314). All of this understandably worries (or at least annoys) philosophers still operating in the Platonic domain of representation and those defending the doctrines and practices of a particular monotheistic (despotic) social machine. However, we need to have this conversation about the value of naturalistic modes of explaining the world and to develop new practices for secularistic modes of inscribing society if we hope to learn how to live together sustainably in our current socio-ecological environment.

# 6

# Strategies for Promoting Safe Sects

In this chapter we return in more detail to the heuristic framework described in Chapter 2 that was designed to guide conversations about how gods are born(e). We humans seem to need sects (or sectioned populations, i.e., groups) to survive, and most of us seem to enjoy this. However, as we have seen in the last few chapters, this preference for hanging out with in-group members all too easily slips over into antagonism and violence towards out-group members. Can we learn how to have safe sects, that is, sectual interactions that do not engender the sorts of superstitious beliefs and segregative behaviours associated with religion (shared imaginative engagement with axiologically relevant supernatural agents)? As we have seen, progress is being made here in contexts where the nomadic atheist machine is contributing to the production of secularising societies that place a high value on naturalistic scientific explanations. Arguably, some progress is also being made in populations where territorial and capitalist machines are at work inscribing the socius, insofar as both challenge the despotic machines that transform religion into theism.

But am I being too harsh in my critique of religion in general and theism in particular? Some of my critics think I am. Among the most friendly of these critics are Brandon Daniel-Hughes and Jeffrey Speaks, who have carefully engaged with some of my earlier proposals in *Theology after the Birth of God* and *Practicing Safe Sects* and offered insightful suggestions for clarifying the project and following out its social implications (Daniel-Hughes, 2018; Speaks, 2018). Both of their critiques were instructive and provocative, providing exactly the kind of critical and constructive commentary that authors hope their work will provoke. We share a great deal in common, including a robustly naturalist metaphysics, an appreciation for the pragmatic philosophical tradition, and a deep (even 'pastoral') concern about the psychological and political shape of future human communities ('sects' in the most general sense). Instead of focusing primarily on these points of agreement, however, in the second and third sections of this chapter I will highlight some of the main differences that remain between us regarding how to *talk* about sects and how to *experiment* with sects. These differences, while not huge, are hugely important for all those of us who would like to enjoy some good, healthy (and sometimes intense) sects without somehow inadvertently making life miserable or impossible for our conspecifics.

The need to talk about – and experiment with – safe sects is becoming increasingly important in light of the pressing global challenges our species faces, such as extreme climate change, excessive consumer capitalism, and escalating cultural conflict. Strategies for discussing how (or whether) to address these challenges will vary greatly depending on whether one's primary goal is to preserve (or adapt) the supernaturally authorised traditions of a particular theistic coalition to which one belongs or to understand and foster the conditions for transforming human minds and cultures in a way that mitigates tendencies towards accepting superstitious beliefs and engaging in segregative behaviours. I lean towards the latter goal. But am I leaning too far? I don't think so. But these two authors have helped me hone some of my rhetorical articulations of theogonic reproduction theory in ways that I hope will be more effective as I attempt to encourage people to have safe sects whenever and wherever they can.

In the fourth and fifth sections of this chapter, I commend the use of 'prebunking' and other debiasing strategies in our attempts to reduce the toxicity of theisms in the body politic. I also propose some concrete strategies for addressing the relevant biases in a way that attends both to the importance of maintaining a healthy continuity between past and future civilisational forms and to the importance of creatively adapting to new social and environmental challenges. I conclude the chapter by exploring the feasibility of promoting sustainable altruism in the Anthropocene. All of this is grounded in the claim that although religious belief–behaviour complexes played an 'adaptive' role in early ancestral environments, and have continued to 'work' throughout most of human history by enhancing the species' capacity for material production and promoting its biological reproduction, today the theistic credulity and conformity biases that surreptitiously shape these kinds of social assemblages have become maladaptive in many contemporary contexts. In other words, theism is producing psychosocial dysfunctions that reduce human flourishing and lower the chances of the long-term survival of the species. Let's begin with another, and in the context of this book a final, summary of the key elements of theogonic reproduction theory as they bear on this provocative claim.

## The (Mal)adaptiveness of Theism

Most contemporary members of our species seem to share a suite of perceptual and affiliative dispositions that encourage them to 'bear' gods: supernatural agents are somewhat easily 'born' in human minds and rather consistently 'borne' across human cultures. Why? Scientific and historical research in a variety of disciplines such as evolutionary biology, cognitive science, cultural anthropology, archaeology, and history of religions has converged to support the general claim that in early ancestral environments the survival advantage went to hominids who quickly detected relevant agents such as predators, prey, protectors, and partners in the natural milieu, and who lived in groups whose cohesion was adequately protected by attachment and surveillance systems that discouraged defecting, cheating, and freeloading in the social milieu.

Although they must be further fractionated when discussing causal dynamics at various explanatory levels, god-bearing mechanisms generally fall into two broad categories: anthropomorphic promiscuity and sociographic prudery. As depicted in the lower left quadrant of Figure 1 (Chapter 2), the aggregation and interactive integration of some of these biases generate 'religion' (in the sense the term is being used here). One can think of the horizontal line in Figure 1 as a continuum on which to mark an individual's tendency to guess 'human-like supernatural force' when confronted with ambiguous or frightening phenomena in the natural environment. The anthropomorphically promiscuous will be on the lookout for hidden intentional agents and find themselves attracted to explanations that appeal to supernatural causes despite – or perhaps because – of their non-falsifiability. The vertical line can be understood as a continuum on which to register how tightly an individual is committed to inscribing the social field in ways that are consistent with the normative evaluations proscribed and prescribed by the supernatural authorities of his or her in-group. Sociographic prudes prefer to remain within their own religious coalitions and are more likely to be suspicious of out-groups.

Here is another way to put it. In early ancestral environments, *error*-management strategies that increased the number of false positives (mistaken beliefs about the presence and prevalence of hidden agents with the power to harm or bless) were naturally selected over strategies that increased the number of false negatives (mistakenly believing that no hidden agents exist when they actually are present and even prevalent). Why? Because those whose cognitive disposition led them to manage their errors in the latter way were more likely to be unprepared to fight, or to miss opportunities for feeding, fleeing, or fucking, than those disposed to manage their errors in the former way. It paid to have *credulity* biases that over-detected agency in one's immediate natural environment. Slowly over the millennia, and then relatively rapidly during the axial age, theistic social machines amplified these credulity biases to infinity (representing an all-knowing, all-powerful hidden agent). This is 'the infinity of religion' that philosophy denounces.

In early ancestral environments, *risk*-management strategies that increased the tendency of individuals to engage in the idiosyncratic rituals and constructed social norms of their own in-group were naturally selected over strategies that increased the tendency of individuals to refuse to participate in such rituals and normative behaviours. Why? Because the presence of too many people in a population with the coalitional disposition to resist opportunities for collective effervescence (as Durkheim would put it) or to trust and tolerate out-group members as much as in-group members would weaken the social cohesion of such a population by rendering it susceptible to cheaters, freeloaders, and invaders. It paid to have *conformity* biases that over-protected the normative rituals of one's immediate social environment. Slowly over the millennia, and then relatively rapidly during the axial age, theistic social machines amplified these conformity biases to eternity (damning out-group members to hell). This is 'the eternity of religion', we might say, which is equally worthy of denunciation.

My main *theoretical* claim here is that religious credulity and conformity biases, which may well have served some adaptive functions up to and throughout most of the Holocene, have now become toxic and are generally maladaptive in the Anthropocene. Here I am using the term (mal)adaptive not only – or even primarily – in a narrow sense that refers to the short-term inclusive fitness of individuals (which blindly follows the non-teleological processes of natural selection at the genetic level) but also – and principally – in a broader sense that refers to the longer-term survival of the human species (which may require foresight and the intentional alteration of ecological conditions that shape social selection). In many contexts today, religious individuals have a higher fertility rate than non-religious individuals and so these biases may well enhance the chances for genetic transmission in some local environments.

When I say that theisms are generally maladaptive in the Anthropocene, I mean that they exacerbate some of the most pressing global challenges our species faces, including those I mentioned above: extreme climate change, excessive consumer capitalism, and escalating cultural conflict. I am not suggesting that all religions – or even all theisms – have always and everywhere been toxic. As we saw in Chapter 2, beliefs and behaviours related to theism – such as those related to racism, classism, and sexism – played a key role in facilitating the emergence and cohesion of large-scale human societies. Without these biases, it is unlikely that our species would have survived or thrived. For a growing number of individuals worldwide, however, it is becoming increasingly obvious that these evolved dispositions are now dysfunctional – at least if our therapeutic goal for society involves widespread human flourishing.

My main *pragmatic* claim is that those who desire to mitigate the toxic effects of these biases would do better to shift some of their energy away from attempts at 'debunking' theism and adopt some of the 'prebunking' and other debiasing strategies that are being constructed and empirically tested by psychologists and policy professionals. As public proponents of the scientific consensus on climate change (for example) have learned, showering people with more and better information about the human role in contributing to this crisis can actually make things worse, activating worldview defence mechanisms and other biases that further strengthen inaccurate beliefs and support inappropriate behaviours. I will focus on some of the practical implications of this research in the later sections of this chapter.

By way of reminder, I have been using the term *religion* in a broad sense to designate 'shared imaginative engagement with axiologically relevant supernatural agents', that is, belief–behaviour complexes conditioned by an aggregate of evolved god-bearing mechanisms that have contributed to the social cohesion of some in-groups. What distinguishes *theistic* social assemblages from other religious assemblages is the way in which the cohesion of the former is also maintained through regular appeals to an infinite supernatural agent, a disembodied (or at least ontologically confused) intentional force that is putatively engaged with through sacerdotally mediated rituals performed by the members (or elites) of a particular in-group (and who eternally rewards or punishes all groups whatsoever). Cognitive and coalitional god-bearing biases, which are part of our phylogenetic inheritance and have been reinforced by millennia of social entrainment practices, now commonly draw contemporary members of *Homo sapiens* into a kind of bio-cultural attractor space within the broader possibility space of human social assemblages. This helps to explain why human beings today so often exhibit a high level of *credulity* towards claims about divine revelations from the gods of their own group and a high level of *conformity* to the norms and rituals regulated by the leaders of their theistic in-groups.

Once again, it is important to highlight the value that these biases provided for our early and even relatively recent ancestors. If they had not offered some survival advantage in the context of challenges in some previous environmental context, the genes whose expression supports traits that engender religious biases would not likely have become widespread in human populations and transmitted through the generations. Moreover, many of the social structures that developed to support religious traditions were also adaptive – in the broader sense that they facilitated the survival of the species. For example, the emergence of priestly elites in the axial age civilisations of west, south, and east Asia helped those societies coordinate and cooperate as their populations increased in size and diversity. Over the last two millennia, theologians and philosophers (as well as rabbis, pastors, and imams) identified with the Abrahamic monotheisms have contributed to the cohesion of these traditions and the cultivation of virtue among their adherents. However, they have also often provided justification and motivation for the exclusion of (and violence towards) out-group members.

Like racist, sexist, and classist biases, theist biases 'worked' in a wide variety of historical and geographical contexts, binding individuals together and motivating them to fight to protect their alliances. Indeed, from the Upper Palaeolithic to the recent past, religious sects have played an important role in the cohesion and expansion of (some) god-bearing human groups. However, we now have good reasons to think that the theist biases that support this sort of social assemblage are becoming increasingly toxic (maladaptive) and no longer promote human flourishing in a growing number of contexts.

Here I point briefly to three of these reasons. First, the constellation of evolved biases and personality factors (such as magical thinking, schizotypy, conspiracy mentality, susceptibility to hallucination, and ontological confusion) that are highly associated with *anthropomorphically promiscuous* individuals in a population render such individuals more prone to making errors in the perception of ambiguous phenomena and less able to detect logical errors – not only in their thinking about gods, but also in their thinking about other paranormal, superstitious, or conspiratorial claims (Breslin and Lewis, 2015; Davies et al., 2001; Lindeman et al., 2015; Pennycook et al., 2014; van Der Tempel and Alcock, 2015; Wlodarski and Pearce, 2016). In other words, theist credulity biases promote not only 'harmless' religious beliefs, but also a host of other beliefs and attitudes that make it more difficult to accept scientific analyses of climate change (for example) and easier to resist calls for compromise and distributed justice in pluralistic social contexts (Bruynell, 2012; Sekerdej et al., 2018; Bakhti, 2018; Kramer and Shariff, 2016; Zmigrod et al., 2019; Ecklund et al., 2017).

The second reason is more directly related to *sociographic prudery*. Here too there are a variety of mental mechanisms that can undergird a preference for the supernaturally authorised norms of one's own in-group, all of which are differentially distributed in human populations. Those that are associated with individual religiosity include higher levels of racial and ethnic prejudice, susceptibility to charismatic leaders, risk-aversion, proclivity to engage in antisocial behaviour towards out-groups, and resistance to innovation (Benabou et al., 2015; Blogowska et al., 2013; Chuah et al., 2014; Coccia, 2014; Dunkel and Dutton, 2016; Schjoedt et al., 2013). In other words, although theist conformity biases enhance in-group cohesion, they are also strongly correlated to societal dysfunction (Delamontagne, 2010; Paul, 2009; Zuckerman, 2010) and can promote intergroup conflict and violent extremism, especially among fundamentalist and dogmatic religious individuals whose sense of self is highly fused with their group (Beller and Kröger, 2017;

Kossowska et al., 2017; Sheikh et al., 2014; Shults, Gore, et al., 2018b; Pretus et al., 2018).

A third reason to worry about the 'toxicity' of theisms in our contemporary, globally interconnected, and ecologically fragile environment has to do with the way in which the two broad types of god-bearing mechanism can *reciprocally reinforce* one another. Like the biases themselves, this mutual intensification operates beneath the level of conscious awareness. Priming studies and other psychological and ethnographic experiments have shown that surreptitiously triggering thoughts about supernatural agents automatically rachets up defensive attitudes and behaviours related to protecting one's own religious coalition, and that activating anxiety about the safety or stability of one's religious in-group ratchets up causal attributions to and beliefs in the relevant 'gods' (Johnson et al., 2010; Wichman, 2010; Routledge et al., 2017; Vail et al., 2012; hundreds of other relevant studies are summarised and analysed in Shults, 2018a).

In other words, mistakenly attributing causality to supernatural agents can amplify segregative behaviours, and fervently affiliating with supernatural coalitions can amplify superstitious beliefs, especially under stressful conditions. All of this makes it more difficult to resolve the major societal and global challenges we face today, rendering these biases 'maladaptive' (in the general sense outlined above).

Theistic sects become toxic when the cognitive and coalitional biases that sustain them no longer function to help support the long-term welfare of the species (even when accounting for short-term gains) or when they propagate conditions that increase the societal dysfunction and material suffering of its members. The good news is that we already seem to be adapting. In recent centuries, both *naturalist* explanations of the causal nexus of the world and *secularist* organisations of the cohesive norms of society have grown in popularity in a wide variety of contexts. As indicated in the upper right quadrant of Figure 2 (Chapter 2), the rise of naturalism and secularism have promoted the contestation of god-bearing biases. Those who are more anthropomorphically prudish resist appeals to supernatural agents in their causal hypotheses. Those who are more sociographically promiscuous resist appeals to supernatural authorities in their social policies. This resistance is typically reinforced by evidence-based scientific training and participation in transparent, democratic, secular societies.

Naturalism and secularism are relatively fragile late modern developments, but they increasingly (albeit tentatively) shape intersubjective and transcommunal discourse in the Anthropocene in a growing number of contexts. For those who are concerned that such developments might too quickly dissolve the virtue-cultivating worldviews and ritual practices upon which the cohesion of their religious sects seem to depend, these changes might seem destructive rather than 'adaptive'. These are valid concerns, and the pursuit of new creative modes of inscribing the socius should be balanced by careful attention to the dignity of individuals and the integrity of communities. Nevertheless, the survival of the species – and the flourishing of more of its individual members – likely depends on the discovery of innovative ways of improving our mental and social health by immunising more of the body politic from toxic forms of theist bias.

## *Talking* about Safe Sects

I turn now to a response to my friendly critics mentioned above, Daniel-Hughes and Speaks, both of whom are naturalists and secularists (in my sense). They both want to have 'the talk' about religious reproduction and facilitate the dissolution of the god-bearing mechanisms. Like me, they are worried about the ease with which linguistic symbols of transcendence erected and protected by priestly elites can activate and amplify imaginative engagement with person-like, coalition-favouring disembodied intentional forces, further intensifying superstitious beliefs. Like me, they are worried about the ease with which in-group religious rituals can activate and amplify anxiety about and antagonism towards out-group members, further intensifying segregative behaviours. Like me, they are worried about the *sacerdotal* trajectory of theology (which flows into the lower left quadrant of Figure 1 in Chapter 2) and are willing to put the necessary energy into promoting the *iconoclastic* forces related to the theolytic mechanisms integrated in the upper right quadrant of Figure 2. That is a lot to hold in common. Our main differences have to do with the ways in which we want to talk about – and to experiment with – participation in *safe* sects.

As both of these authors point out, one of the key hypotheses of theogonic reproduction theory is that the two types of god-bearing mechanisms are *reciprocally reinforcing*. Daniel-Hughes refers to this as my 'automatic reciprocity' thesis, which is understandable since I do write that this mutual amplification can be 'somewhat automatic' in *Theology after the Birth of God*. In *Practicing Safe Sects*, where I discuss the empirical literature in far more detail, I try to avoid the idea of automaticity and emphasise the conditions under which various components of anthropomorphic promiscuity and sociographic prudery are likely to reinforce one another. However, I stand by 'somewhat automatic' because those conditions, which are linked to both individual and contextual variance, are in fact the kind of conditions under which most people on the planet today regularly find themselves. One of the pragmatic implications of the reciprocity hypothesis is that those who want to challenge sociographically prudish tendencies (as most liberal theologians such as Daniel-Hughes and Speaks do) must also challenge anthropomorphically promiscuous ways of engaging with religious symbols, and vice versa.

As both Daniel-Hughes and Speaks emphasise, one of the main bones of contention upon which we are all gnawing is the appropriate use of the highly contentious term 'religion'. This is not the place to rehash the problems related to essentialist and colonialist uses of the term, which all three of us eschew. Speaks helpfully sets this controversy in the broader context of the general differences in the ways in which terms are handled in the academic work of scholars in theology and religious studies, on the one hand, and scholars in the scientific study of religion, on the other. For the latter, the important thing is to operationalise one's terms so that they can function well within testable empirical hypotheses about statistically measurable traits. For the former, the important thing is to clarify one's terms so that they can function well within narrative interpretations of artefacts, institutions, norms, and experiences entangled within complex human traditions. So 'scientists' and 'humanists' have different (albeit often overlapping) concerns about the use of terms in academic research.

Both of my interlocutors accept the basic scientific claims behind my hypotheses about the role of supernatural agents and authorities in the quotidian lives of the laity, as well as the value of my definition of religion (shared imaginative engagement with axiologically relevant supernatural agents) for the purposes of scientific research. However, they seem to prefer a particular humanist-leaning rhetorical strategy when it comes to talking about *religious* sects, especially when 'the talk' is meant to occur in communities that self-identify as religious rather than in scientific journals or conferences. Daniel-Hughes wants to disentangle 'religion' – understood as 'engagement with disembodied intentional agents' – from the 'otherwise valuable axiological dimensions of religious practice' (Daniel-Hughes, 2018: 61). Similarly, Speaks argues that the problem with my 'narrow' definition is that 'belief in, and engagement with supernatural agents is not the only aspect of life that religion offers', and that I 'mistake one aspect of religion for the whole' (Speaks, 2018: 69–70).

Notice, however, that both authors seem to be begging the question. They assume that 'religion' refers to an extremely broad range of phenomena and then complain that my use of the term does not incorporate some variables that they think fall into that range. Speaks prefers definitions that include a more 'comprehensive understanding of their subject', and rejects my definition because it is 'incapable of registering naturalistic forms of religious expression'. Daniel-Hughes worries that I have thrown out the baby (other aspects of 'religion') with the bathwater (beliefs and behaviours related to supernatural agents), and points to the possibility of enjoying those 'exaptive and spandrel-like qualities [of religion] that have little to do with supporting in-group solidarity among non-kin and out-group hostility towards outsiders'. But this simply presupposes the appropriateness of their broad use of the term to refer to the general subject of intense human experiences that are common across narrative traditions.

Of course, one can use terms however one likes, as long as one is clear what one means, but in my view it is important to have good theoretical reasons (I will return to pragmatic reasons below) for one's usage. I prefer my definition because it is able to pick out an empirically relevant and conceptually interesting set of phenomena in human experience, while the broader definitions championed by Daniel-Hughes and Speaks render 'religious' and 'human' almost synonymous. They are not alone. The idea that our species *is* simply *Homo religiosus* is a notion long sponsored by scholars such as Robert Neville and Wesley Wildman, to whom both of my current interlocutors refer.

Speaks alludes briefly to Wildman's 'five elements that religion typically offers its adherents'. Here is Wildman's full list of these elements or 'features' of religion:

> A way to relate every aspect of life to something ultimate and fundamental, in terms of ideas, values, and practices; An answer to concerns about death and immortality, including the ultimate origins, fate, and meaning of human life and all of reality; A means of bonding human beings tightly together through obligation, responsibility, and ritual, in order to stabilize social life and realize relational ideals such as peace, pleasure, power, or prosperity; A solution to the problem of human evil and a means of healing, liberation, social transformation, and personal self-cultivation; A source of orienting narratives by which we discern our place in a cosmological framework and gather the courage to make moral decisions. (Wildman, 2011: 37)

As I have pointed out elsewhere (Shults, 2022b), all five of these features could just as easily apply to individuals and groups committed to atheism or humanism as they do to those committed to the Islamic State or American evangelicalism. The worldview and lifestyle of Richard Dawkins – to pick the standard example of someone who radically rejects religion – seem to contain all of these elements. In fact, these features can be applied to every human being I know, although some people take them more seriously and reflect on them more intensely than others. This approach to defining the term is so broad that it is not clear what analytical work it is doing that similarly vague but less confusing categories such as 'worldview' (or 'lifestyle', 'human culture', 'meaningful life', 'axiological intensity', etc.) could not do equally well.

Second, notice that none of these five features includes any reference to imaginative engagement with *supernatural agents*, that feature that scholars who study these phenomena scientifically almost unanimously agree is that which demarcates the 'religious' from other aspects of human life. Exploratory and confirmatory factor analyses of psychological and sociological datasets have consistently found latent variables tied to *supernatural* beliefs and ritual behaviours. For example, experimental psychological studies found that 'supernatural content' was 'the *only thing* that distinguishes religiosity from non-religiosity' (Lindeman et al., 2016: 225, emphasis added). In fact, a review of the literature suggests that 'supernatural-related belief/practice' is 'the *only unique diagnostic feature* of religiosity … and empirically distinct from sociability, virtue, hope, etc.' (Schuurmans-Stekhoven, 2016: 258, emphasis added).

Factor analyses of online surveys and the International Social Survey Programme dataset have also demonstrated that beliefs and practices related to *supernatural* forces form relatively independent clusters of variables (Schofield et al., 2016; Lemos et al., 2019). The techniques used in the sort of research, including exploratory factor analysis, confirmatory factor analysis, and covariance analysis, are able to tease apart the relationships between variables drawn from responses in surveys or psychological experiments. One might worry that the surveys are biased towards defining religiosity in relation to supernaturalism, but they contain a wide variety of questions, in some cases many dozens of questions, that have nothing to do with supernaturalism. The main point is that variables related to supernatural beliefs and behaviours cluster together and are distinct from other variables related to morality, sense of purpose, community, meaningfulness in life, and other vague categories with which they are often confounded or confused.

But perhaps I am the one begging the question? Am I simply assuming that my narrower definition is correct and inappropriately complaining that 'religious naturalists' are placing too many other phenomena into the category of 'religion'? Of course, there is no abstractly 'right' definition of any term. And again, one can stipulate the use of terms however one likes, but it should be clear (especially for pragmatists) what they are supposed to be *doing* conceptually. The real issue is how terms *work* – in this case, how they work when we *talk about sects*. My goal in using the term 'religion' is to differentiate between ways of participating in human sects that involve ritually engaging with allegedly disembodied, coalition-favouring spirits (which intensifies superstition and segregation under a wide range of conditions) from those that do not. My narrower definition does this differentiating work. How does the fuzzy use of the term preferred by Daniel-Hughes and Speaks work? Whatever else it may do, in my view this kind of liberal permissivism confuses non-scholars and provides cover for the copious fertility of god-bearing conservatives and fundamentalists.

I am not denying the value of the typically 'humanist' approach to terminological usage; it is one I have practised for decades and plan to continue using in my philosophical and historical writings. My concern is with this particular way of using the term *religious* to refer to such a wide swathe of human experience that it encompasses virtually every individual and all human groups, thereby blurring the very important distinction between two ways of holding individuals and coalitions together: those that rely on idiosyncratic inferences about and parochial preferences for imagined supernatural agents and authorities – and those that do not. I can understand why conservative religious apologists would want to use such a vague notion of 'religion': it evokes intense feelings about aspects of being alive that almost everyone finds valuable and obscures that which distinguishes the sort of in-groups to which they belong from other ways of participating in human sects: unfalsifiable beliefs about and ritual practices oriented towards appeasing invisible punitive spirits.

But neither Daniel-Hughes nor Speaks (nor Wildman nor Neville) are conservative apologists. They are scientific naturalists and liberal secularists, eager to discover new ways of understanding the world and to chart new ways of organising the social field that do not depend on supernatural agents or authorities. Continuing to call themselves 'religious' is confusing to everyone who is not already part of an ongoing conversation among a relatively small group of naturalist philosophers who, for one reason or another, value some of the distinctive features of one or more religious traditions. Why do they insist and persist in this unusual use of the term despite all the confusion it engenders? I think their essays engaging with my work make it clear that their motivation is pastoral: they are concerned about the future of their own (and other) religious communities in a world where a growing number of individuals and groups are learning to live together and enjoy sects without worrying about whether any supernatural agents are watching.

## *Experimenting* with Safe Sects

Despite our disagreement over how precisely to talk about sects, Daniel-Hughes, Speaks, and I share an interest in 'sectual' experimentation that does not lead to supernatural agent conceptions. In fact, our pragmatic strategies for promoting 'safe' sects are quite similar. It seems to me that one of our basic differences has to do with the level of optimism we feel about the prospects of engaging in such experimentation within the confines and configurations of traditional 'religious' communities. Daniel-Hughes and Speaks are enthusiastic about the idea. They read me as far less sanguine than I actually am, perhaps, in part, because of the terminological confusion outlined above. Their pressing me on this issue provides a fresh opportunity to clarify my theoretical position and pragmatic orientation.

What Daniel-Hughes considers his 'small contribution' in the conclusion of his article is, in my view, an extremely important contribution, and the moment in this exchange that has had the most profound effect on my thinking around these issues. I believe he is right to alert us to the importance of stressing the continuity between supernaturalist and naturalist chapters in the story of human evolution. '[I]f metaphysically naturalist axiological narratives are to have any chance of competing for even a portion of the popular religious imagination, they must emphasize the *continuities*, not only between multiple traditions and in-groups, but also between the theistic and postpartum chapters of the story' (emphasis added). Daniel-Hughes encourages us to resist the

> impulse to read religious theists as out-group antagonists. The goal should be to narrate naturalist theology, not as a tale of supercessionism in which 'Brights' vanquish 'Supers', but instead as a story of *continuous* axiological ingenuity in which humanity has developed an impressive capacity to solve bio-environmental and bio-cultural problems, to learn from its successes and errors, and to exercise a modicum of personal and communal self-control over its instincts and intuitions. (2018: 64, emphases added)

Daniel-Hughes is fair in his (implied) criticism of me for not adequately emphasising this continuity. He does acknowledge that I explicitly propose interrogating the iconoclastic trajectories of the great theological traditions to extract their god-dissolving resources, a strategy that he refers to as 'ransacking the closets of traditional religions' to find ways of resisting 'theologically incorrect' default inferential habits. And he rightly interprets my postpartum theology as 'an *intensification, rather than a break* with this [naturalist, iconoclastic] tradition of working to bend the cost curve of religious inquiry away from cheap intuitive defaults and towards more promising, but more expensive, creative, living experiments' (2018: 64, emphasis added). However, I read this last section of his article as a gentle, indirect reprimand for my failure to highlight the continuities within the ongoing narrative of the evolution of human modes of configuring social space (having sects).

Indeed, I confess that I have spent more time offering passionate pleas in favour of driving a conceptual wedge between two basic ways of having sects (outlined above) than I have in emphasising that this does not entail driving a demographic wedge between two basic types of people. I do make this latter point in *Theology after the Birth of God* and *Practicing Safes Sects* as well as in other more recent writings (Shults, 2018a; 2019a; Shults, Gore, et al., 2018a). However, if a careful reader such as Daniel-Hughes can imagine a 'strongest reading' of my thesis as suggesting that 'in-group coalition building, even in the name of postpartum axiological experimentation, must be resisted', then clearly I need to stress this point more often and more forcefully. Humans need sects, and I have no desire to dissuade them from enjoying their pleasures. Although I have consistently called for the dissolution of belief–behaviour complexes related to coalition-favouring gods, I have explicitly rejected the idea that religious communities must be dissolved. In *Practicing Safe Sects*, for example, I urge iconoclastic theologians (and activists, and contemplatives) within religious traditions 'to imagine and enact new and creative ways to live in community that do not rely on the [theogonic] mechanisms of the sacerdotal trajectory' (Shults, 2018b: 178).

So, how are theologians (or naturalist philosophers of religion) embedded within particular religious traditions supposed to go about this postpartum pastoral task? Here too Daniel-Hughes is exactly right when he interprets me as 'suggesting that we attempt to intervene in agent-detecting inferential process at the pre-deductive, pre-inductive, post-abductive moment of hypothesis selection (retroduction) and attempt to exercise a kind of communal self-control that would resist our biologically, cognitively, and culturally inherited preference for agent-hypotheses' (2018: 55). I agree with him that axiological experiments involving 'small-scale creative explorations' are the most likely to succeed, and that identifying 'semiotic resources' in the 'venerable' traditions that can be marshalled for 'resisting habitual and traditional domestications of naturalist projects' is a particularly promising strategy. This will be strongly countered, of course, by those whose sense of identity or even livelihood depends on the domesticating forces of the sacerdotal trajectory, but it is still worth the effort.

To be clear: I do see the potentially positive benefits of working with, and within, religious traditions and their sign networks. However, my preference would be for this pastoral work to involve straightforwardly challenging the use of traditional religious symbols that smack of supernaturalism. The scientific study of religion has demonstrated how easily (and covertly) the latter activate superstitious interpretations, which in turn amplify segregative behaviours (under a wide variety of conditions), accelerating a whirlpool of reciprocally reinforcing god-bearing mechanisms. Iconoclastic pastors and philosophers participating in small-scale religious communities have a unique opportunity to help people learn how to see and resist their theistic biases. In fact, I would say that this 'internal' strategy is a healthy and even crucial complement to the broader 'external' strategy of working to increase access to humanist and scientific education and to reduce the dysfunctional socio-economic and political conditions that foster religious beliefs and behaviours.

Speaks also emphasises the value and importance of having 'the talk' *within* religious communities, noting the remarkable power that ministers have to shape the imaginations of their congregants. Like Daniel-Hughes, he is concerned that I am insufficiently attentive to the importance of maintaining continuity within traditions. However, Speaks expresses his worry far more strongly. 'For Shults, there does not seem to be *any way* in which to "practice safe sects" while retaining *any* semblance of *continuity* with existing religious traditions' (2018: 67, emphases added). I am not sure what to make of this reading. At the very least, this tells me that I need to emphasise even more strongly than I have in the two books under discussion that my goal is to *intensify* (rather than ignore) the iconoclastic trajectories in the axial age religious traditions and to *transform* (rather than dissolve) the coalitions in which the vast majority of the human population live and move and have their valuing (Shults, 2014c; 2014b; 2018b).

Speaks's misinterpretation of the pragmatic and normative implications I draw from the empirical findings and theoretical developments behind theogonic reproduction theory demonstrates how easily confusion can arise when one switches back and forth between specific, empirically based, operationalised definitions and broad, narrative-oriented, hermeneutical definitions of religion. This is perhaps best illustrated in his reading of me as promoting an 'abstinence-only' approach to religious education, which he contrasts to his own proposal for 'safe and responsible God-talk'. Of course, I knew I was asking for trouble when I chose to frame theogonic reproduction theory with such *sectsy* metaphors. Like all analogies, the comparison between talking about (and experimenting with) 'sex' and 'sects' eventually breaks down. However, the problem here is not simply that Speaks pushes the analogy too far. It is rather a case of clouding the comparison with a confusion.

Speaks suggests that my narrow definition of religion 'would be akin to defining human sexuality as "the creation of a baby by means of heterosexual intercourse"' (2018: 70). This is mistaken for at least two reasons. First, and most importantly, Speaks's way of framing the analogy presupposes that I see 'religion' only as the act of *conceiving* gods. But it takes a village to raise a god, and this occurs through in-group ritual interactions that are supposed to appease or affirm the imagined anthropomorphic entity in question. His proposed analogue does not adequately take into account the *communal* dimension of my definition of religion: '*shared* imaginative engagement with *axiologically relevant* supernatural agents'. For me the problem is not only the way in which gods are born in human minds but also the way in which they are *borne* in human *societies*. As I have shown in the books under review, theistic credulity and conformity biases engender (and are psychologically and politically entangled within) other socially toxic biases such as sexism, racism, and classism. That to which I want people to 'just say no' (although I realise it is not so easy because of the covert operation of evolved biases) are the affective *and collective* drives that lead to *bearing gods* in cognition *and culture*.

Second, and closely related, Speaks's way of discussing his proposed analogy not only implies that my definition of religion ignores its non-conceptual (extra-copulative) dimensions; it also wrongly suggests that I have disregarded the importance of the intensity and the value of the diversity of ways in which people express themselves in sects *in general*. As I have tried to make clear in several places (see citations above), I am all for intense sectual experimentation and have no qualms about consenting adults (of any gender and culture) engaging in whatever sort of 'intimate', 'life-enriching', and 'existentially gripping' experiences they find satisfying and salubrious. Moreover, I have no interest in regulating the positions people ought to take as they articulate their bodies politic. Speaks is right that abstinence-only approaches to sex education do not work; simply pressuring people to abstain from coitus is not going to help. Neither will forms of religious education that simply tell people not to fantasise about gods (or forbid them to engage in responsible God-talk).

But that is not my project. I am quite happy for people to go on experimenting with creative modes of sectual intercourse within their traditions; however, I want to encourage them to think through the consequences that bearing gods has on their own religious families of origin, as well as on other, non-familiar social coalitions near and far. To be clear: I am not at all against having sects. On the contrary, we humans cannot thrive – or even survive – without them. I am against the reproduction of coalition-favouring supernatural agent conceptions in communities in ways that bind people together by impeding critical thinking and instigating assortative prosociality.

Our desires and fears related to talking about and experimenting with sects are shaped by our personal histories and social contexts. I am certainly no exception. And so time for another confession. I have lived in the US for most of my life, and during that period I pretty much took for granted the relevance and even the necessity of religion for maintaining the social fabric of human life. I agree with Daniel-Hughes and Speaks that all human beings need ways of orienting themselves in the world, narrative frameworks for their lives, ways of managing self-transformation and social interactions, etc. After eighteen years in Norway, however, I am now convinced that 'religious' institutions are not at all necessary for fulfilling these needs. Religious beliefs and church attendance are astonishingly low in Scandinavian populations, and yet these countries are ranked among the highest in the world in terms of happiness, social and gender equality, existential security, and non-parochial altruism.

To put it bluntly, in societal contexts where people have universal access to healthcare, free university education in the humanities and sciences, strong economies, and relatively transparent democratic governments, they don't really need churches or clergy and they certainly don't need theism. They get along fine creating new ways of exploring and enjoying sects without any need for religious symbols. This suggests that working for economic justice and building strong secular institutions are among the most important ways to promote safe sects.

I enthusiastically endorse the commitment by Daniel-Hughes and Speaks (and others) to having 'the talk' about religious reproduction within the coalitions to which they are pastorally connected, but I would encourage them to be even more radical in their promotion of anthropomorphic prudery and sociographic promiscuity in such contexts. When it comes to sects, people are more flexible and adaptive than you might think. Yes, continuity matters, and we should continue to ransack our cultural traditions for resources. We are indeed all part of the same story, and we are in this together. However, the adaptive challenges our species now face are new and the changes in our environment are non-linear; it is imperative that we let go of our religious (theistic) inhibitions and experiment a bit more radically if we want to keep our (and everyone else's) sects safe. What role can philosophy play here?

## Prebunking Theism

Much of the philosophical discussion about the relative value of shared imaginative engagement with axiologically relevant supernatural agents focuses on the extent to which (or even whether) evolutionary accounts can *debunk* religious beliefs about the existence or effects of gods. In other words, do the causal histories of theistic beliefs provided by disciplines such as evolutionary psychology and the cognitive science of religion undermine their plausibility? Non-religious philosophers often point to the peculiar character of supernatural beliefs, which they argue renders them susceptible to evolutionary debunking arguments (Griffiths and Wilkins, 2015; Nola, 2013; Shook, 2015). On the other hand, philosophers who identify with a particular religious coalition (usually Judaism, Christianity, or Islam) commonly warn their interlocutors of the dangers of the genetic fallacy, pointing out that etiological accounts do not entail the falsity of religious beliefs (Johnson et al., 2014; Jong and Visala, 2014; van Eyghen, 2016).

It is important to emphasise that the arguments I have made above (and elsewhere) about beliefs in supernatural agents are not attempts to weaken religious truth claims by problematising their sources or by denigrating those who make them. I do not think theists (or racists, classists, and sexists) are bad people. I do not even think these biases themselves are inherently 'bad'; they are naturally selected tendencies that we now have good reason to contest in some contexts. It is the biased judgements that can be toxic, not the people who make them.

The epidemiological analyses of supernatural conceptions that I have been offering here are aimed not simply at contesting religious beliefs at the level of logical abstraction, but at diagnosing their effects on psychosocial health in relation to the religious behaviours with which they are entangled in theistic traditions. In fact, religious practices, such as rituals whose goal is to successfully engage supernatural agents, are also susceptible to etiological critiques (De Cruz, 2018). My broader point here, however, is that it is necessary to pay as close attention to *context* biases as we do to *content* biases. The former typically trigger and sustain the latter, making them all the more difficult to resist. For example, regular participation in emotionally arousing, synchronic ritual practices involving causally opaque behaviours can downregulate executive function, rendering individuals more susceptible to the non-falsifiable claims of charismatic ritual officers about the putative desires of supernatural agents. The philosophical debates between theists and non-theists rarely lead individuals from one side to convert to the other, and this is due, in part, to the very different ways in which cognitive content biases (such as the tendency to attribute confusing phenomena to gods) are activated – or suppressed – by the very different social contexts within which individuals find themselves (Shults, 2015a; 2018a; 2019).

For this reason, I propose that those concerned with mitigating the toxic effects of theist biases supplement their philosophical efforts with strategies developed in the scientific discussion on cognitive debiasing, which include (relatively) successful *prebunking* techniques. Researchers in these fields often emphasise that debiasing is a kind of applied social epistemology and call for the engagement of individuals in the context of real-life situations involving pragmatic considerations (Aczel et al., 2015; Croskerry et al., 2013; Kenyon, 2014). As policy professionals interested in promoting solutions to global societal challenges have found, debunking strategies that attack biased beliefs are rarely effective and all too often cause people to react defensively and embrace their problematic positions even more strongly. This applies to biased beliefs related to the causes and consequences of conflict, consumerism, and climate change (Campbell and Kay, 2014; Lewandowsky et al., 2013; Lewandowsky and Oberauer, 2016).

Perhaps the most consistent research finding in the psychological literature on debiasing is that it is really, really difficult. This is hardly surprising given the phylogenetic antiquity and sociocultural significance of the evolved dispositions we have been discussing. Nevertheless, there is reason for hope, and a growing number of psychologists are optimistic that debiasing research could positively contribute to human welfare. For example, interventions have been developed that reduce biases affecting anti-Muslim hostility, attribution error, anchoring, social projection, and clinical decision-making (Bruneau et al., 2018; Croskerry, 2003; Jenkins and Youngstrom, 2016; Morewedge et al., 2015). At the most general level, debiasing techniques typically involve the promotion of what some cognitive scientists call 'system 2' processing, which is more controlled and rule-governed, over 'system 1' processing, which is more automatic and intuitive (Lilienfeld et al., 2009; Kahneman, 2013). However, psychologists have drilled down to develop far more specific strategies for debiasing, some of which may be valuable for reducing the deleterious effects of toxic theisms.

For example, the importance of affirming an individual's identity and worldview (insofar as possible) in the context of presenting new information that challenges their bias was one of the earliest – and is now one of the most empirically validated – insights emerging from social psychological studies on this topic. Research based on terror management theory suggests that when people feel uncertain or anxious, they will often respond to worldview-threatening ideas by more intensely defending and justifying their belief systems, and sometimes by increasing their aggressive behaviour towards out-group members (McGregor et al., 1998; Hennes et al., 2012). Research based on self-affirmation theory indicates that motivational biases that increase resistance to persuasion, and decrease sensitivity to argument strength and capacity to objectively evaluate information, can be reduced if individuals first experience affirmations of their self-worth and personal integrity. This is the case even in relation to sensitive topics such as abortion and politics, which are sometimes closely tied to a person's sense of identity (Cohen et al., 2000; 2007; Correll et al., 2004). In other words, debiasing is more likely to occur if individuals feel that their identities are not at risk. This implies that increasing people's open-mindedness to worldview-challenging evidence and arguments will require attention to the social infrastructure within which dialogue occurs.

Another insight emerging from the psychological debiasing literature is that attempts to correct misinformation are more likely to be successful if they involve repeated (and relatively brief) retractions that simultaneously provide an alternative story that fills the coherence gap left by the correction. This is because corrections that are overly complex or that fail to replace the false information with coherent explanations of the phenomena are all too likely to backfire, producing overkill, polarisation, continued influence, or boomerang effects (Hart and Nisbet, 2012; Lewandowsky et al., 2012; 2017). Psychological research suggests that most people have a default expectation that information presented in a conversation is (intended to be) true and pragmatically relevant. This means that attempts to contradict or correct previously presented information is unlikely to work – unless the new account better explains causal features of the events in question and explains why the original (mis)information was presented or is no longer relevant (Seifert, 2002).

A third set of insights derive from experimental evidence indicating that some of the most promising methods for debiasing mistaken beliefs involve inoculation or prebunking strategies (Cook, 2017; Cook et al., 2017). Prebunking or inoculative messages typically include both an explicit warning that biases are at play and a refutation that exposes the fallacy behind the anticipated argument defending the misinformation (e.g., about the scientific consensus on climate change or human evolution). Scholars in this field are candid about the role played by the 'inoculation' metaphor: 'Just as vaccines generate antibodies to resist future viruses, inoculation messages equip people with counterarguments that potentially convey resistance to future misinformation, even if the misinformation is congruent with pre-existing attitudes' (Cook et al., 2017: 4). A meta-analysis of research studies on inoculation or pre-emptive strategies suggests that they are more effective than 'supportive' messages (i.e., those that simply provide new accurate information) at building resistance to misinformation (Banas and Rains, 2010).

Prebunking interventions appear to boost strategic monitoring, which can provide people with a way of fighting back against continued influence-effect biases when they are encoding potential misinformation (Ecker et al., 2010). Experimental research has shown that communications involving explicit warnings about biased arguments that are dismissive of consensual scientific information are better at inoculating individuals from misinformation by comparison with communications that only provide correct content, at least in part because the former encourage people to reflect on the potential role of directed motivational reasoning in their thinking (Bolsen and Druckman, 2015; Linden et al., 2017; Schmid and Betsch, 2019). But critical thinking is not enough. One recent study evaluating the relative success of various strategies for reducing religious (and other epistemically unwarranted) beliefs found that directly addressing problems with particular pseudoscientific claims worked better than teaching general critical thinking skills or research methods. Students who participated in a class that involved specific and explicit warnings about beliefs related to topics such as creationism, anti-vaccination, and alien abductions reported far higher decreases in such beliefs compared to students in control groups (Dyer and Hall, 2019).

What does all of this mean for those interested in reducing the toxic effects of theist biases? I hope readers will have noticed that throughout this chapter I have tried to take advantage of each of the three insights gained from the psychological debiasing literature discussed in this section.

- First, I affirmed the role of religion (in the sense operationalised above) as an identity-enhancing, group-bonding, virtue-building force in human evolution, and recognised the extent to which it still provides the intellectual and practical scaffolding for the worldviews of most contemporary members of our species.
- Second, I also offered (and briefly repeated) an alternative causal account of the basic deliverances of theist credulity and conformity biases that emphasised how and why mistaken beliefs about gods (and costly rituals meant to engage with them) have emerged and prevailed in human populations.
- Third, I went out of my way to include pre-emptive warnings about the role of these biases in the arguments of religious philosophers and apologists. Chapter 7 will focus even more on this latter prebunking strategy.

I have tried to frame this analysis in a way that acknowledges the wisdom of maintaining adequate continuity with religious traditions as we explore our current evolutionary landscape and determine when and where it makes sense to construct socio-ecological niches guided by naturalist and secularist sensibilities. Where do we go from here?

### Sustainable Altruism in the Anthropocene

Why can't we all just get along? Addressing the societal challenges facing humanity today will require new insights into (and new strategies for fostering) cooperative attitudes and behaviours within and across cultures. This will require us to face the sustainability challenges related to the prevalence and persistence of participating in religious and theistic sects. As I have noted in previous chapters, religious individuals are prone to engage in *parochial* altruism, that is, to trust and cooperate with members of their own in-group. The unfortunate dark side of this sort of 'altruism' is the tendency to become antagonistic or even violent towards out-group members, especially under stressful conditions. All of this makes sense in light of human evolution. Religious credulity and conformity biases help to explain why altruism (concern for the well-being of others) is easier for most of us to feel and actively express towards our own kith and kin than towards cultural or (non-)religious others.

However, as socio-ecological environments change, so do organisms – or else they and their offspring do not survive. We have also noted the research showing that non-religious individuals are more likely to engage in *universal* altruism, that is, to trust and cooperate with out-group members. This mode of prosociality fosters and is fostered by contexts that promote naturalism and secularism. What does all of this imply for attempts to find adaptive pathways for the (remarkably prosocial and adaptive) human species in (and possibly through) the Anthropocene?

My argument here is that it is likely that any survival pathways we do find will involve the development of *sustainable* altruism, by which I mean a balance between self-oriented concern for well-being (at the individual or group level) and other-oriented prosocial attitudes and behaviours that can be achieved, maintained, and adapted as socio-ecological systems continue to change during the Anthropocene. In the environments in which most of us currently live the biases that reproduce beliefs in (and behaviours oriented towards) supernatural agents have become maladaptive – at least if we are concerned about the well-being and survival of more than our own cultural in-group. This implies that we may need to discover or invent new forms of social cohesion that are not dependent on religious or theistic supernatural agents or authorities.

As we attempt to adapt and respond to new global challenges, we will need to devote more attention and energy to reducing the toxic effects of theisms on the global body politic. A similar argument is made by Cliquet and Avramov in their book *Evolution Science and Ethics in the Third Millennium: Challenges and Choices for Humankind* (2018). These authors operationalise religion as involving 'the belief in a supernatural agent or power that created the universe, explains its existence and meaning, and often imposes a moral code according to which humans should behave' (2018: 89). Although 'creator' gods are not central in all religions, especially in small-scale societies, the authors' definitional emphasis on *beliefs* in and *behaviours* guided by putative *supernatural* agents and authorities is consistent with the general consensus among scholars working across disciplines in the scientific study of religion, which has informed my discussions and use of the term 'religion' above. They argue that:

> Spirituality/religiosity is part of the human biological heritage that, together with its cultural expressions in the hunter-gatherer and agrarian stages of human history, had adaptive functions in those stages. However, many present

cultural remnants of those stages are no longer well adapted to the exigencies of modernity. They are insufficiently robust to further develop the potential of the human species to reach higher levels of cultural development and biological evolution. (Cliquet and Avramov, 2018: 4)

After reviewing wide swathes of the relevant scientific literature across disciplines, they conclude that 'organized religions and religiosity based on beliefs and in-group morality transmitted though religious institutions are no longer instruments of human survival. They ceased to be adaptive to human survival and have become maladaptive instruments' (2018: 134).

As Cliquet and Avramov make clear throughout their book, it is the supernatural (non-naturalist) aspects of religious beliefs and behaviours that are problematic in our contemporary context. Why? Because such pre-scientific beliefs and in-group behaviours hinder modernisation and enhanced hominisation, which they argue are necessary for responding to the ethical and ecological challenges of the third millennium. As they note, 'there is not much time left to resolve these urgent problems if we want to avoid further damage' (2018: 17). As we have seen in earlier chapters, these arguments about the deleterious consequences of the superstitious beliefs and segregative behaviours promoted by religion are backed by empirical findings from a wide array of disciplines. We are indeed running out of time to address the global challenges of the Anthropocene such as extreme climate change, escalating cultural conflict, and excessive consumer capitalism.

The interaction and acceleration of these three latter crises has had a more profound negative impact in the Global South, where religion plays a powerful role in decreasing openness to scientific solutions to sustainable development and in increasing social conflict and economic inequality. As Rumy Hasan argues in *Religion and Development in the Global South* (2017), belief in doctrines related to putatively supernatural agents is

> necessarily in tension with cognitive thinking for the simple reason that faith obviates the need for evidence and to a significant extent for rational thinking; hence, cognitive faculties are diminished. Criticism, curiosity, critiquing, hypothesizing, theorizing, experimentation and the search for evidence all appear to be suppressed or discouraged. To put it another way, they are not required or desired when truth is thought to emanate from holy texts. (2017: 198)

Hasan interprets the evidence he reviews in this context as suggesting that minds that are not secularised 'are infused with supernatural and irrational thinking, and these powerfully militate against the dynamics of growth, development and the uplifting of people' (2017: 211).

We should resist the temptation to avoid the touchy issue of the (population-level) negative correlation between religion and intelligence, which has been well documented in the scientific literature (e.g., Ganzach and Gotlibovski, 2013; Zuckerman et al., 2013; Dutton and Van der Linden, 2017). Although Cliquet and Avramov focus heavily on the implications of religiosity for fertility and the carrying capacity of the Earth, they do not address the effect that high fertility among the religious could have on the intelligence of the human species at the population level. As Ellis et al. point out, both religiosity and intelligence are substantially influenced by genetics and 'persons with lower IQs and who are most religious are reproducing at substantially higher rates than those who are least religious', which leads them to predict that as religiosity increases 'average intelligence will decline' (2017: 3–4). This is problematic because adapting to current ecological challenges calls for reasoning in 'logical empirically verifiable terms' about complex natural phenomena without 'invoking supernatural "shortcuts"', which in turn 'requires genes for high intelligence and is facilitated by genes for low religiosity' (2017: 15).

Like Cliquet and Avramov, Hasan also points to the positive relationship between widespread religious behaviours motivated or justified by allegedly supernatural authorities and socio-economic dysfunction, a correlation that has been well attested in the literature (Paul, 2009; Zuckerman, 2010). Hasan provides cross-cultural evidence that clearly shows that 'as countries develop, the importance of religion to the population-at-large declines – to the point that a significant percentage self-proclaim to be non-believers and for a rising majority, religion is a declining or unimportant part of their life' (2017: 207). He argues that these findings compel us to acknowledge that if the countries of the Global South are to become developed, they 'must downplay the role of religion in people's lives and institutions writ large and move towards secularizing culture and society. This is not only essential for the cognitive development of children but is also a rational approach to the tasks necessary for economic development and modernization' (2017: 210).

The transdisciplinary community of scholars with expertise in multi-agent artificial intelligence modelling and simulation have a unique opportunity to collaborate and address these challenges by attempting to develop artificial societies capable of uncovering adaptive pathways that can minimise social conflict and maximise cooperation in the face of climate-abetted social and ecological change (Shults, Wildman, et al., 2021). One potentially fruitful direction here would be to link climate models to MAAI models that employ more realistic cognitive architectures informed by social psychology and evolutionary biology and whose agents interact within more realistic social networks. If successful, such efforts could provide policy-relevant insights into the conditions under which conflict and cooperation are likely to emerge in response to climate-related threats, thereby contributing to the achievement of the UN Sustainability Development Goals (Shults and Wildman, 2020b).

Conversations about the exploration of adaptive pathways in the Anthropocene inevitably raise ethical concerns. Pathways for whom? And to what end? Which norms shape the criteria for making such decisions? The capacity for misuse of such models is high, so it matters who defines and controls their 'proper' use. Norms are not distributed universally in human populations, so it matters which norms get attention and which are marginalised. Assumptions about ethical norms operative within social-simulation experiments can significantly impact outputs, which affects the analysis and evaluation of the potential policy interventions explored in such models (Diallo et al., 2021). Although it will not eliminate such ethical quandaries, pressing towards computational architectures that are more deeply informed by the bio-cultural sciences about the moral reasoning equipment bequeathed to humans by evolution and fashioned within cultural settings will at least make the task more tractable by surfacing the assumptions and purposes guiding such conversations.

In this chapter I have argued that while religious and theistic sects (as defined above) have played an 'adaptive' role at least since the Upper Palaeolithic and have continued to 'work' throughout most of human history by enhancing the species' capacity for material production and promoting its biological reproduction, the credulity and conformity biases that surreptitiously shape these social assemblages have now become maladaptive in most contexts in the Anthropocene. Reducing the toxicity of theist biases is no panacea; it will not solve all our social problems and will certainly generate new ones. The same is true for attempts to decrease racism, sexism, and classism. However, learning how to contest these biases can help increase our individual and communal resistance to evolved dispositions that are no longer good for (all of) us, and clear the way for the construction of new, healthy modes of identity formation and social transformation.

I have also highlighted the importance of straightforwardly having 'the talk' about where gods come from – and the consequences of imaginatively nurturing them in communal rituals – and identified ways in which such conversations can be informed by the psychological debiasing literature. This may involve non-anxious personal dialogue that encourages critical thinking about specific cognitive mechanisms, which can diminish the power of god-bearing *content* biases at the individual level. However, the prevalence of religion in human cultures is also influenced by genotypic inheritance patterns and social selection pressures (Turner et al., 2017), forces that shape people's capacity to contest their biases as they engage in such conversations.

As we saw in our discussion of the computational model of 'post-supernatural cultures' (Wildman et al., 2020) in Chapter 5, learning how to practise safe (godless) sects may also be facilitated by non-coercive social policies that promote education, existential security, pluralism, and freedom of expression, which can lower the effect of god-bearing *context* biases at the population level. No doubt these personal conversations and political conversions will be really difficult. However, our species has shown a remarkable capacity to survive and thrive over the millennia. It is not yet clear how (or whether) humans will evolve and adapt in the Anthropocene, but it seems to me that philosophy can play at least a small role. Several Deleuze scholars have explored ways in which the conceptual and pragmatic apparatus of his work bears on the challenges of the Anthropocene (e.g., Dodds, 2012; Lenco, 2013). In the next chapter I attempt something similar but with more explicit attention to the atheist machine driving Deleuzian political philosophy and ethics.

# 7

# A Germ of Tranquil Atheism

The context in which I first developed the ideas articulated in the first part of this chapter was an invitation to participate in a conference at the theological faculty at Lund University on the death of Jesus and the birth of Christianity, which explicitly encouraged discussion about the implications of Deleuze's work for these themes. The posters announcing the conference highlighted Deleuze's claim that:

> For Christianity subjected the form, or rather the Figure, to a fundamental deformation. Insofar as God was incarnated, crucified, ascended to heaven, and so on, the form or the Figure was no longer rigorously linked to essence, but to what, in principle, is its opposite: the event, or even the changeable, the accident. (Deleuze, 2005b: 124)

For Deleuze, ethics has to do with becoming 'worthy of what happens to us' (LOS, 170), and the conference organisers invited contributors to reflect on what it could mean to be worthy of the events of Jesus' death and Christianity's birth.

I began my presentation by playfully inverting (or, Deleuze might say, perverting) the theme, asking instead what it could mean to be 'worthy' of the events of the birth of 'Christ' and the death of 'Christianity'. The title of this chapter is a phrase that appears in the same book (and on the same page) as the quotation above in the context of Deleuze's discussion of Christianity and atheism in *Francis Bacon – The Logic of Sensation*: 'Christianity contains *a germ of tranquil atheism* that will nurture painting; the painter can easily be indifferent to the religious subject he is asked to represent' (Deleuze, 2005c: 124, emphasis added). As I have emphasised at various points in this book, theologians and religious philosophers who find Deleuze fascinating all too often extract his concepts for apologetic purposes and ignore the atheist machine that produces them. My goal here is to bring this machine front and centre and to explore some of its philosophical uses in relation to religion and theism.

The first and second sub-sections of this chapter highlight the significance of Christianity for Deleuze, which has very little to do with Jesus' death (or life, or message), and almost everything to do with the secretion of atheism. Building on the arguments above, I summarise how Deleuze's critique of the repressive and oppressive mechanisms of Christianity (the poster child for the despotic machine) and of the symbol of Christ (the poster child for the White Face) can be complemented and strengthened by insights from the bio-cultural sciences of religion. The notion of 'Christ' was *born* in human minds and *borne* in human cultures in the same basic way that every other supernatural agent imaginatively engaged in rituals by a religious in-group has been conceived and nurtured throughout history. Moreover, like all social assemblages held together by shared belief in imagined punitive gods, Christianity will eventually die – either sooner (if we take demographic projections seriously) or later (if we take astronomical projections seriously). The question, then, is whether we can be worthy of *that* event: the death of Christianity, whose timely demise, ironically, is hurried along by that 'germ of tranquil atheism' that it could not help but secrete.

The third and fourth sub-sections take 'philosophy of religion' as a case study of the function of the atheist machine in philosophy. This sub-discipline of philosophy is increasingly disenfranchised in the modern secular academy, in part because of the extent to which religious franchises have been the benefactors and beneficiaries of the philosophising of so many of its practitioners. Religious (and especially Christian) apologists have dominated this sub-discipline for such a long time, even within some non-sectarian universities, that many worry it is no longer (if it ever was) really philosophy of religion but rather philosophy *for* religion. It is an open question whether this field can change its image as a haven for philosophers trying to defend their own in-group's interpretation of a particular monotheistic religion and define itself clearly as philosophy *of* (i.e., bias-challenging critical reflection on, rather than bias-confirming justification for) *religion* (i.e., empirically tractable quotidian beliefs and behaviours related to putative supernatural agents and authorities, rather than the abstract quodlibetal arguments of ecclesiastical and theological elites). I describe several ways in which computational modelling and simulation can help.

The final sub-section summarises some of the achievements of Deleuze's 'meta-ethics', both in relation to the 'secretion of atheism' as well as to the developments in CMS we have been exploring throughout this book. As we have seen, in *What is Philosophy?* Deleuze asserts that Christianity secretes 'atheism more than any other religion' (WIP, 92). Why more than any other? In the wider context of this quotation from WIP, and in light of Deleuze's discussion of the death(s) of God in Chapter 5 of his book on Nietzsche (Deleuze, 1983), it is clear that he has in mind the concrete way in which Christianity introduced the idea of the death of God (on the cross of Christ) into the world. This atheism that Christianity secretes is wholly negative, saturated with ressentiment, a 'clerical atheism' whose 'image of the master is a slavish one' (NP, 196). Neither Nietzsche nor Deleuze want anything to do with this atheism, promoting instead an active, affirmative, joyful 'atheism'. In this context, however, I want to suggest another reason why Christianity secretes atheism more than any other religion. The theological notion of an infinite supernatural intentional agent who eternally determines and judges all human intensity whatsoever presses religious credulity and conformity biases so far that their plausibility simply collapses, thereby liberating an affirmative atheist machine that can produce the 'image of a free person' (LOS, 314).

## How Christ was Born(e)

As noted above, the main focus of the conference at which I first analysed the implications of Deleuze's identification of 'a germ of tranquil atheism' in Christianity was on the death of Jesus and the role it might have played in the emergence of the Christian religion. To be more precise: how did reflection on the trauma of this event shape the formation of the early followers of Jesus into a recognisable religious sect? Even if I were convinced that a man called Jesus of Nazareth was crucified in a way that resembled one of the (contradictory) Gospel narratives (even after elements such as dead people wandering around Jerusalem had been excised by scholarly biblical criticism), I would have no reason to think that this event was qualitatively different in its cosmological impact than the death of other members of our species.

This is not to deny the value of scholarship on the late Second Temple period and the New Testament that contributes to debates over the extent to which stories about the *death* of Jesus may have impacted the earliest (Pauline) followers of 'the Way'. Bradley McLean helpfully tackles this latter task in his book on *Deleuze, Guattari and the Machine in Early Christianity: Schizoanalysis, Transformation and Multiplicity*, where he adopts and adapts concepts developed in *Anti-Oedipus* and *A Thousand Plateaus* in order to shed light on the 'rise of the Christ machines' in early Christianity (McLean, 2022).

Here, however, I am tackling a different task. I am interested in the cognitive *conception* of 'Christ' and the role it played in the construction of early Christian sects and their ritual practices. The key, in my view, is to understand how this notion was *born* in the minds of early followers of Paul and other apostles, and how it was *borne* in the rituals and devotional behaviours that came to characterise diverse expressions of this religious sect. 'Christ' was born(e) in the same basic way that all other supernatural agent conceptions are engendered and sustained: as a result of the natural deliverances of cognitive and coalitional biases that once provided a survival advantage to (some) hominids in an early human ancestral environment, biases that have been passed on to us. From the point of view of scholars who study religion using empirical data and theoretical frameworks in fields such as cognitive science, evolutionary biology, archaeology, experimental psychology, and cultural anthropology, the conception of 'Christ' is just the sort of counter-intuitive or ontologically confused idea that one would expect to find widely shared among members of a newly formed religious in-group.

As we have seen, research in the bio-cultural sciences of religion suggests that supernatural agent conceptions are *born* in human minds as the result of evolved hyper-active *cognitive* mechanisms that are part of our phylogenetic inheritance. Although the tendency to over-detect human-like agents regularly leads to mistaken perceptions, such as seeing faces in the clouds, it would have been naturally selected in the upper Palaeolithic environment of our early ancestors because it would have given survival advantage to those who, when confronted by an ambiguous pattern or movement in the forest, immediately jumped at the guess 'hidden agent'. Those who lazily guessed 'just the wind' when it was really a predator (or prey) would have been more likely to be eaten (or have failed to eat). Notions of hard-to-detect, disembodied intentional forces lurking around are relatively naturally conceived and easily remembered in the human mind.

However, when it comes to *raising* gods, as I have repeatedly emphasised, it takes a village. This is why I have argued that we also need to recognise that supernatural agent conceptions are *borne* in human groups as a result of evolved hyper-active *coalitional* mechanisms that are also part of our phylogenetic (and cultural) inheritance. Ideas about gods multiply like rabbits in the human Imaginarium, reproducing rapidly in fertile cognitive fields cultivated by participation in religious rituals. But only some of these ideas have been domesticated and bred across generations; the most easily reproduced god-conceptions are typically those that somehow facilitate a rigid protection of in-group norms among those engaged in religious sects.

If the members of a coalition really believe that there are disembodied punitive agents around who are watching out for cheaters, freeloaders, or potential defectors, they are more likely to cooperate and stay committed to the norms of the group. These sorts of beliefs are reinforced by regular participation in emotionally arousing rituals that involve synchronic and causally opaque movements, and allegedly provide a way of engaging with or manipulating such mysterious agents (e.g., ancestor ghosts, saints, or the spirit of a deceased saviour). Groups whose members continually shared in this kind of ritual would have been more likely to cooperate and hold together in the upper Palaeolithic, and thus would have been better able to out-compete groups that could not 'bear' gods.

Supernatural agents who are cared for and ritually nurtured within a coalition then become imaginative targets for the easily triggered agency-detection mechanisms of each new generation. In the environment of our early ancestors the selective advantage went to hominids whose cognitive capacities led them to quickly *infer* the presence of hidden (possibly punitive) agents and to strongly *prefer* the parochial norms monitored by the supernatural authorities of their coalition, especially when they felt confused or threatened. The early believers in 'Christ' and followers of 'the Way', evolved hominids like the rest of us, felt extremely confused by the death of a man whom the leaders of their sect took to be supernaturally sanctioned, and felt extremely threatened by ridicule and persecution from all sides.

Jesus Christ. Yes, he is just the type of supernatural agent that one would expect to find born(e) in the mental and social space of a religious coalition under this sort of pressure. Within two or three decades after his death, stories about the birth, ministry, and resurrection of 'the Christ' emerged in which Jesus was portrayed in very much the same way as other gods are portrayed; contingently embodied (walking through walls, walking on water, ascending to the clouds) and morally concerned about the behaviour of the members of the group (watching, preparing, coming soon to judge, etc.). Such conceptions are easy to remember and transmit from one generation to another – as long as they are reinforced by rituals that consistently motivate coalition members to display costly signals of their commitment to the in-group.

And this is exactly what we find in the ritual commonly called the 'Eucharist'. Paul's warnings to the Corinthians about their practice of the 'Lord's Supper' are illuminating in this regard (1 Cor. 11:17–32). He is not surprised at the factions among them, since such conflict is necessary to determine who among them is 'genuine'. Participation in the ritual is a proclamation of 'the Lord's death until he comes'. However, Paul admonishes them for not examining themselves adequately before participating and insists that they are eating and drinking 'judgment against themselves'. 'For this reason', he explains, 'many of you are weak and ill, and some have died.' Paul concludes: 'if we judged ourselves we would not be judged, but when we are judged by the Lord we are disciplined so that we may not be condemned along with the world'.

In other words, early Christians were warned that their weaknesses and illnesses were caused by their failure to detect the real presence of a judgemental supernatural agent who was returning soon to reveal who was genuinely part of the in-group and who would be eternally condemned. Although it promotes anxious self-judgement and antipathy towards out-groups, this is just the sort of ritual that holds a new religious movement together.

Even before Christianity took over the empire, patristic theologians engaged with (and even contributed to) the philosophical debates of their era, shaped as it was by Neo-Platonic obsession with the One. How could Christ the Logos be both the same substance as the man Jesus and the same substance as the One (Eternal Father)? As we noted in Chapter 2, the concept of an infinite intentional supernatural agent makes no sense, and trying to articulate the Identity of two (and later, when theologians became more interested in the Holy Spirit, three) such agents did not help. Nevertheless, Christianity was able to survive for the same reason that other large-scale religions that developed primarily doctrinal modes of ritual engagement have survived: laypeople concerned about their own quotidian thriving pretty much ignored the irrelevant quodlibetal arguments of the theologians, content to rely on and even celebrate their appeals to mystery.

The mental conception of (and ritual engagement with) 'Christ' led to the emergence of the cluster of religious in-groups typically referred to as 'Christianity'. The regular arrival of new claims to have (re)discovered the 'correct' understanding of this supposedly transcendent religious figure helps to explain the ongoing fragmentation of Christianity throughout Church history. However, as long as some groups of *Homo sapiens* continue to imaginatively engage in shared ritual interactions that they interpret as mediating some relationship with a supernatural agent associated with one of these fragmented traditions, Christianity will survive.

### How Christianity Will Die

All religions eventually die. No one takes Baal or Zeus seriously any more. Of course, there may well be a new religious movement whose recent emergence I have missed, whose members are devoted to supernatural agents they call 'Baal' or 'Zeus', but it is highly unlikely that they engage with them using the same sort of animal sacrifices common among the ancient Canaanites or the ancient Greeks. Most of the manifold expressions of the Christian tradition over the centuries have also died, and those that remain continually reinvent themselves to survive. Eventually all forms of Christianity will die. What would it mean to become worthy of *this* event – the death of Christianity?

But first, let's back up and clarify how and why this religion (among others) is already dying, at least in the West, and what this has to do with the 'germ of tranquil atheism' that Deleuze perceived as secreting from Christianity. As I argued in Chapter 2, the emergence of *theology* in the wake of the axial age (800–200 BCE) introduced a conceptual (and political) crack out of which atheism could grow and eventually thrive. For most of human history, supernatural agents were typically imagined as finite in knowledge and power, and with relatively provincial interests (e.g., animal spirits, ancestor ghosts, and war gods). For most of human history, supernatural rituals were typically performed only within relatively small groups, and had relatively provincial purposes (e.g., mediating the group's success in hunting, child-raising, and battle).

As we saw in Chapter 2, however, a new sort of god-concept was born in the minds of intellectual and priestly elites in the largest and most complex literate states across east, south, and west Asia during the first millennium BCE. These elites imagined an all-encompassing supernatural agency that conditioned all things and in relation to which all behaviour was punished (or rewarded). In east and south Asia, some of the most common ideas about an axiologically relevant ultimate Reality were 'Dao' and 'Dharma', but neither of these was typically conceived primarily as person-like or coalition-favouring. The priestly elite of the monotheistic religions that flowed out of the *west* Asian axial age, on the other hand, did depict 'God' (Yahweh, the Father of Jesus Christ, Allah) as an ultimate person who favoured a specific coalition. Most theologians in these Abrahamic (or Adamic) traditions have claimed that the supernatural agent revealed in the curated holy texts of their in-group is the one true 'God', the Creator upon whom all of creation is wholly dependent and whose *infinite* knowledge and power is the basis for the punishment (or reward) of everyone for all *eternity*.

This supernatural agent conception was tentatively born(e) in the minds of theologians who pressed the anthropomorphic and ethnocentric biases (described above) as far as they would go – but pressing them to infinity (and eternity) turned out to be too far. If God is so transcendent that he is beyond representation, then he cannot be conceived at all, much less as a human-like, coalition-favouring agent. If everything is eternally foreknown and pre-ordained by God, then praying to or ritually engaging with him seems superfluous. Throughout the centuries, monotheistic theologians have worked hard to defend hypotheses about the existential conditions for human life that utilise symbols (or icons) of the divine that try to uphold both the infinite transcendence of God and his immanence within (or to) a finite world.

The theological concept of Christ as the Logos (image, son, face, etc.) of God was intended to solve this dilemma, but this led to interminable debates among philosophical factions within the Church, and an increasing chasm between lay piety towards Jesus and 'theologically correct' notions of an infinite Son of God. I discuss these issues in detail in *Iconoclastic Theology: Gilles Deleuze and the Secretion of Atheism* (Shults, 2014b). In the current context, I want to suggest that the 'germ of tranquil atheism' within Christianity also has to do with the impossible task of trying to *represent* 'Christ' in doctrine – as well as in painting – in such a way that he is supposed to depict both the 'essence' of an infinite Father in the arguments of theologians, while simultaneously being 'besieged, even replaced' (Deleuze, 2005b: 101) by 'accidents', in ways that can be made relevant for the everyday lives of laypeople.

The problem (for priests and theologians invested in keeping their in-group's religious doctrines and rituals alive) is that the evolved cognitive tendency to detect hidden finite supernatural agents crumples under the pressure of trying to think an infinite intentional entity. The evolved coalitional biases for protecting in-groups sustained by idiosyncratic religious rituals implode (or explode) under the stress of trying to live together in complex, pluralist, secular social contexts. Does it really make sense that claims about the gods (or God) worshipped by one particular in-group (mine) just happen to be correct, while the claims of my neighbours, which are no more intrinsically strange, are incorrect? These other groups claim unique and exclusive divine revelation for their sects just as vigorously as we do. Defending these claims is exhausting, not to mention antagonising to my neighbour. Moreover, the abstract descriptions of the Divine upon which rabbis, priests, and imams insist seem to have little if any relevance for daily life. Might it be possible to make sense of the world and act sensibly in society without appeals to supernatural agents, whether finite or infinite? As the atheist machine was assembled during the axial age, new lines of flight opened up in ways that were previously unimaginable. More and more minds and cultures were freed of god-bearing cognitive and coalitional biases, and atheist machinic assemblages expanded in mental and social spaces previously dominated by the despotic machines of Abrahamic monotheism.

Atheism is in fact being secreted and spreading throughout the globe, especially in the West, where the intellectual plausibility and political dominance of Christianity continues to be undermined as naturalistic explanations of the world and secular inscriptions of society grow in popularity. Demographic projections, mathematical modelling, and computer simulations support the claim that non-religious worldviews will continue to expand in the human population (Bruce and Voas, 2023; Funk and Smith, 2012; Kosmin and Keysar, 2013; Pew Research Center, 2015; Shults, Gore, et al., 2018a; Stinespring and Cragun, 2015; Twenge, 2015; Voas, 2009; Voas and Chaves, 2016), at least in contexts where people have access to education and value pluralism and where governments provide a basic sense of existential security and freedom of expression.

The secret is out: none of the (contradictory) supernatural ideas proposed by competing religions are necessary for interpreting nature and none of the (contradictory) supernatural norms authorised by their holy texts are needed for organising the social field. Segregative inscriptions of the latter based on superstitious beliefs about punitive (or otherwise axiologically relevant) gods are becoming more and more problematic in our pluralistic, globalising context. A growing number of people, especially young people, are finding it increasingly easy to evaluate explanatory hypotheses and normative proposals without the need for supernatural agents as causal powers or moral regulators.

In other words, the secretion of atheism (from Christianity and other religions) has facilitated the production of *naturalism* and *secularism*. These god-dissolving forces help people challenge the evolved god-bearing biases discussed above. They learn to solve problems related to initially confusing natural phenomena through critical reflection and the scientific method. They learn to resolve problems related to initially frightening social phenomena by constructing and maintaining non-religious legislative and judicial institutions. They learn to lay out plan(e)s of immanence within socio-ecological niches in which survival no longer depends on the detection and protection of the gods of any particular in-group.

In such contexts, day by day, Christianity dies a thousand little deaths. Theologians with expertise in the anatomy of this moribund monotheism have at least two options. They can struggle to keep (some version of) it on life support by constantly repairing or replacing its exhausted despotic religious machinery. Or they can nurture the germ of atheism that is being secreted by its demise, releasing and spreading naturalism and secularism, which are increasingly contagious in populations characterised by relatively easy access to scientific education and social welfare provided by relatively transparent, stable governments.

Deleuze urged us to create rhizomes, not to prop up and idealise arboreal religious figures. For me, the question is not whether we can be worthy of the event of someone else's crucifixion. It is whether we can be worthy of what Deleuze called *Eventum tantum*, the 'eternal return' of the Different, the infinite expression of accidental singularities, the univocity of being that flattens any and all hierarchical claims to represent a transcendent Logos (in painting, thought, or politics). Atheist tranquillity is slowly germinating across the plane of pure immanence in which we live and move and have our psycho-social becoming. We do not yet know all that naturalistic-secularistic bodies can do. But we are learning.

In the context of the quotations with which I began this chapter, Deleuze emphasised that he 'only took Christianity as a first point of reference that it would be necessary to look beyond'. Looking beyond. This, for Deleuze, is the only point in referring to Christianity. Instead of remaining transfixed by the image of a crucified (or resurrected) Jesus, or any other religious figure for that matter, constantly trying to reinterpret the privileged icons of one's in-group in light of the latest scientific findings and philosophical fashions, as liberal theologians are wont to do, we can take Christian traditions and other monotheistic molarities seriously enough to extract the atheist machine they contain (and constrain) and then look beyond them, philosophically extending the lines of flight opened up by their molecularisation.

## Theist Credulity and Conformity Biases in Philosophy of Religion

What role can philosophy play in all of this? Professional philosophers, like professional scientists, are far less likely to believe in God (or gods) than the rest of the population. The most recent results of the relevant poll on PhilPapers.org, for example, show that 72.8% of responding philosophers accept or lean towards atheism, while only 14.6% accept or lean towards theism (https://philpapers.org/surveys). This is rather unsurprising since, as we noted above, high levels of intelligence, education, and critical thinking style have been shown to correlate with low levels of religiosity (e.g, Dutton and Van der Linden, 2017; Ellis et al., 2017; Ganzach et al., 2013; Ganzach and Gotlibovski, 2013; Gervais and Norenzayan, 2012; Hungerman, 2014; Lewis, 2015; Lindeman and Svedholm-Häkkinen, 2016; McLaughlin and McGill, 2017; Stoet and Geary, 2017).

When one analyses the survey results by focus area, however, it turns out that philosophers *of religion* are an exception to this rule. In fact, the results of the poll mentioned above indicate that, compared to philosophers in general, the ratio of believers to non-believers in that sub-field is almost reversed: 72.3% accept or lean towards theism, while only 19.1% accept or lean towards atheism. Other survey analyses have produced similar results. Bourget and Chalmers found that 72.3% of philosophers of religion in their sample leaned towards or accepted theism, while only 11.7% of philosophers outside that field fell into those categories (Bourget and Chalmers, 2014). The same asymmetry was found in the sample of philosophers recently surveyed by De Cruz and De Smedt; 73% of philosophers of religion leaned towards theism, compared to 23.9% of philosophers with other specialisations (De Cruz and De Smedt, 2016). The authors hypothesise that their sampling method was responsible for the relatively high percentage (compared to other surveys) of philosophers in general (those not specialising in philosophy of religion) who leaned towards theism in their survey.

In a more detailed survey that focused only on North American philosophers of religion, Wildman and Rohr found that among those in their sample who operated in institutions that require assent to a statement of religious faith (to keep their job), 71.5% believed that 'philosophy of religion' was either complementary or identical to 'theology', and 0% prized comparison with other religions as a vital component of the philosophy of religion (Wildman and Rohr, 2018). All of this suggests that philosophers of religion are more religious than other philosophers, and that *religious* philosophers of religion are primarily interested in studying and defending their *own* religion. It is important to note that in the context of this chapter I am less concerned about the rationality of belief in God or gods than I am in the reasonableness of providing cover within the academy for apologetically oriented philosophical approaches to the study of religion, although these issues are clearly interrelated (Shults, 2015a).

How are we to make sense of this difference between philosophers of religion and philosophers in general? Draper and Nichols argue that both 'cognitive biases operating at the nonconscious level' as well as 'group influence' and 'coalitional features' of religious participation are among the factors contributing to the prevalence of theistic belief among religious philosophers of religion. They note the pervasive role historically played by apologetics in this philosophical sub-field and suggest that this has led to a paradoxical situation for *religious* philosophers of religion: '[A]pologists, unlike philosophers engaged in genuine inquiry, seek to justify their religious beliefs (as opposed to seeking to have beliefs that are justified). This implies that their inquiry ... is *inevitably biased* ... [T]o obtain justification, one must directly seek, not justification, but truth' (Draper and Nichols, 2013: 439, emphasis added). These authors also point to contextual factors that can reinforce (or at least reduce interest in contesting) religious biases among theistic philosophers of religion: it is difficult to think clearly and critically about beliefs the rejection of which would endanger one's income and livelihood (if one teaches at a religious institution that requires a statement of faith), not to mention one's relationship to believing spouses, children, parents, and lifelong friends.

The extent to which evolved biases that engender theistic beliefs and behaviours shape arguments within philosophy of religion, and related fields such as 'natural theology' that have traditionally overlapped this sub-discipline of philosophy, has been well documented (De Cruz and De Smedt, 2010; De Smedt and De Cruz, 2011; Shults, 2015a; Teehan, 2013). Theologians and religious apologists are not immune to the error-producing distortions that are associated with religious belief in general (Barlev et al., 2017; Breslin and Lewis, 2015; Davies et al., 2001; Pennycook et al., 2014; Slone, 2007; van Der Tempel and Alcock, 2015; Wlodarski and Pearce, 2016). For example, a study exploring the question 'Does Religious Belief Infect Philosophical Analysis?' showed that theists are more likely (than non-theists) to make mistakes about the logical validity of formal arguments when the conclusion has to do with the existence of God (Tobia, 2016).

Our discussion in previous chapters of some of the findings in the bio-cultural sciences of religion helps to explain why this is the case. It is important to emphasise that all human beings, non-theist philosophers included, have biases. However, empirical research and experimental results from a wide variety of cognitive, psychological, and social scientific disciplines have demonstrated that *theists* tend to be *more* susceptible to the two broad types of bias I outlined in Chapter 2: anthropomorphic promiscuity and sociographic prudery (see Figure 1). This conceptual grid does not capture all of the nuances in this literature, but it does serve the heuristic purpose for which it was created: providing a framework for discussing the cognitive and coalitional mechanisms that engender (or enervate) beliefs and behaviours related to putative supernatural agents and authorities.

In other words, understanding the mechanisms underlying these religious biases helps to explain where gods come from – and why some people keep them around. Remember that the horizontal line in Figure 1 represents a continuum on which to indicate the extent to which a person tends to *infer* that some natural phenomena (especially ambiguous or anxiogenic phenomena) are the result of human-like supernatural forces (or 'gods' in the general sense, whether animal spirits and ancestor ghosts, or deities such as Xiuhtecuhtli, Yahweh, or Zeus). The vertical line, on the other hand, represents a continuum on which to indicate the extent to which an individual tends to *prefer* the supernaturally authorised norms of the religious coalition with which he or she primarily identifies.

As a result of the natural selection of cognitive biases for *detecting* hidden agents and *protecting* in-groups in early ancestral environments, gods are relatively easily *born* in human minds that are characterised by high levels of mentalising, schizotypy, and ontological confusion, and relatively easily *borne* in human cultures that are characterised by costly signalling through credibility-enhancing religious displays, risk-aversion strategies activated by ecological duress, and low levels of existential security. Those who are anthropomorphically promiscuous and sociographically prudish will somewhat automatically *rely* on appeals to supernatural causes when explaining confusing events and *comply* with the supernatural conventions of their in-group when inscribing the social field. From the perspective of scientific disciplines such as cognitive science, evolutionary psychology, and cultural anthropology, 'religion' can be understood as the result of aggregates of these two types of evolved biases (which, of course, must be further fractionated within the relevant disciplines). In other words, religiosity – as operationalised by many scientists in these fields – *is* the outcome of the confluence of these reciprocally reinforcing content and context biases.

Although my focus is on philosophy *of* religion, in the sense defined above, it is important to note that some apologists have suggested that CMS might be useful for supporting what we might call philosophy *for* religion (or theology). In an article proposing 'Simulation as a Method for Theological and Philosophical Inquiry' (Donaldson and McConnell, 2015), for example, the authors acknowledge that the use of CMS tools to study God as an 'agent' in an artificial world would be resisted by most theologians, for whom divine action is mysterious and cannot be studied scientifically. However, they fail to acknowledge that their proposals for using CMS in 'theological inquiry' beg the question of divine existence and intervention, and evade the question of how the variables and behaviours of a supernatural agent could be empirically verified and validated in relation to a computational model. It is not surprising that the few examples of the application of computational tools to 'theological' questions do not typically address divine action of the sort that would be of interest to laypeople, but deal instead with abstract logical issues such as the validity of various versions of the ontological argument for the existence of a perfect divine being (e.g., Benzmüller and Paleo, 2016; Kirchner et al., 2019).

The majority of contemporary philosophers offer non-religious hypotheses about the big questions of metaphysics, epistemology, and ethics, that is, *naturalistic* hypotheses that are intended to be empirically tractable or at least intersubjectively and intercommunally contestable in *secularistic* contexts. Theistic philosophers of religion, on the other hand, typically offer answers that directly or indirectly appeal to the putative revelation of an empirically intractable and inherently mysterious intentional force that allegedly communicates with (at least some of) the intellectual and priestly elite of *their own* religious coalition. Given the way in which god-bearing biases can amplify superstition and segregation, and the general consensus that expunging these sorts of biases from one's thinking and writing is a desideratum for philosophers and, indeed, for scholars in any discipline, it is not unreasonable to expect that the renewal of philosophy of religion will require its participants to more explicitly promote anthropomorphic prudery and sociographic promiscuity.

It seems to me that the future of philosophy of religion is in doubt. I mean this in two senses. First, it is doubtful whether this philosophical sub-field will thrive (or even survive) as an academic discipline over the next few decades. Professional academic positions in the field have dwindled markedly in recent decades (even, albeit less so, in church-sponsored colleges and denominational seminaries). It is deeply fractured and in danger of falling apart or fading away in contemporary Western universities. Such a loss would not necessarily be devastating. Disciplinary boundaries are constantly overlapping, dissolving, and reforming, and philosophical reflection on religion would certainly carry on (and perhaps intensify) in other academic fields. On the other hand, there might be good theoretical or even pragmatic reasons for carving out and maintaining professional academic space dedicated to philosophical reflection on these issues.

Second, I mean that if philosophy of religion is to survive (and even thrive) in the academy, its representatives and stakeholders must do what the members of every other sub-discipline in philosophy have done: acknowledge and even highlight the dubitability of claims that refer to supernatural agents and appeal to supernatural authorities. Like scholars in every other field in the modern academy, most philosophers carry out their intellectual tasks without inserting 'gods' into their explanatory hypotheses and without relying on special pleading references to 'revelation' to which only their in-group has access. If philosophy of religion has a future as a coherent and generative discipline, it is one in which there is no place for confessional apologetics. The latter is not philosophy *of* religion, but philosophy *for* religion (or philosophy *co-dependent* on the religious coalition to which the apologist belongs), and therefore has no place in the secular academy. The good news is that some scholars are working hard to renew this beleaguered discipline and secure its place in the secular academy by exorcising apologetics and incorporating insights from the comparative and scientific study of religion into their philosophical analysis (Knepper, 2013; Schilbrack, 2014; Wildman, 2018; Maitzen, 2017; Knepper, 2022).

## Computer Modelling and Philosophy of Religion

How might the developments in computational modelling and social simulation that we have been discussing in this book contribute to the revisioning of philosophy of religion? At the very least, the scientific literature behind the conceptual framework outlined in Chapter 2, which informs several of the computer models described in Chapters 4 and 5, exerts pressure on philosophers of religion to become more self-critical about the religiously salient content and context biases that play a unique role in their discipline. But what will happen to this sub-discipline if, as intimated at the end of Chapter 1, the use of these tools for thinking continues to grow in philosophy throughout the twenty-first century? Here I argue that computer modelling and simulation (CMS) can contribute to the reformation of the philosophy of religion in at least two ways: by facilitating conceptual clarity about the role of biases in the emergence and maintenance of phenomena commonly deemed 'religious', supplying methods and techniques that enhance our capacity to link philosophical analysis and synthesis to empirical data in the psychological and social sciences; and by providing material insights for metaphysical hypotheses and meta-ethical proposals that rely solely on immanent resources.

First, the process of developing a computational model and designing simulation experiments to test hypotheses presses scholars to be explicit about their assumptions and to seek exceptional conceptual clarity as they articulate their logical or causal claims. Most philosophers welcome this sort of pressure, and some might even view it as a *sine qua non* for philosophy itself. All too often in philosophy of religion, however, scholars operate with inadequately defined or abstract notions of 'religion' and fail to acknowledge (or recognise) the theistic *biases* that are shaping their analyses and arguments. How could computer modelling help? By providing techniques for integrating theoretical insights from multiple disciplines into the scientific study of religion within conceptual architectures that can be implemented in computer models and drive simulation experiments in (more or less religious) artificial societies. CMS introduces new tools and methodologies that can enable philosophers to make their arguments more concrete and more explicitly tied to empirical data (Grim, 2019a).

In the case of philosophy of religion, this means tying arguments to theories and real-world data about how human beings imaginatively engage in shared rituals with the contingently embodied, human-like, coalition-favouring intentional forces of their own religious in-group. Engaging with CMS might help to establish the respectability of this sub-field of philosophy in the academy by providing computational tools for linking its philosophical reflection to empirical findings and theoretical frameworks within the relevant *sciences* that study the mechanisms and dynamics in the complex adaptive systems that constitute and regulate phenomena commonly deemed 'religious'. Throughout its history, philosophy (at least its vanguard) has rigorously engaged with the most advanced scientific inquiry of its day. All too often, however, philosophy of religion has been in the rearguard, defending traditional theological claims about supernatural agents and authorities until they become so implausible that their reformulation is necessary for the survival of the relevant religious coalition.

The bulk of the discussion among scholars in this discipline focuses on abstract notions such as the possibility of divine action or the ontological status of divine ideas, rather than on concrete beliefs and actual ritual practices aimed at appeasing or accessing axiologically relevant supernatural agents. In other words, the bulk of what happens under the disciplinary label in question is philosophy of *theology* rather than philosophy of *religion*. Granted, theological reflection is a part of religion, but this sub-field of philosophy has focused almost entirely on the abstract arguments of religious elites and has mostly ignored the concrete beliefs and behaviours of religious people.

Philosophers of religion all too often use vague definitions of 'religion' that allude to a sense of transcendence, the binding force of cultural norms, or the capacity for meaning-making – or simply fail to define their subject matter at all. This makes it relatively easy for apologists or theologians to dominate the field by keeping the focus on abstract ideas and possible worlds that have little to do with the idiosyncratic beliefs and causally opaque practices that characterise actual religious minds and cultures. Incorporating computational methodologies and findings from simulation techniques into philosophy of religion would encourage and further enable scholars in this field to focus on the actual subject matter that appears in the discipline's self-designation.

A second way in which CMS methodologies can help renew philosophy of religion is by materially informing broader discussions within the classical loci of philosophy. I limit myself here to a brief exploration of some of the implications for debates in metaphysics, epistemology, and ethics. These issues have already been discussed in the chapters above and by other scholars elsewhere (e.g., DeLanda, 2011; Floridi, 2002; Grim et al., 2013; Humphreys, 2006; Squazzoni, 2009; Tolk, 2015; Weisberg, 2012; Winsberg, 2010). My focus here is on the implications of what I have been calling metaphysical (not merely methodological) naturalism and secularism on philosophy of religion in particular. Today, most philosophers (just like other reflective academics) have learned how to contest biases associated with anthropomorphic promiscuity and sociographic prudery – at least when they are making philosophical arguments. In other words, they do not appeal to supernatural agents or authorities when providing warrants for their philosophical claims. They do not insert 'gods' into their construction or critique of hypotheses about the existential conditions or evaluative criteria for human knowing, acting, and being.

What criteria should one use for evaluating claims about the grounds for – and dynamics of – human rationality, morality, and causality? What makes these modes of human engagement possible or actualisable? As I noted in Chapter 3, most answers to these kinds of questions have been more or less 'Platonic'. Plato was certainly not alone in privileging notions of idealised transcendence in philosophy, but his formulations have had a profound influence on the way in which most Western metaphysicians have tried to explain the existential conditions for actual entities or events. Up until the last couple of centuries, the majority of philosophers operating in the wake of the west Asian axial age posited the existence of some kind of (more or less) anthropomorphic, eternally transcendent Being whose character is somehow relevant for organising and orienting the temporal lives of human beings who (more or less) resemble it (the Form of the Good, the Unmoved Mover, the Divine Creator, etc.). Despite its apparent philosophical sophistication, this approach remains an expression of the naturally evolved bias towards interpreting ambiguous events or phenomena (in this case, 'all things') as caused by some person-like force.

In this sense, philosophers in these traditions have still been anthropomorphically promiscuous (although perhaps less so than non-philosophers). Belief in unchanging transcendent causes (such as Platonic Ideas or the monotheistic notion of a divine Mind or Will) among philosophers and theologians flourished within a thought world overshadowed and regulated by the categories of *substance*, *stasis*, and *sameness*. However, most contemporary philosophers (and virtually all scientists) prefer to work with *relational*, *dynamic*, and *differential* concepts. For computer scientists, especially those engaged in modelling and simulation, this means exploring dynamic relations among variables in complex systems. The success of scientific methodologies such as computer modelling has accelerated the 'reversal of Platonism', that is, the dissolution of the myth of transcendence that has surreptitiously shaped the bulk of Western thought, a myth whose dominance allowed theistic content and context biases to run naked and unchallenged in (most of) philosophy and (all of) theology for over two millennia.

As Manuel DeLanda explains in *Philosophy and Simulation*, the success of CMS technologies (e.g., cellular automata, neural nets, multi-agent modelling) has shown that it is possible to account for the emergence and behaviour of complex entities or 'assemblages' by describing the *immanent* intensive processes that actually generate them and simulating such processes in computational models (DeLanda, 2011). As explained in Chapter 4, in DeLanda's use of the term, an *assemblage* is an emergent whole that is irreducible and decomposable (DeLanda, 2006; 2016). Every actual assemblage is an *individual singularity* whose properties are the product of a historical process. Every assemblage is actualised in relation to a *universal singularity* whose real, mechanism-independent, structured possibility space defines the tendencies and capacities of the assemblage. Finally, every assemblage is part of a *population* with distributed variables whose alteration is conditioned by *parameters* such as (de)territorialisation and (de)coding.

The fact that computer models can simulate the emergence of assemblages (from thermodynamic systems to organisms to societies) suggests that the morphogenesis of the latter can be explained by referring to resources and mechanisms immanent to the world of matter and energy, without any need to postulate transcendent essences, types, or creators. There are no gods in (or outside) the machine. We no longer need *Deus ex machina* explanations to make sense of the emergence of new forms. Moreover, the successful simulation of topological events in computer models suggests that we do not even need gods (or God) to make sense of the emergence (or even the existence) of any forms at all.

This has rather obvious implications for philosophers of religion, especially those focused on defending (or denouncing) theistic interpretations of the origin, order, or orientation of the cosmos. The successful application of CMS methodologies provides warrant for – and demonstrates the explanatory power of – an anthropomorphically prudish metaphysics of immanence. Philosophers of religion are running out of excuses for not embracing metaphysical naturalism. They are also running out of excuses for not embracing metaphysical secularism. By including appeals to the general or special revelation of a transcendent supernatural agent as grounds or guidance for ethics, theist philosophers of religion foster both moral evasion and moral confusion. If philosophers of religion can promote anthropomorphic prudery and sociographic promiscuity (like most of their philosophical and scientific peers), they have a unique opportunity to use their subject-matter expertise to unveil the implicit tribalism and parochialism of religious ethics and, by incorporating insights from the bio-cultural sciences, to contribute materially to conversations in neighbouring sub-disciplines such as moral psychology and political philosophy.

CMS provides us with tools that can facilitate such conversations by rendering more tractable the complex adaptive ethical systems within which we behave and interact. We can begin to imagine a future in which a robustly naturalistic and secularistic philosophy of religion contributes alongside other disciplines to the production of new knowledge about our world and to the construction of new pragmatic solutions to the global challenges facing human societies. As we have seen in earlier chapters, computational techniques also have the capacity to elicit the emergence and analyse the alteration of divergent cultural norms within the 'flat ontology' of an artificial society. This also provides a point of contact with Deleuze's philosophical efforts to articulate the conditions for an ethics of pure immanence.

## The Achievement of Deleuze's Meta-ethics

Analogous to my discussion of Deleuze's metaphysics and meta-epistemology in Chapters 3 and 5 respectively, my interest here is less in the details of his ethics and more in the ways in which he used the philosophical atheist machine to articulate the conditions for ethical discourse and practice. In other words, how did he move beyond Christianity's secretion of negative, clerical atheism towards a purely immanent and affirmatively atheistic understanding of the criteria for evaluating human acting? Unlike most philosophers, Deleuze's meta-ethics is almost coterminous with his ethics and so we cannot simply ignore the latter. In *The Logic of Sense* he argued that

'Either ethics makes no sense at all, or this is what it means and has nothing else to say: not to be unworthy of what happens to us' (LOS, 169). He spells this out in relation to 'the actor' (such as the Stoic sage) who is like an 'anti-god' (*contradieu*) who belongs to the Aion and counter-actualises the event, rather than getting caught in the contracting divine present of Chronos. Assessments of Deleuze's ethical and political arguments in his work with and without Guattari abound in the secondary literature (e.g., Buchanan, 2008; 2013; Lambert, 2021; Nail, 2012; Patton, 2002; Van Heerden, 2019).

My goal in this context, however, is not to unpack Deleuze's Stoic-inspired ethics (and politics), which I have done in Chapters 4 and 5 of *Iconoclastic Theology: Gilles Deleuze and the Secretion of Atheism* (Shults, 2014b), but to explore possible connections between his meta-ethics and insights derived from the bio-cultural sciences of religion and implemented in computational modelling and social simulations. To guide this exploration I am going to use a meta-ethical framework developed elsewhere with Wesley Wildman (Shults and Wildman, 2019). We proposed this framework as way of guiding discussions within and around collaborative teams developing computational models in which human (all too human) factors play a significant role. These factors are particularly relevant when developing models of (non-)religiosity because ethics and moral foundations have been associated with religion for most of human history. Our framework has three distinct but interrelated elements: the philosophical, the scientific, and the practical.

The *philosophical* aspect of this framework calls for clarification and invites contestation of philosophical claims about the nature (or existence) of 'the good' and 'the right'. As noted above, scholars and practitioners in the computer sciences quite often discuss the ethical implications of their work. However, treatments of more abstract questions related to the conditions and criteria for understanding the nature of moral thought and practice are less common. This first element of the framework, therefore, aims to encourage computer modellers (and especially those involved in social simulation) to attend to the meta-ethical assumptions that often surreptitiously shape ethical discussions about which moral rules we should follow or which moral goals we should pursue. Proponents of deontological and teleological (or consequentialist) approaches to ethics, for example, differ in their understanding of the relationship between 'the right' and 'the good'. The textbook example of the deontological approach is Kant's Categorical Imperative, which unites the right and the good and grounds both in the moral law of a transcendent divine being. The textbook example of the teleological approach is Mill's Utilitarianism, which distinguishes between the good (well-being for the greatest number of people) and the right (actions whose consequences promote that goal). Insofar as the construction of computational architectures for social simulation are always purposeful, most modellers (*qua* modellers) seem to be naturally drawn towards consequentialism.

In my view, the capacity of CMS techniques to simulate the emergence and expansion of divergent human norms, including 'ethical' or 'unethical' behaviours (e.g., altruism or violence), in a population of agents (Conte et al., 2014; Haynes et al., 2017; Lemos et al., 2020; Mascaro, 2010; Xenitidou and Edmonds, 2014) lends warrant to moral non-realism or amoralist philosophy. In other words, just as emergent assemblages can be explained without appealing to transcendent supernatural agents, so emergent norms can be explained without appealing to transcendent supernatural authorities. It seems to me that Deleuze falls into this broad meta-ethical camp of 'amoralism'. This is not immoralism, of course, which would presuppose (and negate) moralism, but rather a rejection of the false premises on which the whole debate about transcendent moral facts that can guide ethical judgements is grounded. In other words, the 'amoralist' position sees

> dialectically wrangling with a theist or a moralist on theistic or moralist grounds [as] a tar baby, precisely because, in the realm of fantasy, anything goes … hence there can never be a resolution … Thus, normative ethics is as pointless a pursuit as theology, inasmuch as both seek to determine the truths about a fictitious entity. (Marks, 2016: 9, 17)

Not all modellers, social scientists, or stakeholders will find a philosophically amoralist meta-ethical position easy to accept, but having the conversation at least opens up the possibility for linking Deleuze's reflections on ethics and politics to wider policy-relevant deliberations. And it is important to remember that even if we did achieve widespread acceptance of meta-ethical amoralism that would obviously not solve all our problems. We will still need to argue about what attitudes and behaviours to recommend as we connect our desiring-machines and transform our social machines. However, embracing a methodological (at least, and metaphysical at best) amoralist stance would help cut down on the amount of time wasted arguing about which in-group's supernaturally authorised (or even secularly secured) social norms provide a transcendent starting point for ethical debate.

The *scientific* aspect of our meta-ethical framework calls for more serious consideration of the findings of the bio-cultural evolutionary sciences and their incorporation into computational models that aim to simulate religious (or secular) minds and groups. It makes sense to think about the conditions and criteria for ethical behaviour in light of knowledge gained from these sciences devoted to the study of the evolution of human morality. As a hypersocial species, we humans survive and thrive by cooperating and coordinating in groups. Traits that fostered these sorts of 'altruistic' behaviours or 'moral' dispositions were naturally selected in early ancestral environments because they improved inclusive fitness and are now part of our phylogenetic inheritance. These traits included the tendency to infer the presence of morally interested supernatural agents and the tendency to prefer the supernaturally authorised norms of the religious coalition that constitutes and regulates the social context in which one is raised or to which one converts.

For the vast majority of the history of our species, moral norms have been justified and enforced by appeals to supernatural agents who are putatively engaged in rituals performed by the members (or elites) of an in-group. This dependence on the 'judgement of God' (or gods) for regulating ethical behaviour and defending political decisions might have helped humans survive, but, as I have been arguing throughout the preceding chapters, surviving the Anthropocene may require the discovery (or generation) of other tendencies and capacities within the structured possibility space of human and social assemblages. Believing that uncooperative behaviours could be punished by animal spirits, ancestor ghosts, or monotheistic deities helped keep cheaters and freeloaders in line even when they thought none of their actual affines were watching. Unfortunately, the dark side of in-group altruism is out-group antagonism, and so it is not surprising that religious beliefs and behaviours can ratchet up intergroup conflict and slow down psychologically and sociologically salutogenic developments in modern cultures.

Scientific knowledge about the evolution of our moral equipment can inform our reflections about the best way to organise the intersecting social fields of our contemporary local and global contexts. Many people think we need religion (or theism) as a basis for ethical discourse and social cohesion, but this is demonstrably false: countries and regions in which affiliation to religion is low score higher on a host of 'moral' issues, including economic equality, gender equality, healthcare, infant mortality, environmental protection, lack of crime and corruption, etc. (e.g., Paul, 2009; Zuckerman, 2009; 2010). Religion worked well in small-scale societies to activate and constrain the 'collective effervescence' (Durkheim, 1912) that helped hold them together. Today, however, in large-scale, pluralist social organisations characterised by high levels of information technology, existential security, population density, and decentralisation, populations are able to acquire emotional energy that promotes social cohesion through what we might call 'distributive effervescence' (McCaffree and Shults, 2022). To put this in Deleuzian terms, desiring-machines are able to thrive without the moralism of territorial and despotic social machines.

This brings us to the third and final element of our meta-ethical framework, which highlights the *practical* import of the first two elements. The philosophical element is practical insofar as it focuses our attention on the pragmatic value of consistent ethical reasoning that does not evade responsibility by defending normative proposals with appeals to allegedly transcendent moral realities. The scientific element is practical insofar as it reminds us to take account of the limitations as well as the capacities of the moral equipment bequeathed to us by millions of years of natural selection and reinforced by social entrainment. Attending to each of these elements more carefully in our meta-ethical reflections can help us avoid – or at least mitigate – moral evasion (e.g., appealing to unfalsifiable supernatural revelations about a particular in-group's moral code) and moral confusion (e.g., failing to account for the actual cognitive and moral equipment that is part of our phylogenetic inheritance).

We cannot fully understand (much less address) most of the major challenges facing global society without accounting for the role played by various forms of religious belief and behaviour in contemporary worldviews and lifeways. As I have argued throughout these chapters, adapting in the Anthropocene will require us to learn new ways to challenge cognitive tendencies that promote superstition and segregation, a task that might be facilitated by adopting depolarising polices and debiasing strategies. CMS approaches can construct and explore wholly immanent socio-material 'state spaces' within which we can discover topological facts about the ethical and political capacities and tendencies of networked agents with heterogeneous norms under a diversity of parameterised conditions (Diallo et al., 2021; Shults and Wildman, 2020a). Such tools make it possible for us to design and execute simulation experiments that tease out the propensities and probabilities of various ethical and political behaviours and interactions in the complex systems whose immanent dynamics they study. As I have consistently emphasised, these methods will not solve all of our problems and will no doubt produce new ones. But they do provide us with new ways of conceiving and hooking up to atheist machines that clear the ground of theist biases and open up novel opportunities for living together on the plane of immanence.

# 8

# How Do You Make Yourself an Atheist Body without Organs?

As we noted in Chapter 1, Deleuze followed a line of philosophers that he traced from some of the ancient Greeks through Spinoza and Nietzsche in distinguishing (and linking) the speculative and the practical purposes of (naturalist, atheist) philosophy.

> The speculative purpose and the practical purpose of philosophy as Naturalism, science and pleasure, coincide on this point: it is always a matter of denouncing the illusion, the false infinite, the *infinity of religion* and all of the theologico-erotic-oneiric myths in which it is expressed. To the question 'what is the use of philosophy?' the answer must be: what other subject would have an interest in erecting the image of a *free person*, and in denouncing all of the forces which need myth and troubled spirit in order to establish their power? (LOS, 314, emphases added, translation emended)

In the context of this quotation, which is an exposition of Lucretius' Naturalism, Deleuze recommends a philosophy of affirmation and joy in the truly infinite diverse production of Nature, rather than a philosophy of anxiety tied to the false infinite of myth, 'the myth of a false philosophy totally impregnated by theology' (LOS, 315).

Deleuze also distinguished (while linking) what he referred to as the 'negative' and 'positive' tasks of schizoanalysis (micropolitics, rhizomatics, pragmatics, etc.). On the one hand, 'the task of schizoanalysis goes by way of destruction – a whole scouring of the unconscious, a complete curettage. Destroy Oedipus, the illusion of the ego, the puppet of the superego, guilt, the law, castration (AO, 342). On the other hand, and at the same time, schizoanalysis performs the positive tasks of 'causing the desiring machines to start up again' (AO, 373) and attaining 'a nonfigurative and nonsymbolic unconscious ... flows-schizzes or real-desire, apprehended below the minimum conditions of identity' (AO, 385). There is a reactive mode of destruction that merely conserves and perpetuates the 'established order of representation, models, and copies', but Deleuze highlights another productive mode of destruction in which the models and copies are destroyed 'in order to institute the chaos which creates, making the simulacra function and raising a phantasm – the most innocent of all destructions, the destruction of Platonism' (LOS, 303). Throughout this book I have highlighted the role of the atheist machine and atheist assemblages in the destructive-creative production of philosophy.

In this final chapter, I discuss these distinctions in relation to Deleuze's use of the phrase 'Body without Organs' (BwO), especially in the *Capitalism and Schizophrenia* project with Guattari, but in other writings as well. Given our discussion of the role of atheism in Deleuze's work and his understanding of atheism as philosophy's achievement and the philosopher's serenity, it should not be surprising that all BwOs are atheist. The last three sub-sections spell out some of the ways in which the practice of making oneself a BwO helps shed light on the achievements of Deleuze's atheist metaphysics, meta-epistemology, and meta-ethics, each of which we discussed in the central chapters of the book. Although computational modelling and social simulation are not the focus here, I will include a brief discussion of the potential explanatory and experimental role they might play in constructing a BwO in the context of expositing Deleuze's proposals related to 'becoming-sorcerer', 'brain-subject', and 'the philosopher's serenity'.

Sorcery? Subjectivity? Serenity? Such concepts bring us to a question that might have arisen in the minds of some readers as I discussed Deleuze's understanding of atheism as 'philosophy's achievement' in the preceding chapters: Even if one accepts that a philosophy of immanence requires clearing the ground of transcendent religious figures, might the creative laying out of planes and following of nomadic lines of flight, etc., still involve some sort of *spirituality*? In other words, can the atheist machine produce an intensive spirituality (or distribute spiritual intensities that take shape as minoritarian mysticism, esotericism, shamanism, etc.) while simultaneously dissolving theism and religion (in the sense we have been defining the latter in this book)? It depends, of course, on what one means by 'spirituality', a term almost as contentious as 'religion'. Whether or not one calls it spirituality, Deleuze's corpus clearly includes critical engagement with concepts and ordeals that have been commonly associated with that term; this aspect of his work has attracted growing interest in the secondary literature (e.g., May, 2000; Kerslake, 2007; Behum, 2010; Smith, 2010; Delpech-Ramey, 2010; Gangle, 2010; Ramey, 2012; Kerslake, 2019).

Exploring these issues in detail is beyond the scope of the current book, but I hope that my arguments so far have made it clear that whatever is going on here in Deleuze's philosophy, it has nothing to do with the promotion of priestly-mediated ritual engagement with the axiologically relevant supernatural agents of a religious in-group. Still, it might have something to do with the distribution of intensities on the plane of immanence in a way that some philosophers (and perhaps even some social scientists and computer modellers) might want to call 'spirituality'. As we have seen, for Deleuze, the speculative and practical purposes of philosophy are 'always a matter' of denouncing the infinity of religion and creating the image of a free person. And so in the first two sub-sections of this final chapter I briefly describe the relationship of these 'negative' and 'positive' tasks to the process of constructing a BwO, spelling out the destruction required (to be done with the judgement of God) in the creative production of a free life (a joy immanent to desire).

### To be Done with the Judgement of God

First, then, let us spell out the negative task of philosophy in light of Deleuze's understanding of the relationship between the BwO and the 'judgement of God'. He had already been playing with Artaud's idea of the BwO in *The Logic of Sense* (e.g., LOS, 147, 216), but in his collaboration with Guattari it takes on a far more significant role. *A Thousand Plateaus* treats the BwO in several places, but it makes sense to begin with the chapter 'How Do You Make Yourself a Body without Organs?', which is associated with 28 November 1947. This is the date when 'Artaud declares war on the organs: *To be done with the judgment of God* … Experimentation: not only radiophonic but also biological and political, incurring censorship and repression. Corpus and Socius, politics and experimentation. They will not let you experiment in peace' (ATP, 166). So, the BwO has something to do with experimenting in a way that overcomes the judgement of God. But what is it exactly?

> At any rate, you have one (or several) … At any rate, you make one, you can't desire without making one … It is not at all a notion or a concept but a practice, a set of practices. You never reach the Body without Organs, you can't reach it, you are forever attaining it, it is a limit. People ask, So what is this BwO – But you're already on it, scurrying like a vermin, groping like a blind person, or running like lunatic. (ATP, 166)

Deleuze emphasises in several places that the BwO is not opposed to the organs, but rather to the organism and that which is 'organised' by the judgement of God. In the context of discussing Artaud's novels, he argues that the 'true organs' of the BwO,

> which must be composed and positioned, are opposed to the organism, the organic organization of the organs. The *judgment of God*, the system of the judgment of God, the theological system, is precisely the operation of He who makes an organism … The judgment of God uproots it [the BwO] from its immanence and makes it an organism, a signification, a subject. (ATP, 176)

It might help to make more explicit the relationship between the BwO and assemblages, which we have discussed in earlier chapters. In the opening pages of *A Thousand Plateaus*, Deleuze explains that 'One side of a machinic assemblage faces the strata, which doubtless make it a kind of organism, or signifying totality ... it also has a side facing a *body without organs*, which is continually dismantling the organism, causing asignifying particles or pure intensities to pass or circulate...' (ATP, 4). Strata, territory, plane of organisation on one side, BwO, deterritorialisation, and plane of consistency on the other. For Deleuze, 'The BwO is the *field of immanence* (of desire), the *plane of consistency* specific to desire (with desire defined as a process of production without reference to any exterior agency, whether it be a crack that hollows it out or a pleasure that fills it)' (ATP, 170). We will return to the link between the BwO and desire below, but the important point here is that the plane of organisation (stratification, the 'judgement of God') is 'constantly working away at' the plane of consistency (BwO, field of immanence), 'always trying to plug the lines of flight'; and, conversely, the plane of consistency is 'constantly extricating itself' from the plane of organisation, 'causing particles to spin off the strata ... breaking down functions by means of assemblages or microassemblages' (ATP, 297–8).

In *Anti-Oedipus* Deleuze had noted that 'An apparent conflict arises between desiring-machines and the body without organs ... Beneath its organs it [the BwO] senses there are larvae and loathsome worms, and a God at work messing it all up or strangling it by organizing it' (AO, 9). Keep in mind that the concept of 'desiring-machines' in *Anti-Oedipus* is eventually replaced by the concept of machinic assemblages in *A Thousand Plateaus*. In both cases, they are organised (or strangled, plugged up, judged) by 'God'. *A Thousand Plateaus* depicts God as 'a Lobster, or a double pincer, a double bind' (ATP, 45), a principle of double articulation: deducting from molecular particle-flows and establishing molar compounds. In *Anti-Oedipus*, God is depicted as 'the master of the disjunctive syllogism, or as its a priori principle (God defined as the *Omnitudo realitatis*, from which all secondary realities are derived by a process of division)' (AO, 14). In either case, we may think of the 'judgement of God' as that which organises by dividing, the negative use of the disjunctive syllogism, the segmentation of intensities, and the strangling of desire.

It should be increasingly clear how all of this is related to Deleuze's insistence that denouncing the infinity of religion is an essential task of philosophy. As I argued in Chapter 2, when Deleuze attacks the infinity of 'religion' he has in mind what I have been calling 'theism', that is, theologically segmented and sacerdotally policed collective imaginative engagement with a supernatural agent who is imagined to be an infinite intentional entity that is the origin, condition, and goal of all finite intensities whatsoever. We have already seen how such a figure cannot be borne logically, psychologically, or politically. All BwOs are atheist in the same way that the 'regions of the auto-production of the unconscious' (AO, 66) and the nomadic 'sense of the absolute' (ATP, 422) are atheist: they experiment in order to be free of the judgement of God. For Deleuze, constructing a BwO involves revolting against any imagined superior, original, final intentionality and liberating bodies in their intensity, that is, following the lines of flight drawn by infinite intensities populating and traversing the plane of immanence. Of course, one has to be careful, a point to which we will return below.

Unsurprisingly, Spinoza and Nietzsche are in the background of Deleuze's philosophical denunciation of the judgement of God. In the conclusion of *A Thousand Plateaus*, in the section dealing with the BwO, both are listed as 'surveyors' of the plane of consistency, 'never unifications, never totalizations, but rather consistencies or consolidations' (ATP, 558). Deleuze refers to Spinoza's *Ethics* as 'the great book of the BwO'. Sometimes BwO is singular (the BwO) and sometimes plural (BwOs). But is there a 'totality' of all BwOs? Deleuze's answer explicitly utilises Spinozist terminology:

> There is a continuum of all of the attributes or genuses of intensity under a single substance, and continuum of the intensities of a certain genus under a single type or attribute. A continuum of all substances in intensity and of all intensities in substance. The uninterrupted continuum of the BwO, immanence, immanent limit. (ATP, 170)

As in so much of his work, Deleuze appeals to Nietzsche when illustrating key philosophical concepts or movements, such as deterritorialisation, nomad thought, haecceities, and the production of speeds and slownesses between particles, all of which are components of a 'Cosmos philosophy' in which the BwO plays a key role.

Spinoza and Nietzsche are also prominent in Deleuze's late essay 'To Have Done with Judgment', where they join D. H. Lawrence, Kafka, and Artaud as examples of thinkers for whom the 'logic of judgment merges with the psychology of the priest, as the inventor of the most somber organization: I want to judge, I have to judge...' (Deleuze, 1997: 127). The process of undoing the judgement of God is not only atheist, it is 'antijudicative, understood as Antichrist'. We are reminded of his distinction in *The Logic of Sense* between the order of God and 'the order of the Antichrist, which is opposed point for point to the divine order'. The order of the Antichrist is 'characterized by the death of God, the destruction of the world, the dissolution of the person, the disintegration of bodies, and the shifting function of language which now expresses only intensities' (LOS, 334). For Nietzsche, challenging the divine order involved expressing the creative power of pure affirmation. Like Artaud, Nietzsche intuited that only an organised body could be judged by God. The body without organs, on the other hand,

> is an affective, intensive, anarchist body that consists solely of poles, zones, thresholds, and gradients. It is transversed by a powerful, nonorganic vitality ... the way to escape judgment is to make yourself a body without organs, to find your body without organs. This had already been Nietzsche's project: to define the body in its becoming, in its intensity, as the power to affect or to be affected, that is, as *Will to power*. (Deleuze, 1997: 131)

This essay also provides more insight into why Deleuze thinks that Christianity secretes more atheism than any other religion. Early religions, which may have been characterised by a 'system of cruelty' in which bodies 'are marked by each other, and the debt is inscribed directly on the body following the *finite blocks* that circulate in a territory', were not yet under the control of the theological doctrine of judgement. In the latter, 'our debts are inscribed in an autonomous book without our even realizing it, so that we are no longer able to pay off an account that has become infinite' (Deleuze, 1997: 128). Here we are clearly dealing with what Deleuze elsewhere calls the despotic social machine of monotheism. Humans are given 'lots', which means they are fit for a particular 'form' and organic 'end'. Deleuze refers to the 'final bifurcation' that occurs with Christianity:

> there are no longer any lots, for it is our judgments that make up our only lot; and there is no longer any form, for it is the judgment of God that constitutes the infinite form ... Nothing is left but judgment, and every judgment bears on another judgment ... we are no longer debtors of the gods through forms or ends, but have become in our entire being the infinite debtors of a single god. (1997: 128–9)

The gravity of an infinite judgemental Being is unbearable, but the atheist machine escapes with celerity; atheism secretes and philosophy begins.

How can we be done with the judgement of God? The secret is

> to bring into existence and not to judge. If it is so disgusting to judge, it is not because everything is of equal value, but on the contrary because what has value can be made or distinguished only by defying judgment ... it is not a question of judging other existing beings, but of sensing whether they agree or disagree with us, that is, whether they bring forces to us, or whether they return us to the miseries of war, to the poverty of the dream, to the rigors of organization. (Deleuze, 1997: 135)

Philosophy is always a matter of denouncing the infinity of religion (theism), which involves clearing the ground of religious figures, of a false (transcendent) infinite: 'Wherever there is transcendence, vertical Being, imperial State in the sky or on earth, there is *religion*; and there is *Philosophy* only where there is immanence ... only friends can set out a plane of immanence as a ground from which idols have been cleared' (WIP, 43, emphases added). Philosophy tears down the myths of Being and the One, attacks the negative, and establishes the 'multiple as multiple' as the object of affirmation and the 'diverse as diverse' as the object of joy (LOS, 315). All three of the quotations in this paragraph illustrate the way in which, for Deleuze, the positive (or creative) task of philosophy is always and already at work alongside – or as the other side of – its negative (or destructive) task.

## A Joy Immanent to Desire

The positive task of philosophy is 'always a matter' of erecting an image of the free person. It is linked to the negative task of denouncing the infinity of religion because determining the distinction between the true infinite and the false infinite is 'the necessary means of ethics and practice'. The liberation of desire is produced in (or as) the wake of the escape from the theological, erotic, and oneiric illusions of the infinite capacity of the body for pleasure and the infinite duration of the soul, which together produce anxiety about infinite suffering after death. 'And the two illusions are linked: the idea of infinite punishment is the natural price to be paid for having unlimited desires.' Infinity in all the wrong places, the false infinite of theistic myth, strangling desire through avidity and anguish, covetousness and culpability, a 'strange complex that generates crimes' (LOS, 309). Deleuze's emphasis on putting philosophy to use in the creation of the free human being can also be traced to his appreciation of the same line of philosophers mentioned at the beginning of this chapter, including Lucretius, Spinoza, and Nietzsche (Ansell-Pearson, 2016; Johnson, 2016; Montag, 2016; Roberts, 2019).

In this context, however, I want to focus primarily on how we can spell out the positive task of philosophy, the creative use of the atheist machine, in light of Deleuze's call to make oneself a BwO. Here is the place to confess that my favourite quotation from *A Thousand Plateaus*, and indeed my favourite quotation from the whole of Deleuze's corpus, appears in the chapter on 'How to Make Yourself a Body without Organs'.

> There is, in fact, a *joy* that is *immanent* to *desire* as though desire were filled by itself and its contemplations, a joy that implies no lack or impossibility and is not measured by pleasure since it is what distributes *intensities* of pleasure and prevents them from being suffused by anxiety, shame, and guilt. (ATP, 172, emphases added)

In this sub-section I will briefly unpack some of the key concepts in this quotation in the context of outlining the role of the BwO in Deleuze's setting forth of an image of a person freed from the judgement of God. We have already touched on the relation between the BwO and the plane of immanence, and so here I'll focus on the other three terms italicised above: joy, desire, and intensities.

In Chapter 1 I noted that Deleuze often highlighted the role (expression, affirmation) of joy in the works Spinoza and Nietzsche (e.g., Deleuze, 1992: 262; 1983: 135), but he also emphasised its productive power and effects in the writings of other authors. In his book with Guattari on *Kafka: Toward a Minor Literature*, for example, Deleuze observed that 'There is a Kafka laughter, a very joyous laughter ... He is an author who laughs with a profound joy, a joie de vivre, in spite of, or because of, his clownish declarations that he offers like a trap or a circus' (Deleuze and Guattari, 1986: 41). In his book on *Proust and Signs*, he notes that 'reminiscence raises questions about the source of the extraordinary joy that we already feel in the present sensation ... A joy so powerful that it suffices to make us indifferent to death' (Deleuze, 2000: 56). Deleuze suggests that although the repeated return to certain 'memories' in *In Search of Lost Time* may well be of a particular suffering, 'the repetition itself is always joyous, the phenomenon of repetition forms a general joy. Or rather, the phenomena are always unhappy and particular, but the idea extracted from them is general and joyous.' Under a constraint of sensibility, the intelligence can transmute 'our suffering into joy at the same time that it transmutes the particular into the general ... [it] can discover generality and find it a source of joy' (Deleuze, 2000: 74–5).

This is not the kind of 'joy' that implies a desire has now been pleasurably satiated by an idealised object that its subject once lacked. Every time we encounter these assumptions we know that desire has been 'betrayed, cursed, uprooted from the field of immanence', and that 'a priest is behind it'. Whether in religious or psychoanalytic garb, the priest finds ever new ways of 'inscribing in desire the negative law of lack, the external rule of pleasure, and the transcendent ideal of phantasy' (ATP, 171). The joy Deleuze has in mind is immanent to desire, 'as though desire were filled by itself and its contemplations', a wholly productive and purely immanent joy. Later in that chapter he makes the link between the BwO, desire, and the plane of consistency more explicit. 'The BwO is desire; it is that which one desires and by which one desires. And not only because it is the plane of consistency or the field of immanence of desire ... There is desire whenever there is the constitution of a BwO under one relation or another' (ATP, 183).

Unsurprisingly, the priestly curse on desire is related to the way in which monotheisms attempt to 'organise' human bodies and 'judge' human souls or, to use the terminology of *Anti-Oedipus*, the way in which the despotic social machine falls back upon and overcodes desiring-machines. However, making oneself a BwO does not mean completely escaping the social formation in which one is embedded. Rather, it involves seeing 'how it is stratified for us and in us and at the place where we are; then descend from the strata to the deeper assemblage within which we are held; gently tip the assemblage, making it pass over to the side of the plane of consistency'. What is the point of all this seeing, descending, tipping, and passing over to the plane of consistency? Because '[i]t is only there that the BwO reveals itself for what it is: connection of desires, conjunction of flows, continuum of intensities' (ATP, 178). Constructing the BwO requires the overcoming of the habituated patterns of affect and socially entrained behaviours that are bound up in the organismically ordered (Oedipalised) body, and the following of lines of flight and waves of intensities in the production of something new (desiring-production).

In *Anti-Oedipus*, the BwO is described as a 'naked' full body in contrast to the 'clothed' full bodies of the socius: the earth, the body of the despot, and capital-money (correlated to the territorial, despotic, and capitalist social machines that 'fall back upon' desiring-machines in the distinctive ways we outlined in Chapter 2). The BwO is 'the limit of the socius, its tangent of deterritorialization, the ultimate residue of a deterritorialized socius ... [the BwO] exists at the limit, at the end, not at the origin' (AO, 309). To switch back to the terminology of *A Thousand Plateaus*, the BwO is the limit of the process of destratification just as the organism is the limit of the process of stratification. As John Protevi points out in his analysis of the BwO, one never really gets to the (actual) organism or the (virtual) BwO because these are the limits of opposed and never-ending processes. '"An organism" is only a representation of pure molar fixity, just as "a BwO" is only a representation of pure molecular flow' (Protevi, 2018: 107). A life (more or less joyful or anxious) is lived swinging in the tension between these two processes of territorialisation and deterritorialisation.

The concept of 'intensities' is crucial for understanding the BwO and, indeed, for understanding the motivation of the *Capitalism and Schizophrenia* project as a whole. As noted above, for Deleuze, the joy that is immanent to desire is not measured by pleasure but is that which distributes intensities of pleasure and 'prevents them from being suffused by anxiety, shame, and guilt' (ATP, 172). The making of a BwO occurs 'in such a way that it can be occupied, populated only by intensities. Only intensities pass and circulate ... The BwO causes intensities to pass; it produces and distributes them in a *spatium* that is itself intensive, lacking extension' (ATP, 169). In both volumes, the BwO is described as an egg. However, it is the 'full egg before the extension of the organism and the organization of the organs … the intense egg defined by axes and vectors, gradients and thresholds' (ATP, 170). The BwO is

> an egg, crisscrossed with axes, banded with zones, localized with areas and fields, measured off by gradients, traversed by potentials, marked by thresholds … In this sense, we believe in a biochemistry of schizophrenia … that will be progressively more capable of determining the nature of this egg and the distribution of field–gradient–threshold. (AO, 93)

Field–gradient–threshold? These are terms familiar to scientists engaged in computer modelling, who utilise (virtual) state spaces to experiment with (actual) simulated events under various parametric conditions. Rather than revisiting our discussion (in Chapters 3 and 4) of these developments and the mathematical innovations that led to them, here I simply want to point out that the connection I have been trying to make between Deleuze and CMS is not as far-fetched as it might initially have seemed. To cite Protevi's discussion of the BwO again,

> behavior patterns emerge at a singularity or threshold in the differential relations [rates of change in the body, the world, and body–world interaction]. Over time, the repetition of a number of such actualisations provides a temporary structure to the singular virtual BwO, a virtually available response repertoire, a set of capacities for the politically formed body. (Protevi, 2018: 113)

In a similar way, Daniel Smith describes the BwO as 'the full set of capacities or potentialities of a body prior to its being given the structure of an organism, which only limits and constrains what it can do' (Smith, 2018: 107), and emphasises that Deleuze's 'non-mechanical mechanism, which is also a vitalism of the inorganic, highlights not the form or structure that bodies *actually have*, but rather the virtual capacities that bodies have to do something different' (2018: 109). As we have seen throughout this book, computational modelling and simulation provides tools for exploring the virtual structures, singularities, and attractors within a multi-dimensional phase space in order to discover the conditions under which – and the mechanisms by which – various thresholds are reached and simulated events are immanently actualised. This is one way to experiment with BwOs.

Another way is mysticism. Here we can point to some of the resources Deleuze finds for erecting an image of the free person in the work of Bergson, especially in the latter's understanding of creativity and emotion as they converge in the experience of the mystic.

> And what is this creative emotion, if not precisely a cosmic Memory, that actualizes all the levels at the same time, that liberates man from the plane

(plan) or the level that is proper to him, in order to make him a creator, adequate to the whole movement of creation? (Deleuze, 1988: 111)

Here again we are presented with Cosmos philosophy. Although Deleuze does not utilise the term BwO in this context, we can sense it in the background of his discussion of Bergson:

> At the limit, it is the mystic who plays with the whole of creation, who invents an expression of it whose adequacy increases with its dynamism ... Undoubtedly philosophy can only consider the mystical soul from the outside and from the point of view of its lines of probability. But it is precisely the existence of mysticism that gives a higher probability to this final transmutation into certainty, and also gives, as it were, an envelope or a limit to all the aspects of method. (1988: 112)

Of course, one has to be careful, whether experimenting through models or mysticism or in some other mode. The BwO can be 'botched' in several ways, including destratifying so wildly that one is plunged into demented or suicidal collapse. In addition to 'empty' BwOs, which are like flotsam and jetsam on the strata, there is also the danger of constructing 'cancerous' BwOs, fascist, totalitarian, or despotic fabrications that invade the entire social field (ATP, 180–1). On the other hand, one can fail to destratify adequately, so that 'nothing is produced on it, intensities do not pass or are blocked'. Well, then, how *does* one make oneself an atheist BwO?

> This is how it should be done: Lodge yourself on a stratum, experiment with the opportunities it offers, find an advantageous place on it, find potential movements of deterritorialization, possible lines of light, experience them, produce flow conjunctions here and there, try out continuums of intensities segment by segment, have a small plot of new land at all times. (ATP, 178)

A small plot of new land? What is Deleuze talking about here? The answer is the experimentation of sorcerers.

## Becoming-sorcerer

Sorcerers? Mystics are worrisome enough. But sorcerers? Why in the world would Deleuze link philosophy to sorcery? In fact, one of the most common ways in which Deleuze illustrates how to make oneself a BwO is the sorcerer's experimentation. As I hope to show in the next few pages, this plays a far more pervasive role in *A Thousand Plateaus* than might initially appear. It is most obvious in the 'Memories of a Sorcerer' sections of the chapter '1730: Becoming-intense, becoming-animal, becoming-imperceptible…', to which I will return below. However, Deleuze appeals to Carlos Castaneda's experimentation with the Indian sorcerer Don Juan throughout the chapter 'November 28, 1947: How do You Make Yourself a Body without Organs?' and in several other places in *A Thousand Plateaus* (sometimes without explicitly mentioning Castaneda). In what follows, I try to show how the concept (or practice) of becoming-sorcerer plays a role in Deleuze's metaphysical reversal of Platonism.

Clearly, if we want to maintain that sorcerers hook up to (use, and feel the effects of) the atheist machine, then we must not think of them as dealing with 'supernatural agents' as imaginatively engaged with in religious in-groups (i.e., as entities whose intentionality does not supervene upon biologically evolved nervous systems). But this is no reason to deny that sorcerers might well be experimenting with material distributions of intensities and with multiplicities of emergent intentionalities (their own and those of others) in ways that most people find hard to believe – or worrisome enough to resist or oppress. Those familiar with the history of the persecution of witches and sorcerers in the history of the Christian Church are well aware that the rhizomatic and molecular flows of the former are perceived as extremely dangerous to the arboreal and molar segmentations of the socius by the latter. And so it is no surprise that 'false philosophy totally impregnated by theology' (LOS, 315) of the sort that we criticised in Chapter 7 will do all it can to protect its Platonic icons of transcendence from the simulacra unleashed on the plane of immanence by experimental sorcery. One more preliminary point. Although Deleuze refers to the 'Memories of a Sorcerer' relatively early in the chapter mentioned above, further along he switches from memories to becomings. 'Wherever we used the word "memories" in the preceding pages, we were wrong to do so; we meant to say "becoming", we were saying becoming' (ATP, 324). And so I will refer throughout to this mode of constructing a BwO as 'becoming-sorcerer'.

Sorcery already appears in 'Introduction: Rhizome', the first chapter of *A Thousand Plateaus*, although it is easy to miss. Without stating the source in the text, Deleuze quotes Castaneda's report of Don Juan's instructions to him:

> Go first to your old plant and watch carefully the watercourse made by the rain. By now the rain must have carried the seeds far away. Watch the crevices made by the runoff and from them determine the direction of the flow. Then find the plant that is growing at the farthest point from your plant. All the devil's weed plants that are growing in between are yours. Later … you can extend the size of your territory by following the watercourse from each point along the way. (ATP, 12)

Interestingly, this entire quotation is repeated later in *A Thousand Plateaus* in the chapter '1227: Treatise on Nomadology – The War Machine', again without informing the reader that these are Don Juan's instructions to his disciple (ATP, 411).

In the chapter '587 B.C. – A.D. 70: On Several Regimes of Signs', Deleuze explicitly expresses the profound interest he has in Castaneda's books, particularly in the way in which the sorcerer Don Juan 'manages to combat the mechanisms of interpretation and instill in the disciple a presignifying semiotic, or even an asignifying diagram'. Paraphrasing Don Juan, Deleuze writes: 'Stop! You're making me tired! Experiment, don't signify and interpret! Find your own places, territorialities, deterritorializations, regimes, lines of flight. Semiotize yourself instead of rooting around in your prefab childhood and Western semiology' (ATP, 153). In the chapter '1933: Micropolitics and Segmentarity', Castaneda's Don Juan is credited with identifying four dangers (fear, clarity, power, disgust) that can arise when tracing the 'lines' associated with primitive segmentarity, the State apparatus, and the war machine. In the case of the (less obvious) danger of 'clarity', Deleuze notes Castaneda's illustration of 'the existence of a molecular perception to which drugs give us access (but so many things can be drugs): we attain a visual and sonorous microperception revealing spaces and voids, like holes in the molar structure' (ATP, 250–1).

But let's focus on the two places in *A Thousand Plateaus* where Deleuze deals with sorcery in the most detail. First, in the chapter on making yourself a BwO, he explicitly illustrates the latter by appealing to Castaneda's depictions of the sorcerer Don Juan.

> Castaneda describes a long process of experimentation ... let us recall for the moment how the Indian forces him first to find a 'place', already a difficult operation, then to find 'allies', and then gradually to give up interpretation, to construct flow by flow and segment by segment lines of experimentation, becoming-animal, becoming molecular, etc. (ATP, 178–9)

Deleuze has an extended discussion of the distinction between 'tonal' and the 'nagual' described in Castaneda's fourth book, *Tales of Power*. The former 'seems to cover many disparate things: it is *the organism*, and also all that is organized and organizing'. The tonal is everything, including God, the *judgement of God*, since it 'makes up the rules by which it apprehends the world'. In the sense that it 'creates' the world, the tonal is everything. However, the nagual is also everything, but in a different sense. '[I]t is the same everything, but under such conditions that the *body without organs* has replaced the organism and experimentation has replaced all interpretation, for which it no longer has any use' (ATP, 179, emphases added).

In this context, Deleuze also explicitly links the experimentation involved in becoming-sorcerer to the distribution of intensities that overcomes the judgement of God as the BwO is constructed. 'Flows of intensity, their fluid, their fibers, their continuums and conjunctions of affects, the wind, fine segmentation, microperceptions, have replaced the world of the subject.' He spells this out in terms of the relation between the tonal and the nagual, and the importance of being careful as one experiments with the latter's dismantling of the former. The tonal 'includes all of the strata and everything that can be ascribed to the strata, the organization of the organism, the interpretations and explanations of the signifiable, the movements of subjectification'. The plane of the nagual, however, dismantles the strata as it constructs a BwO. However, it is important 'not to dismantle the tonal by destroying it all of a sudden. You have to diminish it, shrink it, clean it, and that only at certain moments. You have to keep it in order to survive, to ward off the assault of the nagual.' Why is this so important? Because 'a nagual that erupts, that destroys the tonal, a body with organs that shatters all the strata, turns immediately into a body of nothingness, pure self-destruction whose only outcome is death'. As Don Juan warns, 'The tonal must be protected at any cost' (ATP, 179–80).

The second and most obvious place in *A Thousand Plateaus* where Deleuze deals with sorcery is in the three sections called 'Memories of a Sorcerer' in the chapter '1730: Becoming-intense, becoming-animal, becoming-imperceptible…' The first section begins: 'A becoming-animal always involves a pack, a band, a population, a peopling, in short, a multiplicity. We sorcerers have always known that' (ATP, 264). This is one of the few places where Deleuze and Guattari use the first person plural (we) to identify themselves as members of a population (another example being writers). They do it again a few pages later. 'This is how we sorcerers operate. Not following a logical order, but following alogical consistencies or compatibilities.' Deleuze cites several examples of becoming-animal: werewolves, leopard-men, crocodile-men, goat-men. We should note that not only sorcerers but also shamans in a wide variety of contexts report becoming-animal (Balzer, 2017; Eliade, 2020; Fonneland, 2017; Winkelman, 2010). Of course, one never knows in advance whether a particular experiment, a distribution of intensities, a crossing of one multiplicity into another, will go well. Here too one has to be wary of botching the BwO. 'No one can say where the line of flight will pass: Will it let itself get bogged down and fall back to the Oedipal family animal, a mere poodle? Or will it succumb to another danger, for example, turning into a line of abolition, annihilation, self-destruction, Ahab, Ahab…?' (ATP, 276).

Deleuze associates sorcerers not only with the pack – the 'contagion of the pack, such is the path becoming-animal takes' – but also with the 'exceptional individual', the anomalous, with which a 'monstrous alliance' is formed. 'There is always a pact with a demon' (ATP, 268). Sorcerers do not operate through filiation, but through alliances and contagion. 'Sorcerers have always held the anomalous position, at the edge of the fields or woods ... the sorcerer has a relation of alliance with the demon as the power of the anomalous' (ATP, 271). Sorcerers do not fit into the segmentations of families, religions, or despots. 'There is an entire politics of becomings-animal, as well as a politics of sorcery, which is elaborated in assemblages that are neither those of the family nor of religion nor of the State.' The social assemblages associated with sorcerers are expressions of 'minoritarian groups, or groups that are oppressed, prohibited, in revolt, or always on the fringe of recognized institutions'. Here too we can hear echoes of *Anti-Oedipus*, of the movement of schizz-flows breaking free of the Oedipalising forces of society. Becoming-animal 'takes the form of a Temptation and of monsters aroused in the imagination by the demon [because] it is accompanied, at its origin as in its undertaking, by a rupture with the central institutions that have established themselves or seek to become established' (ATP, 272–3).

Deleuze observes that Castaneda's books illustrate the evolution (or involution) through which 'becomings-molecular take over where becomings-animal leave off'. In the first of his books, *The Teaching of Don Juan*, the eponymous sorcerer has Carlos experiment with drugs, which introduce him to microperceptions that were previously unavailable. '[T]he affects of a becoming-dog, for example, are succeeded by those of a becoming-molecular, microperceptions of water, air, etc.' In *Tales of Power*, when another sorcerer moves from one door to the next and disappears, Don Juan says to Carlos: 'All I can tell you is that we are fluid, luminous beings made of fibers.' Deleuze points out that

> all the so-called initiatory journeys include these thresholds and doors where becoming itself becomes, and where one changes becoming depending on the 'hour' of the world, the circles of hell, or the stages of a journey that sets scales, forms, and cries in variation. From the howling of animals to the wailing of elements and particles. (ATP, 274)

In case there is any doubt left about the importance of becoming-sorcerer in *A Thousand Plateaus*, in the 'Conclusion: Concrete Rules and Abstract Machines', Deleuze explicitly links sorcery to the pragmatic utilisation of multiplicities: 'At the level of *pathos*, these multiplicities are expressed by psychosis and especially schizophrenia. At the level of pragmatics, they are utilized by sorcery. At the level of theory, the status of multiplicities is correlative to that of spaces...' (ATP, 557). Making oneself a BwO: this is what sorcerers *do*, this *is* becoming-sorcerer. A BwO comes into play in individuation by haecceity, in the production of intensities beginning at a degree zero, in the matter of variation, in the medium of becoming or transformation, and in the smoothing of space. A powerful nonorganic life that escapes the strata, cuts across assemblages, and draws an abstract line without contour, a line of nomad art and itinerant metallurgy. (ATP, 558–9)

Making oneself an atheist BwO involves liberating lines of flight, extending rhizomes, feeling the movement of the pack, while maintaining enough relation to the strata to hold oneself together. Such experimentation is threatening to despotic monotheist machines, which use their massive arsenal to ban or marginalise it. But like the nomads, we sorcerers have weapons of mass secretion that clear the ground of transcendent icons (inverting Platonism) every time we open them up, lay out a plane of immanence, and follow the witch's flight.

## The Brain-subject

'To think', Deleuze asserts in *What is Philosophy?*, 'is always to follow the witch's flight' (WIP, 41). We are moving beyond sorcery in this section, but things will not get any less weird. Here I focus less on the metaphysical and more on some of the meta-epistemological insights connected to the BwO. Throughout his work, Deleuze challenges the 'dogmatic' image of thought, which presupposes that thought has a subject (man) oriented towards truth, and argues instead that we must begin with the crack (or ungrounding) of thought, the encounter with the sensible, which forces us to think, putting thought into motion. As he puts it in *A Thousand Plateaus*, in this approach, 'Philosophy is no longer synthetic judgment; it is like a thought synthesizer functioning to make thought travel, make it mobile, make it a force of the Cosmos (in the same way as one makes sound travel)' (ATP, 379). In this penultimate sub-section, however, I will focus mainly on *What is Philosophy?*, in which Deleuze expands on an idea he had already outlined in *The Logic of Sense* a quarter of a century earlier (LOS, 255), the idea that it is not 'man' but 'the brain' that 'becomes subject, Thought-brain' (WIP, 210).

Before diving in, it is important to make a preliminary comment about Deleuze's use of the term 'subject'. Although he is well known for his critique of a certain sort of 'subjectification' – indeed the latter is what the BwO destratifies – this does not mean that Deleuze does not have a theory of the subject in a more general sense. It is simply that the subject is not prior to, or the origin of, thought; rather it is an effect (or superject) of the movement of thought. In a variety of places Joe Hughes (2008a; 2008b; 2012) has clarified the overarching structure of Deleuze's theory of the subject, demonstrating a certain isomorphism in his treatment of this topic in writings as diverse as *Difference and Repetition*, *The Logic of Sense*, *Nietzsche and Philosophy*, *Expressionism and Philosophy*, and even the books on cinema (Deleuze, 2013; 2019). Without denying the dangers of subjectification (Oedipalisation, etc.), in this context I will, without further qualification, use the term 'subject' (brain-subject) to refer to that which creates concepts and invents conceptual personae that it lays out on the pre-philosophical plane of immanence.

These latter phrases require some unpacking. In the third chapter of *What is Philosophy?*, Deleuze writes that:

> Philosophy presents three elements, each of which fits with the other two but must be considered for itself: *the prephilosophical plane it must lay out (immanence), the persona or personae it must invent and bring to life (insistence), and the philosophical concepts it must create (consistency)*. Laying out, inventing, and creating constitute the philosophical trinity – diagrammatic, personalistic, and intensive features ... The three activities are strictly simultaneous and have only incommensurable relationships. The creation of concepts has no other limit than the plane they happen to populate; but the plane itself is limitless, and its layout only conforms to the concepts to be created that it must connect up, or to the personae to be invented that it must maintain. (WIP, 76–8)

The key point to make here is that these three elements (features, activities) of philosophy are produced (and can only be produced) by atheist assemblages (to switch back briefly to the language of *A Thousand Plateaus*) whose edges of deterritorialisation are conjugated by the abstract machine of atheism (a plateau of variation placing variables of godless content and godless expression in continuity) as they liberate atheist bodies and achieve the atheism of the concept.

We have already seen how the plane of immanence is linked to the negative task of the atheist machine, clearing the ground of transcendent icons. Philosophers, argues Deleuze, are 'those who institute a plane of immanence like a sieve stretched out over the chaos', in contrast to priests, who institute an 'always transcendent order imposed from outside by a great despot or by one god higher than the others' (WIP, 43). For Plato and his successors, immanence is always '"immanent "to" the One ... whenever immanence is interpreted as immanent *to* Something, we can be sure that this Something reintroduces the transcendent' (WIP, 44–5). What about conceptual personae? For Deleuze, the latter and the plane of immanence 'presuppose each other'. Throughout chapter 3 of *What is Philosophy?*, he outlines the features of conceptual personae whose role is to '*show thought's territories*' as 'thought-events on the plane laid out by thought' (WIP, 69–70). The key point for my argument in this context is that conceptual personae intervene 'between chaos and the diagrammatic features of the plane of immanence and also between the plane and the intensive features of the concepts that happen to populate it' (WIP, 75).

The third element or activity of philosophy, which always co-occurs and overlaps with the other two, is the creation of concepts. Concepts are solutions, but solutions whose corresponding problems lie in their 'intensional conditions of consistency'. The conditions of philosophical problems are 'found on the plane of immanence presupposed by the concept (to what infinite movement does it refer in the image of thought?) ... and the unknowns of the problem are found in the conceptual personae that it calls up (what persona, exactly?)' (WIP, 80–1). As already noted in the epigraph with which I started this book: 'Atheism is not a problem for philosophers or the death of God. Problems begin only afterward, when the *atheism of the concept* has been attained' (WIP, 92, emphasis added). Philosophical engagement with problems (the creation of concepts) begins with atheism or, to put it the other way around, atheism is the achievement of philosophy.

But where does the 'brain-subject' come in? 'At the same time that the brain becomes subject – or rather "superject", as Whitehead puts it – the concept becomes object as created, as event or creation itself; and philosophy becomes the plane of immanence that supports the concepts and that the brain lays out' (WIP, 211). Here Deleuze is talking explicitly about philosophy, but throughout *What is Philosophy?* he describes the former's relationship with science and art, the other 'daughters of chaos'. On the one hand, as we saw in Chapter 1, what these three share in common (as opposed to religion) is that they cast planes over the chaos instead of invoking gods as 'figures of an *Urdoxa* from which opinions stem' (WIP, 202). On the other hand, the elements of the planes cast by these three 'daughters' are irreducible: '*plane of immanence of philosophy, plane of composition of art, plane of reference or coordination of science; form of concept, force of sensation, function of knowledge; concepts and conceptual personae, sensations and aesthetic figures, figures and partial observers*' (WIP, 216).

Deleuze plays with these ideas throughout *What is Philosophy?*, but for our purposes here the details are less important than the point that these three planes 'join up in the brain' (WIP, 216); in other words, '*The brain is the junction* – not the unity – *of the three planes* (WIP, 208). Deleuze is critical of phenomenologists for whom 'Man thinks, not the brain.' In such an approach, 'thought depends on man's relations with the world – with which the brain is necessarily in agreement because it is drawn from these relations'. As Deleuze points out, however, this does not get us out of 'the sphere of opinions. It leads us only to an *Urdoxa* posited as original opinion, or meaning of meanings.' He urges us to look instead for the place where 'the brain is "subject", where it becomes subject ... It is the brain that thinks and not man – the latter being only a cerebral crystallization.' Here we are not dealing with a brain 'behind' the brain, but with

> a state of survey without distance, at ground level, a self-survey that no chasm, fold, or hiatus escapes ... an absolute consistent form that surveys *itself* independently of any supplementary dimension, which does not appeal therefore to any transcendence, which has only a single side whatever the number of its dimensions. (WIP, 210)

In this approach, the three fields or disciplines of philosophy, art, and science 'are not the mental objects of an objectified brain but the three aspects under which the brain becomes subject, Thought-brain. They are the three planes, the rafts on which the brain plunges into and confronts the chaos' (WIP, 210). Whether in the concepts of philosophy, the functives of science, or the percepts of art, thought 'does not depend upon a brain made up of *organic* connections and integrations' (WIP, 209, emphasis added). In other words, Deleuze's atheist meta-epistemology does not begin with the 'organisation' wrought by the 'judgement of God', but with the ongoing construction of a BwO on (or as) the plane of immanence. The brain-subject has three aspects or 'layers', namely form of concept, force of sensation, and function of knowledge, which are correlated to the planes laid out by philosophy, art, and science respectively. Each of these planes and their elements is fragile and can interfere with one another in a variety of ways, a chaotic transdisciplinarity that all too often tempts us back into the safety of *Urdoxa*.

In *Francis Bacon*, Deleuze notes a similarity between Artaud and Bacon (the painter); in both cases,

> the Figure is the body without organs ... the body without organs is flesh and nerve; a wave flows through it and traces levels upon it; a sensation is produced when the wave encounters the Forces acting on the body, an 'affective athleticism', a scream-breath ... Bacon has not ceased to paint bodies without organs, the intensive fact of the body. (Deleuze, 2005c: 40)

Discussing the way in which geometry and the figure function in Gothic painting and in Bacon, Deleuze notes that if the pictorial line

> encounters the animal, if it becomes *animalized*, it is not by outlining a form but, on the contrary, by imposing, through its clarity and nonorganic precision, a zone where forms become indiscernible. It also attests to a high *spirituality*, since what leads it to seek the elementary forces beyond the organic is a spiritual will. But this spirituality is a spirituality of the body; the spirit is the body itself, the body without organs... (2005c: 41)

Here we have it all again: spirituality, sorcery, and subjectivity laid out (and played out) on the plane of immanence.

Once more, and for the last time in this book, let me suggest that computer modelling and simulation can play a heuristic role in understanding and a pragmatic role in furthering the atheist achievements of Deleuze's philosophy. Let's also make this my final confession (in this context). As we have seen, CMS tools enable philosophers (and social scientists) to create virtual worlds, mechanism-independent structured state spaces in which the actualisation (or emergence) and alteration of various social assemblages, along with their tendencies and capacities, can be studied through simulation experiments. My experience in this process has indeed often felt like following a witch's flight, drawing diagrammatic lines across virtual planes, unfolding and enfolding variables and vectors, exploring multi-dimensional phase spaces by putting them in motion, testing thresholds and analysing attractors, creating forms of concepts and functions of knowledge, as well as the occasional force of sensation.

Computational methods such as multi-agent artificial intelligence modelling involve casting all sorts of planes in a statistical and simulated confrontation with the Chaosmos in order to discover the conditions under which – and the mechanisms by which – we might gently tilt various socio-ecological assemblages, making them pass over to the plane of consistency. We can experiment with ways of tipping such assemblages that foster the human capacity for freedom without triggering suicidal, fascist, or other self-destructive tendencies. What is the difference between laying out thought-events on the plane of immanence when exploring a model's multi-dimensional phase space and when exploring my affective powers and behavioural prospects in the 'real world'. If we follow Deleuze in rejecting the dualism between the artificial and the natural, then these two modes of experimentation may well weave into one another in potentially creative ways. Why not blur the boundaries between becoming brain-subject *in situ* and *in silico*? After all, according to Deleuze, all thought is engendered by simulation.

## The Philosopher's Serenity

'Atheism is not a drama but the *philosopher's serenity* and philosophy's achievement' (WIP, 92, emphasis added). We began the book with this quotation, and throughout the preceding chapters I have been focusing primarily on atheism as the achievement of philosophy. However, as promised, I want to return here at the end to briefly explore the relationship between the atheist machine and the serenity of the philosopher. Here we are dealing quite clearly with the 'positive' task of philosophy, erecting the image of the free person, although, as we have seen, it cannot be separated from the 'negative' task of denouncing the sad passions generated by the false infinity of religion. To reiterate, these two tasks are linked because determining the distinction between the true infinite and the false infinite is 'the necessary means of ethics and practice' (LOS, 309). And so in this final section, I will touch more explicitly on some of the meta-ethical insights and implications involved in making oneself a BwO.

Now, we should begin by acknowledging that not all atheist philosophers are serene and not all serene philosophers are atheist. Moreover, not all serene people are philosophers. As I emphasised in Chapter 1, I am not claiming that atheism is 'better' than theism in any transcendent 'moral' sense, nor that pursuing philosophy is the only or best way to achieve 'the good life'. I am not making moral judgements, but rather recommending experimentation in a mode of becoming-philosopher that is also a becoming-serene produced by the atheist machine. Here too we can follow the line traced by Deleuze from some of the ancient Greek philosophers through Spinoza and Nietzsche.

> In the affirmation of the multiple lies the practical joy of the diverse. Joy emerges as the sole motive for philosophising. To valorise negative sentiments or sad passions – that is the mystification on which nihilism bases its power. (Lucretius, then Spinoza, already wrote decisive passages on this subject. Before Nietzsche, they conceived philosophy as the power to affirm, as the practical struggle against mystifications, as the expulsion of the negative). (Deleuze, 2005b: 84)

These philosophers are not the only sources in which Deleuze finds insights and inspiration for serene experimentation. For example, in *Dialogues II*, written with Claire Parnet between the publication of *Anti-Oedipus* and *A Thousand Plateaus*, Deleuze appeals to the writings of F. Scott Fitzgerald as a resource for understanding and pursuing the molecular fluxes that motivate rhizomatics (micro-politics, pragmatics, diagrammatism, cartography, etc.). It starts with a crack. Everything may be going well on the old lines of rigid segmentarity, when

> a crack happens on this new line – secret, imperceptible, marking a threshold of lowered resistance, or the rise of a threshold of exigency ... the distribution of desires has changed in us, our relationships of speed and slowness have been modified, a new type of anxiety comes upon us, but also a new *serenity*. (Deleuze and Parnet, 2002: 95, emphasis added)

Deleuze also finds resources in the work of other philosophers such as Foucault. He is fascinated, for example, by the 'searing phrase' that appears in the latter's book *The Uses of Pleasure*, that is, 'to get free of oneself'. Is an image of the free person being erected? In Foucault's *The History of Sexuality*, Deleuze finds hints at a new axis, different from the axes of 'both knowledge and power. Could this axis be the place where a sense of *serenity* would be finally attained and life truly affirmed?' (Deleuze, 1999: 79–80, emphasis added).

In this context, however, it makes sense to highlight another important philosophical resource for Deleuze's serenity-generating meta-ethics – the Stoics. The latter, he argues in *The Logic of Sense*, were 'the first to reverse Platonism' (LOS, 9). They are also the inspiration for his claim that 'Either ethics makes no sense at all, or this is what it means and has nothing else to say: not to be unworthy of what happens to us' (LOS, 169). In Chapter 4 of *Iconoclastic Theology: Gilles Deleuze and the Secretion of Atheism*, I spelled out Deleuze's Stoic-inspired atheist ethics by focusing on the point–line–surface motif that he develops throughout *The Logic of Sense*. For Deleuze, the capacity for ethics (intentionality) is engendered by the pure becoming of the infinity of intensities or singularities-events that are emitted at the metaphysical surface by the endless movement of the aleatory point in both directions along the unlimited line of the Aion. The Stoic sage belongs to the Aion and skirts the metaphysical surface (or frontier) counter-actualising (or releasing) the events distributed by the aleatory point (or paradoxical instance).

Here I want to focus instead on another Stoic-inspired ethical motif that spreads across the series that compose *The Logic of Sense*: humour. Deleuze is not talking here about joking or laughing at funny things. Although becoming-serene may often include such things, we are dealing here not with the philosopher's sense of humour but with humour in a philosophical sense. See what I did there? Deleuze explicitly links humour to the ethics of the Stoic sage. While other Greek philosophers had used humour as a weapon against Socratic irony, 'with the Stoics, humor found its dialectics, its dialectical principle or its natural place and its pure philosophical concept' (LOS, 11). Humour, in this sense, is 'the art of the surfaces and of the doubles, of nomad singularities and of the always displaced aleatory point...' (LOS, 159–60). The wise person finds at the surface

> pure singularities, an emission of singularities considered from the perspective of their aleatory element, independent of the individuals and persons which embody them or actualise them. This adventure of humor, its two-fold dismissal of height and depth to the advantage of the surface is, in the first instance, the adventure of the Stoic sage. (LOS, 155)

What Deleuze provides here is a *philosophical* analysis of the Stoic concept and practice of humour, especially as it can be distinguished from irony

(Socratic, schizophrenic, obsessed with the heights) and satire (pre-Socratic, depressive, obsessed with the depths).

> We call '*satiric*' the process by which regression regresses itself; that is, it is never a sexual regression at the surface without its also being a digestive alimentary regression in depth, stopping only at the cesspool and pursuing the withdrawn voice as it uncovers the excremental soil that this voice leaves behind. (LOS, 284)

Is this why poop jokes and sex jokes can be amusing and appalling at the same time? *Irony*, on the other hand,

> appears each time language deploys itself in accordance with relations of eminence, equivocity, or analogy ... There is, for example, a primordial form of Platonic irony, redressing height, disengaging it from depth, repressing and hemming in satire or the satirist, and employing all its 'irony' in asking whether, by chance there could be an Idea of mud, hair, filth, or excrement. (LOS, 284)

In distinction from the satiric descent of the pre-Socratics or the ascent in Socratic irony (both of which are in search of essences), *humour* is

> the art of surfaces and of the complex relation between the two surfaces [being and language, bodies and events]. Beginning with one excessive equivocation, humor constructs all univocity; beginning with the properly sexual equivocation which ends all equivocity, humor releases a desexualised Univocity – a speculative univocity of Being and language.

The humorous philosophical act (or counter-actualisation) makes 'the energy of sexuality pass into the pure asexual', affirming the neutral (pre-individual, impersonal) *eventum tantum*, composing the pure infinitive, grasping language as the 'total expresser of a unique expressed – the event' (LOS, 285).

All of this is related to erecting an image of the free person. Deleuze describes 'a change of will, a sort of leaping in place of the whole body which exchanges its *organic* will for a *spiritual* will'. But what is willed, what is selected? Philosophical serenity involves willing not 'exactly what occurs, but something *in* that which occurs, something yet to come which would be consistent with what occurs, in accordance with the laws of an obscure, humorous conformity: the Event'. It is only in this sense that 'the *Amor fati* is one with the struggle of free men' (LOS, 170). Liberated from the limits of individuality and personhood, the Stoic sage engages with the communicating singularities of the event; 'the actor [*l'acteur*] delimits the original, disengages from it an abstract line, and keeps from the event only its contour and its splendor, becoming thereby the actor [*comédien*] of one's own events – a counter-actualization' (LOS, 171). This is why, Deleuze insists, only the free person can comprehend every wound, every violent act, 'every mortal event *in a single Event* which no longer makes room for the accident, and which denounces and removes the power of *ressentiment* within the individual as well as the power of oppression within society' (LOS, 173). In other words, humour plays a key role in the process of making oneself an atheist BwO in the sense we have explored in the earlier parts of this chapter.

But what does humour have to do with atheism? The 'humor-actor' is 'anti-god [*contradieu*]' (LOS, 170). The serene traversal of the surface, of the divergent as such, follows the aleatory point 'which circulates throughout singularities, and emits them as pre-individual and impersonal, does not allow God to subsist. It does not tolerate the subsistence of God as an original individuality, nor the self as a Person, nor the world as an element of the self and as God's product' (LOS, 201). To switch back to the terminology of *A Thousand Plateaus*, making oneself a BwO is to be done with the judgement of God, but also with human judgement and the judgement of the world.

It all comes down to how one understands and practises the relationship between infinity, intensity, and intentionality. Sacerdotal theologies protected and promoted by monotheistic social machines operate within Plato's Eidetic framework insofar as they select one image (icon) among others as representing an intentional infinite entity who creates all finite intensities whatsoever and determines the regulative ideals for human morality. The achievement of philosophy is the inversion of this dualist domain of religious representation through a pure affirmation of the rising of the simulacra and the movement of sense *from the infinity of intensities to intentionality*. The genetic conditions for the real experience of axiological engagement are not transcendent or intentional (gods or a God above us, whom we resemble). For Deleuze, intentionality (Oedipal or otherwise) is engendered by the pure becoming of the infinity of intensities or singularities-events that are emitted at the metaphysical surface by the endless movement of the aleatory point in both directions along the unlimited line of the Aion. The philosopher who achieves serene (humorous) atheism has come to terms with the true infinite, affirming the infinity of intensities that engender her intentionality, producing a joy immanent to desire, a life on the metaphysical surface.

Let's finish with a brief reference to Deleuze's final publication, an essay titled 'Immanence: A Life' (from which I have already quoted a few paragraphs above), written the year before his death. 'We will say of pure immanence that it is A LIFE, and nothing else. It is not immanence to life, but the immanent that is in nothing is itself a life. A life is the immanence of immanence, absolute immanence: it is complete *power*, complete *bliss*'

(2005b: 27, emphases added). Echoing or resounding themes from *The Logic of Sense*, Deleuze writes that such a life is

> a haecceity no longer of individuation but of singularization: a life of pure immanence, neutral, beyond good and evil, for it was only the subject that incarnated it in the midst of things that made it good or bad. The life of such individuality fades away in favor of the singular life immanent to a man who no longer has a name, though he can be mistaken for no other. (2005b: 28–9)

A life is 'made up of virtualities, events, singularities'. Here the distinction between the virtual and the actual continues to be central. 'The event considered as non-actualized (indefinite) is lacking in nothing.' A joy immanent to desire even though – or because – there are cracks. 'A wound is incarnated or actualized in a state of things or a life; but it is itself a pure virtuality on the plane of immanence that leads us into a life' (2005b: 31).

My first main goal in this book was to demonstrate Deleuze's productive and destructive use of the atheist machine throughout his corpus. For him, atheism is philosophy's achievement and the philosopher's serenity. Philosophy begins when and where atheism is secreted from religion. But getting to this starting point is not as easy as Deleuze sometimes seems to imply. This is why I have brought his philosophy into explicit dialogue with the bio-cultural sciences of religion, which disclose the god-bearing coalitional and coalitional biases that engender religious mystifications, as well as new strategies for contesting these evolved tendencies by creating the conditions for the emergence and maintenance of naturalist explanations of the world and secularist inscriptions of society. My other main goal was to bring Deleuze's atheist philosophy into dialogue with recent advances in computational social simulation, especially multi-agent artificial intelligence modelling, which provides resources for articulating a flat ontology that can account for the morphogenesis of existing things (or the becoming of assemblages) without any appeal to transcendence, and for experimenting with the conditions and mechanisms involved in the actualisation of socio-ecological assemblages in relation to the virtual planes of immanence in the structured phase space of a computational architecture. Of course, modelling is not for everyone. Some might prefer sorcery, mysticism, or some other way of following the witch's flight. Experiment. Create. Find your own way of making yourself an atheist Body without Organs.

# References

Acselrad, H., and Bezerra, G. (2010). Book Review: Manuel DeLanda, *A New Philosophy of Society: Assemblage Theory and Social Complexity*. *Planning Theory*, *9*(1), 88–93.
Acuto, M., and Curtis, S. (eds) (2014). *Reassembling International Theory: Assemblage Thinking and International Relations*. Palgrave.
Aczel, B., Bago, B., Szollosi, A., Foldes, A., and Lukacs, B. (2015). Is it time for studying real-life debiasing? Evaluation of the effectiveness of an analogical intervention technique. *Frontiers in Psychology*, *6*. https://doi.org/10.3389/fpsyg.2015.01120
Adkins, B. (2015). *Deleuze and Guattari's A Thousand Plateaus*. Edinburgh University Press.
Ahrweiler, P., Gilbert, G. N., and Pyka, A. (2016). *Joining Complexity Science and Social Simulation for Innovation Policy: Agent-based Modelling using the Skin Platform*. Cambridge Scholars Publishing.
Alcorta, C. S., and Sosis, R. (2013). Ritual, religion and violence: An evolutionary perspective. In M. Juergensmeyer, M. Kitts, and M. Jerryson (eds), *The Oxford Handbook of Religion and Violence*, 571–96. Oxford University Press.
Allen, J. (2011). Powerful assemblages? *Area*, *43*(2), 154–7.
Altamirano, M. (2015). Deleuze's reversal of Platonism, revisited. *Deleuze Studies*, *9*(4), 503–28.
Alvarado, R. (2022). Computer simulations as scientific instruments. *Foundations of Science*, *27*, 1183–1205. https://doi.org/10.1007/s10699-021-09812-2.
Alvarez, R. M. (ed.) (2016). *Computational Social Science: Discovery and Prediction* (reprint edition). Cambridge University Press.
Anderson, B., Kearnes, M., McFarlane, C., and Swanton, D. (2012a). Materialism and the politics of assemblage. *Dialogues in Human Geography*, *2*(2), 212–15.
Anderson, B., Kearnes, M., McFarlane, C., and Swanton, D. (2012b). On assemblages and geography. *Dialogues in Human Geography*, *2*(2), 171–89.
Anderson, B., and McFarlane, C. (2011). Assemblage and geography. *Area*, *43*(2), 124–7.
Aning, K., and Abdallah, M. (2013). Islamic radicalisation and violence in Ghana. *Conflict, Security and Development*, *13*(2), 149–67. https://doi.org/10.1080/14678802.2013.796206
Annas, J. (2009). *Plato*. Sterling.
Ansell-Pearson, K. (2016). Naturalism as a joyful science: Nietzsche, Deleuze, and the art of life. *Journal of Nietzsche Studies*, *47*(1), 119–40.
Antosz, P., Puga-Gonzalez, I., Shults, F. L., Lane, J. E., and Normann, R. (2022). Documenting data use in a model of pandemic 'emotional contagion' using the rigour and transparency reporting standard. In M. Czupryna and B. Kaminski (eds), *Advances in Social Simulation*, 20–4. Springer.
Arnason, J. P., Eisenstadt, S. N., and Wittrock, B. (eds) (2004). *Axial Civilizations and World History*. Brill.
Ash, J., Kitchin, R., and Leszczynski, A. (2018). Digital turn, digital geographies? *Progress in Human Geography*, *42*(1), 25–43.
Atkinson, Q. D., and Whitehouse, H. (2011). The cultural morphospace of ritual form: Examining modes of religiosity cross-culturally. *Evolution and Human Behavior*, *32*(1), 50–62. https://doi.org/10.1016/j.evolhumbehav.2010.09.002
Atran, S. (1993). *Cognitive Foundations of Natural History: Towards an Anthropology of Science* (reprint edition). Cambridge University Press.

# REFERENCES

Atran, S. (2002). *In Gods We Trust: The Evolutionary Landscape of Religion*. Oxford University Press.

Atran, S. (2010). *Talking to the Enemy: Faith, Brotherhood, and the (Un)Making of Terrorists* (reprint edition). HarperCollins e-books.

Atran, S., and Axelrod, R. (2008). Reframing sacred values. *Negotiation Journal*, 24(3), 221–46. https://doi.org/10.1111/j.1571-9979.2008.00182.x

Atran, S., and Ginges, J. (2008). Humiliation and the inertia effect: Implications for understanding violence and compromise in intractable intergroup conflicts. *Journal of Cognition and Culture*, 8(3–4), 281–94. https://doi.org/10.1163/156853708X358182

Avalos, H. (2013). Religion and scarcity: A new theory for the role of religion in violence. In M. Juergensmeyer, M. Kitts, and M. Jerryson (eds), *The Oxford Handbook of Religion and Violence*, 554–70. Oxford University Press.

Bacevic, J. (2019). With or without U? Assemblage theory and (de)territorialising the university. *Globalisation, Societies and Education*, 17(1), 78–91.

Badham, J., Barbrook-Johnson, P., Caiado, C., and Castellani, B. (2021). Justified stories with agent-based modelling for local COVID-19 planning. *Journal of Artificial Societies and Social Simulation*, 24(1), 1–28.

Bainbridge, W. (2006). *God from the Machine: Artificial Intelligence Models of Religious Cognition*. AltaMira Press.

Baker, T., and McGuirk, P. (2017). Assemblage thinking as methodology: Commitments and practices for critical policy research. *Territory, Politics, Governance*, 5(4), 425–42.

Bakhti, R. (2018). Religious versus reflective priming and susceptibility to the conjunction fallacy. *Applied Cognitive Psychology*, 32(2), 186–91. https://doi.org/10.1002/acp.3394

Balzer, M. M. (2017). *Shamanism: Soviet Studies of Traditional Religion in Siberia and Central Asia*. Routledge.

Banas, J. A., and Rains, S. A. (2010). A meta-analysis of research on inoculation theory. *Communication Monographs*, 77(3), 281–311.

Bankes, S., Lempert, R., and Popper, S. (2002). Making computational social science effective: Epistemology, methodology, and technology. *Social Science Computer Review*, 20(4), 377–88.

Banyasz, A. M., Tokar, D. M., and Kaut, K. P. (2014). Predicting religious ethnocentrism: Evidence for a partial mediation model. *Psychology of Religion and Spirituality*, 8(1), 25–34. https://doi.org/10.1037/rel0000020

Barlev, M., Mermelstein, S., and German, T. C. (2017). Core intuitions about persons coexist and interfere with acquired Christian beliefs about God. *Cognitive Science*, 41, 425–54. https://doi.org/10.1111/cogs.12435

Beheim, B., Atkinson, Q. D., Bulbulia, J., Gervais, W., Gray, R. D., Henrich, J., Lang, M., Monroe, M. W., Muthukrishna, M., Norenzayan, A., Purzycki, B. G., Shariff, A., Slingerland, E., Spicer, R., and Willard, A. K. (2021). Treatment of missing data determined conclusions regarding moralizing gods. *Nature*, 595(7866), E29–E34. https://doi.org/10.1038/s41586-021-03655-4

Behum, W. (2010). The body of light and the body without organs. *SubStance*, 39(1), 125–40.

Bell, J. A. (2006). *Philosophy at the Edge of Chaos: Gilles Deleuze and the Philosophy of Difference*. University of Toronto Press.

Bellah, R. N. (2011). *Religion in Human Evolution: From the Paleolithic to the Axial Age*. Harvard University Press.

Beller, J. (2017). Religion and militarism: The effects of religiosity, religious fundamentalism, religious conspiracy belief, and demographics on support for military action. *Peace and Conflict: Journal of Peace Psychology*, 23(2), 179–82. https://doi.org/10.1037/pac0000250

Beller, J., and Kröger, C. (2017). Religiosity, religious fundamentalism, and perceived threat as predictors of Muslim support for extremist violence. *Psychology of Religion and Spirituality*, 10(4), 345–55. https://doi.org/10.1037/rel0000138

# REFERENCES

Benabou, R., Ticchi, D., and Vindigni, A. (2015). Religion and innovation. *American Economic Review*, 105(5), 346–51.

Benioff, M. R., and Lazowska, E. D. (2005). *Computational Science: Ensuring America's Competitiveness*. National Coordination Office for Information Technology Research and Development. https://www.nitrd.gov/pitac/reports/20050609_computational/computational.pdf

Bennett, M. J. (2019). *Deleuze and Ancient Greek Physics: The Image of Nature*. Bloomsbury.

Benzmüller, C., and Paleo, B. W. (2016). The inconsistency in Gödel's ontological argument: A success story for AI in metaphysics. In Subbarao Kambhampati and G. Brewka (eds), *Proceedings of the Twenty-Fifth International Joint Conference on Artificial Intelligence*, 936–42. AAAI Press. https://www.ijcai.org/Proceedings/16/Papers/137.pdf

Bjørgo, T., and Gjelsvik, I. (2015). *Norwegian Research on the Prevention of Radicalisation and Violent Extremism: A Status of Knowledge*. PHS Forskning.

Blogowska, J., Lambert, C., and Saroglou, V. (2013). Religious prosociality and aggression: It's real. *Journal for the Scientific Study of Religion*, 52(3), 524–36. https://doi.org/10.1111/jssr.12048

Blok, A., and Farías, I. (2016). *Urban Cosmopolitics: Agencements, Assemblies, Atmospheres*. Routledge.

Bolsen, T., and Druckman, J. N. (2015). Counteracting the politicization of science. *Journal of Communication*, 65(5), 745–69. https://doi.org/10.1111/jcom.12171

Borum, R. (2011a). Radicalization into violent extremism I: A review of social science theories. *Journal of Strategic Security*, 4(4), 7–36. https://doi.org/10.5038/1944-0472.4.4.1

Borum, R. (2011b). Radicalization into violent extremism II: A review of conceptual models and empirical research. *Journal of Strategic Security*, 4(4), 37–62. https://doi.org/10.5038/1944-0472.4.4.2

Bourget, D., and Chalmers, D. J. (2014). What do philosophers believe? *Philosophical Studies*, 170(3), 465–500. https://doi.org/10.1007/s11098-013-0259-7

Boyer, P. (1994). *The Naturalness of Religious Ideas: A Cognitive Theory of Religion*. University of California Press.

Boyer, P. (2002). *Religion Explained: The Evolutionary Origins of Religious Thought* (reprint edition). Basic Books.

Braun, B. (2006). Environmental issues: Global natures in the space of assemblage. *Progress in Human Geography*, 30(5), 644–54.

Breslin, M. J., and Lewis, C. A. (2015). Schizotypy and religiosity: The magic of prayer. *Archive for the Psychology of Religion*, 37(1), 84–97. https://doi.org/10.1163/15736121-12341300

Briassoulis, H. (2017). Response assemblages and their socioecological fit: Conceptualizing human responses to environmental degradation. *Dialogues in Human Geography*, 7(2), 166–85.

Bridge, G. (2020). On pragmatism, assemblage and ANT: Assembling reason. *Progress in Human Geography*, 45(3), 417–35. https://doi.org/10.1177/0309132520924710

Brubaker, R. (2015). Religious dimensions of political conflict and violence. *Sociological Theory*, 33(1), 1–19. https://doi.org/10.1177/0735275115572153

Bruce, S., and Voas, D. (2023). Secularization vindicated. *Religions*, 14(3), 301.

Brumbaugh, R. S. (1991). *Plato for the Modern Age*. University Press of America.

Bruneau, E., Kteily, N., and Falk, E. (2018). Interventions highlighting hypocrisy reduce collective blame of Muslims for individual acts of violence and assuage anti-Muslim hostility. *Personality and Social Psychology Bulletin*, 44(3), 430–48.

Bruynell, M. (2012). The dangers of modern day belief in the supernatural: International persecution of witches and albinos. *Suffolk Transnational Law Review*, 35, 393.

Bryant, P. R. (2003). *Difference and Givenness: Deleuze's Transcendental Empiricism and the Ontology of Immanence*. Loyola University Press.

# REFERENCES

Bryden, M. (2001). *Deleuze and Religion*. Routledge.
Buchanan, I. (2008). *Deleuze and Politics*. Edinburgh University Press.
Buchanan, I. (2013). Schizoanalysis: An incomplete project. In B. Dillett (ed.), *The Edinburgh Companion to Poststructuralism*, 163–85. Edinburgh University Press.
Buchanan, I. (2015). Assemblage theory and its discontents. *Deleuze Studies*, 9(3), 382–92.
Buchanan, I. (2017). Assemblage theory, or, the future of an illusion. *Deleuze Studies*, 11(3), 457–74.
Buchanan, I. (2020). *Assemblage Theory and Method: An Introduction and Guide*. Bloomsbury.
Bulbulia, J. (2012). Spreading order: Religion, cooperative niche construction, and risky coordination problems. *Biology and Philosophy*, 27(1), 1–27.
Bulbulia, J., and Schjoedt, U. (2010). Religious culture and cooperative prediction under risk: Perspectives from social neuroscience. *Religion, Economy, and Cooperation*, 49, 35.
Burrai, E., Mostafanezhad, M., and Hannam, K. (2017). Moral assemblages of volunteer tourism development in Cusco, Peru. *Tourism Geographies*, 19(3), 362–77.
Caldwell-Harris, C. L., Wilson, A. L., Lotempio, E., and Beit-Hallahmi, B. (2011). Exploring the atheist personality: Well-being, awe, and magical thinking in atheists, Buddhists, and Christians. *Mental Health, Religion and Culture*, 14(7), 659–72. https://doi.org/10.1080/13674676.2010.509847
Callimachi, R. (2016). How do you stop a future terrorist when the only evidence is a thought? *The New York Times*, 21 June. http://www.nytimes.com/2016/06/22/world/europe/france-orlando-isis-terrorism-investigation.html
Campbell, T. H., and Kay, A. C. (2014). Solution aversion: On the relation between ideology and motivated disbelief. *Journal of Personality and Social Psychology*, 107(5), 809–24. https://doi.org/10.1037/a0037963
Cederman, L.-E., Gleditsch, K. S., and Wucherpfennig, J. (2017). Predicting the decline of ethnic civil war. *Journal of Peace Research*, 54(2), 262–74. https://doi.org/10.1177/0022343316684191
Cederman, L.-E., and Weidmann, N. B. (2017). Predicting armed conflict: Time to adjust our expectations? *Science*, 355(6324), 474. https://doi.org/10.1126/science.aal4483
Chabbert, M. (2018). On becoming secular: Gilles Deleuze and the death of God. In D. Gudmunsen and G. Dellacasa (eds), *The Sacred in the Secular in European Literature*, 50–9. Modern Humanities Research Association.
Christmann, K. (2012). *Preventing Religious Radicalisation and Violent Extremism: A Systematic Review of the Research Literature*. Applied Criminology Centre, University of Huddersfield. http://dx.doi.org/10.13140/2.1.4641.6169
Chuah, S.-H., Hoffmann, R., Ramasamy, B., and Tan, J. H. W. (2014). Religion, ethnicity and cooperation: An experimental study. *Journal of Economic Psychology*, 45, 33–43. https://doi.org/10.1016/j.joep.2014.07.002
Clarke, S., Powell, R., and Savulescu, J. (2013). Religion, intolerance, and conflict: Practical implications for social policy. In S. Clarke, R. Powell, and J. Savulescu (eds), *Religion, Intolerance, and Conflict: A Scientific and Conceptual Investigation*, 266–72. Oxford University Press.
Cliquet, R. L., and Avramov, D. (2018). *Evolution Science and Ethics in the Third Millennium: Challenges and Choices for Humankind*. Springer.
Cliquet, R. L., and Avramov, D. (2021). Evolution science and ethics in the third millennium: Challenges and choices for humankind. *Religion, Brain and Behavior*, 11(1), 65–78.
Clough, P., Han, S., and Schiff, R. (2007). Book review: *A New Philosophy of Society: Assemblage Theory and Social Complexity* by Manuel DeLanda. *Theory, Culture and Society*, 24(7–8), 387–93.
Coccia, M. (2014). Socio-cultural origins of the patterns of technological innovation: What is the likely interaction among religious culture, religious plurality and innovationα Towards

a theory of socio-cultural drivers of the patterns of technological innovation. *Technology in Society*, *36*(1), 13–25. https://doi.org/10.1016/j.techsoc.2013.11.002

Coe, K., VanPool, C. S., and Palmer, C. T. (2012). Figurines, religion, and tradition in human evolution. In P. McNamara and W. J. Wildman (eds), *Science and the World's Religions, Volume 1: Origins and Destinies*, 91–116. Praeger.

Cohen, G. L., Aronson, J., and Steele, C. M. (2000). When beliefs yield to evidence: Reducing biased evaluation by affirming the self. *Personality and Social Psychology Bulletin*, *26*(9), 1151–64.

Cohen, G. L., Sherman, D. K., Bastardi, A., Hsu, L., McGoey, M., and Ross, L. (2007). Bridging the partisan divide: Self-affirmation reduces ideological closed-mindedness and inflexibility in negotiation. *Journal of Personality and Social Psychology*, *93*(3), 415.

Colebrook, C. (2016). 'A grandiose time of coexistence': Stratigraphy of the Anthropocene. *Deleuze Studies*, *10*(4), 440–54.

Conte, R., Andrighetto, G., and Campennì, M. (2014). *Minding Norms: Mechanisms and Dynamics of Social Order in Agent Societies*. Oxford University Press.

Conte, R., Gilbert, N., Bonelli, G., Cioffi-Revilla, C., Deffuant, G., Kertesz, J., Loreto, V., Moat, S., Nadal, J., Sanchez, A., Nowak, A., Flache, A., San Miguel, M., and Helbing, D. (2012). Manifesto of computational social science. *The European Physical Journal Special Topics*, *214*(1), 325–46. https://doi.org/10.1140/epjst/e2012-01697-8

Cook, J. (2017). Understanding and countering climate science denial. *Journal and Proceedings of the Royal Society of New South Wales*, *150*, 207.

Cook, J., Lewandowsky, S., and Ecker, U. K. H. (2017). Neutralizing misinformation through inoculation: Exposing misleading argumentation techniques reduces their influence.(Research Article). *PLoS ONE*, *12*(5), e0175799. https://doi.org/10.1371/journal.pone.0175799

Correll, J., Spencer, S. J., and Zanna, M. P. (2004). An affirmed self and an open mind: Self-affirmation and sensitivity to argument strength. *Journal of Experimental Social Psychology*, *40*(3), 350–6.

Cragun, R., McCaffree, K., Puga-Gonzalez, I., Wildman, W., and Shults, F. L. (2021). Religious exiting and social networks: Computer simulations of religious/secular pluralism. *Secularism and Nonreligion*, *10*(2), 1–20. https://doi.org/10.5334/snr.129.

Crone, M. (2014). Religion and violence: Governing Muslim militancy through aesthetic assemblages. *Millennium – Journal of International Studies*, *43*(1), 291–307. https://doi.org/10.1177/0305829814541166

Croskerry, P. (2003). Cognitive forcing strategies in clinical decisionmaking. *Annals of Emergency Medicine*, *41*(1), 110–20.

Croskerry, P., Singhal, G., and Mamede, S. (2013). Cognitive debiasing 2: Impediments to and strategies for change. *BMJ Quality & Safety 22*(Suppl 2), ii65–ii72.

Currie, C. S., Fowler, J. W., Kotiadis, K., Monks, T., Onggo, B. S., Robertson, D. A., and Tako, A. A. (2020). How simulation modelling can help reduce the impact of COVID-19. *Journal of Simulation*, *14*(2), 83–97.

Dalton, C. M. (2019). Rhizomatic data assemblages: Mapping new possibilities for urban housing data. *Urban Geography*, *41*(8), 1–19.

Daniel-Hughes, B. (2018). Postpartum theology: Axiological experimentation at the margins. *American Journal of Theology and Philosophy*, *39*(3), 48–64.

Dávid-Barrett, T., and Carney, J. (2015). The deification of historical figures and the emergence of priesthoods as a solution to a network coordination problem. *Religion, Brain and Behavior*, *6*(4), 307–17. https://doi.org/10.1080/2153599X.2015.1063001

Davies, M. F., Griffin, M., and Vice, S. (2001). Affective reactions to auditory hallucinations in psychotic, evangelical and control groups. *British Journal of Clinical Psychology*, *40*(4), 361–70. https://doi.org/10.1348/014466501163850

# REFERENCES

De Beistegui, M. (2004). *Truth and Genesis: Philosophy as Differential Ontology*. Indiana University Press.
De Beistegui, M. (2010). *Immanence – Deleuze and Philosophy*. Edinburgh University Press.
De Beistegui, M. (2012). The Deleuzian reversal of Platonism. In D. Smith and H. Somers-Hall (eds), *The Cambridge Companion to Deleuze*, 55–81. Cambridge University Press.
De Cruz, H. (2018). Etiological challenges to religious practices. *American Philosophical Quarterly*, 55(4), 329–40.
De Cruz, H., and De Smedt, J. (2010). Paley's iPod: The cognitive basis of the design argument within natural theology. *ZYGON*, 45(3), 665–84. https://doi.org/10.1111/j.1467-9744.2010.01120.x
De Cruz, H., and De Smedt, J. (2016). How do philosophers evaluate natural theological arguments? An experimental philosophical investigation. In H. De Cruz, R. Nichols, and J. R. Beebe (eds), *Advances in Religion, Cognitive Science, and Experimental Philosophy*, 119–42. Bloomsbury.
De Smedt, J., and De Cruz, H. (2011). The cognitive appeal of the cosmological argument. *Method and Theory in the Study of Religion*, 23(2), 103–22. https://doi.org/10.1163/157006811X567715
Delamontagne, R. G. (2010). High religiosity and societal dysfunction in the United States during the first decade of the twenty-first century. *Evolutionary Psychology*, 8(4), 617–57.
DeLanda, M. (1991). *War in the Age of Intelligent Machines*. Zone Books.
DeLanda, M. (1995). Virtual environments and the concept of synergy. *Leonardo*, 28(5), 357–60.
DeLanda, M. (2002). *Intensive Science and Virtual Philosophy*. Bloomsbury.
DeLanda, M. (2005). Virtual environments and the emergence of synthetic reason. In J. Dixon and E. Cassidy (eds), *Virtual Futures: Cyberotics, Technology and Posthuman Pragmatism*, 85–101. Routledge.
DeLanda, M. (2006). *A New Philosophy of Society: Assemblage Theory and Social Complexity*. Continuum.
DeLanda, M. (2011). *Philosophy and Simulation: The Emergence of Synthetic Reason*. Continuum.
DeLanda, M. (2012a). Emergence, causality and realism. *Architectural Theory Review*, 17(1), 3–16.
DeLanda, M. (2012b). IO Deleuze, mathematics, and realist ontology. In D. Smith and H. Somers-Hall (eds), *The Cambridge Companion to Deleuze*, 220–38. Cambridge University Press.
DeLanda, M. (2016). *Assemblage Theory*. Edinburgh University Press.
DeLanda, M., and Crary, J. (1997). *A Thousand Years of Nonlinear History*. Zone Books.
Deleuze, G. (1983). *Nietzsche and Philosophy*. Trans. J. Tomlinson. Columbia University Press.
Deleuze, G. (1985). *Kant's Critical Philosophy: The Doctrine of the Faculties*. University of Minnesota Press.
Deleuze, G. (1988). *Bergsonism*. Trans. H. Tomlinson. Urzone.
Deleuze, G. (1992). *Expressionism in Philosophy: Spinoza*. Trans. M. Joughin. Zone Books.
Deleuze, G. (1995a). *Difference and Repetition*. Trans. P. Patton (rev. edn). Columbia University Press.
Deleuze, G. (1995b). *Negotiations, 1972–1990*. Columbia University Press.
Deleuze, G. (1997). To have done with judgment. In *Essays Critical and Clinical*, 126–35. University of Minnesota Press.
Deleuze, G. (1999). *Foucault*. Continuum.
Deleuze, G. (2000). *Proust and Signs*. Trans. R. Howard. University of Minnesota Press.
Deleuze, G. (2001a). *Spinoza: Practical Philosophy*. Trans. R. Hurley. City Lights.
Deleuze, G. (2001b). *Empiricism and Subjectivity*. Trans. C. V. Boundas. Columbia University Press.

Deleuze, G. (2004). *The Logic of Sense*. Continuum.
Deleuze, G. (2005a). Pericles and Verdi: The philosophy of François Chatelet. *The Opera Quarterly*, 21(4), 716–24.
Deleuze, G. (2005b). *Pure Immanence: Essays on a Life* (2nd edn). Zone Books.
Deleuze, G. (2005c). *Francis Bacon: The Logic of Sensation*. University of Minnesota Press.
Deleuze, G. (2007). *Two Regimes of Madness: Texts and Interviews 1975–1995*. Semiotext(e).
Deleuze, G. (2013). *Cinema II: The Time-Image*. Bloomsbury.
Deleuze, G. (2019). Cinema I: The movement-image. In C. Kul-Want (ed.), *Philosophers on Film from Bergson to Badiou: A Critical Reader*, 152–76. Columbia University Press.
Deleuze, G., and Guattari, F. (1983). *Anti-Oedipus: Capitalism and Schizophrenia*. University of Minnesota Press.
Deleuze, G., and Guattari, F. (1986). *Kafka: Toward a Minor Literature*. University of Minnesota Press.
Deleuze, G., and Guattari, F. (1988). *A Thousand Plateaus: Capitalism and Schizophrenia*. Continuum.
Deleuze, G., and Guattari, F. (1996). *What is Philosophy?* Trans. H. Tomlinson and G. Burchell. Columbia University Press.
Deleuze, G., and Parnet, C. (2002). *Dialogues II*. Trans. H. Tomlinson and B. Habberjam. Continuum.
Delpech-Ramey, J. (2010). Deleuze, Guattari, and the 'politics of sorcery'. *SubStance*, 39(1), 8–23.
Desai, A. (ed.). (2012). *Simulation for Public Policy*. Springer.
Develaki, M. (2019). Methodology and epistemology of computer simulations and implications for science education. *Journal of Science Education and Technology*, 28(4), 353–70.
Devellennes, C. (2021). *Positive Atheism: Bayle, Meslier, D'Holbach, Diderot*. Edinburgh University Press.
Diallo, S. Y., Shults, F. L., and Wildman, W. J. (2021). Minding morality: Ethical artificial societies for public policy modeling. *AI and Society*, 36(1), 49–57.
Diallo, S. Y., Shults, F. L., and Wildman, W. J. (under review). Minding morality: Ethical artificial societies for public policy modeling.
Diallo, S. Y., Wildman, W. J., Shults, F. L., and Tolk, A. (eds) (2019). *Human Simulation: Perspectives, Insights, and Applications*. Springer.
Dignum, F., and Dignum, V. (2014). *Perspectives on Culture and Agent-based Simulations: Integrating Cultures*, Vol. 3. Springer International.
Dittmer, J. (2014). Geopolitical assemblages and complexity. *Progress in Human Geography*, 38(3), 385–401.
Dodds, J. (2012). *Psychoanalysis and Ecology at the Edge of Chaos: Complexity Theory, Deleuze, Guattari and Psychoanalysis for a Climate in Crisis*. Routledge.
Donaldson, S., and McConnell, M. (2015). Simulation as a method for theological and philosophical inquiry. *Theology and Science*, 13(3), 354–70. https://doi.org/10.1080/14746700.2015.1053763
Doosje, B., Moghaddam, F. M., Kruglanski, A. W., de Wolf, A., Mann, L., and Feddes, A. R. (2016). Terrorism, radicalization and de-radicalization. *Current Opinion in Psychology*, 11, 79–84. https://doi.org/10.1016/j.copsyc.2016.06.008
Dovey, K., and Ristic, M. (2017). Mapping urban assemblages: The production of spatial knowledge. *Journal of Urbanism: International Research on Placemaking and Urban Sustainability*, 10(1), 15–28.
Draper, P., and Nichols, R. (2013). Diagnosing bias in philosophy of religion. *The Monist*, 96(3), 420–46. https://doi.org/10.5840/monist201396319
Duff, C. (2022). The ends of an assemblage of health. *Social Science and Medicine*, 115636. https://doi.org/10.1016/j.socscimed.2022.115636

# REFERENCES

Duffy, P., and Stojanovic, T. (2018). The potential for assemblage thinking in population geography: Assembling population, space, and place. *Population, Space and Place*, 24(3), e2097.

Duffy, S. (2013). *Deleuze and the History of Mathematics: In Defense of the 'New.'* Bloomsbury.

Dunkel, C. S., and Dutton, E. (2016). Religiosity as a predictor of in-group favoritism within and between religious groups. *Personality and Individual Differences*, 98, 311–14. https://doi.org/10.1016/j.paid.2016.04.063

Durkheim, E. (1912). *The Elementary Forms of Religious Life*. Trans. K. E. Fields. Free Press.

Dutton, E., and Van der Linden, D. (2017). Why is intelligence negatively associated with religiousness? *Evolutionary Psychological Science*, 3(4), 392–403. https://doi.org/10.1007/s40806-017-0101-0

Dyer, K. D., and Hall, R. E. (2019). Effect of critical thinking education on epistemically unwarranted beliefs in college students. *Research in Higher Education*, 60(3), 293–314.

Ecker, U. K., Lewandowsky, S., and Tang, D. T. (2010). Explicit warnings reduce but do not eliminate the continued influence of misinformation. *Memory and Cognition*, 38(8), 1087–100.

Ecklund, E. H., Scheitle, C. P., Peifer, J., and Bolger, D. (2017). Examining links between religion, evolution views, and climate change skepticism. *Environment and Behavior*, 49(9), 985–1006.

Edmonds, B. (2017). Different modelling purposes. In B. Edmonds and R. Meyer (eds), *Simulating Social Complexity*, 39–58. Springer.

Eisenstadt, S. N. (ed.) (1986). *The Origins and Diversity of Axial Age Civilizations*. State University of New York Press.

Ekblom, P. (2012). Conceptual and methodological explorations in affordance and counter terrorism. In M. Taylor and P. M. Currie (eds), *Terrorism and Affordance*, 33–48. Continuum.

Ekblom, P., Sidebottom, A., and Wortley, R. (2016). Evolutionary psychological influences on the contemporary causes of terrorist events. In M. Taylor, J. Roach, and K. Pease (eds), *Evolutionary Psychology and Terrorism*, 42–69. Routledge.

Eliade, M. (2020). *Shamanism: Archaic Techniques of Ecstasy*, Vol. 76. Princeton University Press.

Ellis, L., Hoskin, A. W., Dutton, E., and Nyborg, H. (2017). The future of secularism: A biologically informed theory supplemented with cross-cultural evidence. *Evolutionary Psychological Science*, 3(4), 224–42. https://doi.org/10.1007/s40806-017-0090-z

Elsenbroich, C., and Gilbert, N. (2014). *Modelling Norms*. Springer Netherlands.

Elwood, S. (2021). Digital geographies, feminist relationality, Black and queer code studies: Thriving otherwise. *Progress in Human Geography*, 45(2), 209–28.

Epstein, J. M. (2006). *Generative Social Science: Studies in Agent-Based Computational Modeling*. Princeton University Press.

Epstein, J. M. (2014). *Agent_Zero: Toward Neurocognitive Foundations for Generative Social Science*. Princeton University Press.

Etengoff, C., and Lefevor, T. G. (2021). Sexual prejudice, sexism, and religion. *Current Opinion in Psychology*, 40, 45–50.

Everton, S. (2016). Social networks and religious violence. *Review of Religious Research*, 58(2), 191–217. https://doi.org/10.1007/s13644-015-0240-3

Fellman, P. V., Bar-Yam, Y., and Minai, A. A. (eds) (2015). *Conflict and Complexity: Countering Terrorism, Insurgency, Ethnic and Regional Violence*. Springer.

Fishwick, P. A. (2018). A humanities based approach to formally defining information through modelling. *Historical Social Research/Historische Sozialforschung. Supplement*, 31, 154–62.

Floridi, L. (2002). *Philosophy and Computing: An Introduction*. Routledge.

Floridi, L. (2013). *The Philosophy of Information*. Oxford University Press.

Fonneland, T. (2017). *Contemporary Shamanisms in Norway: Religion, Entrepreneurship, and Politics*. Oxford University Press.

# REFERENCES

Forney, J., Rosin, C., and Campbell, H. (2018). Introduction: Agri-environmental governance as assemblage. In J. Forney, C. Rosin, and H. Campbell (eds), *Agri-environmental Governance as an Assemblage: Multiplicity, Power, and Transformation*, 1–32. Routledge.

French, S. (2017). *The Structure of the World: Metaphysics and Representation*. Oxford University Press.

Funk, C., and Smith, G. (2012). 'Nones' on the rise. *Pew Research Center*. https://www.pewresearch.org/religion/2012/10/09/nones-on-the-rise/

Galen, L., Gore, R., and Shults, F. L. (2021). Modeling the effects of religious belief and affiliation on prosociality. *Secularism and Nonreligion*, 10(6), 1–21.

Gangle, R. (2010). Divinatory chances. *SubStance*, 39(1), 76–86.

Gangle, R. (2015). *Diagrammatic Immanence: Category Theory and Philosophy*. Edinburgh University Press.

Ganzach, Y., Ellis, S., and Gotlibovski, C. (2013). On intelligence, education and religious beliefs. *Intelligence*, 41(2), 121–28. https://doi.org/10.1016/j.intell.2013.01.001

Ganzach, Y., and Gotlibovski, C. (2013). Intelligence and religiosity: Within families and over time. *Intelligence*, 41(5), 546–52. https://doi.org/10.1016/j.intell.2013.07.003

Garcia, H. A. (2015). *Alpha God: The Psychology of Religious Violence and Oppression*. Prometheus Books.

Gervais, W. M., and Norenzayan, A. (2012). Analytic thinking promotes religious disbelief. *Science*, 336(6080), 493–96. https://doi.org/10.1126/science.1215647

Ghoddousi, P., and Page, S. (2020). Using ethnography and assemblage theory in political geography. *Geography Compass*, 14(10). https://doi.org/10.1111/gec3.12533

Gilbert, N., Ahrweiler, P., Barbrook-Johnson, P., Narasimhan, K. P., and Wilkinson, H. (2018). Computational modelling of public policy. *Journal of Artificial Societies and Social Simulation*, 21(1), 1–19.

Gilbert, N., and Conte, R. (eds) (1995). *Artificial Societies: The Computer Simulation of Social Life*. UCL Press.

Ginges, J., and Atran, S. (2011). War as a moral imperative (not just practical politics by other means). *Proceedings of the Royal Society B*, 278(1720), 2930–8. https://doi.org/10.1098/rspb.2010.2384

Ginges, J., Atran, S., Medin, D., and Shikaki, K. (2007). Sacred bounds on rational resolution of violent political conflict. *Proceedings of the National Academy of Sciences of the United States of America*, 104(18), 7357–60.

Ginges, J., Atran, S., Sachdeva, S., and Medin, D. (2011). Psychology out of the laboratory. *American Psychologist*, 66(6), 507–19. https://doi.org/10.1037/a0024715

Gore, R., Lemos, C., Shults, F. L., and Wildman, W. J. (2018). Forecasting changes in religiosity and existential security with an agent-based model. *Journal of Artificial Societies and Social Simulation*, 21, 1–31.

Gorur, R. (2011). Policy as assemblage. *European Educational Research Journal*, 10(4), 611–22.

Gräbner, C. (2018). How to relate models to reality? An epistemological framework for the validation and verification of computational models. *Journal of Artificial Societies and Social Simulation*, 21(3). https://doi.org/10.18564/jasss.3772

Graeber, D., and Wengrow, D. (2021). *The Dawn of Everything: A New History of Humanity*. Penguin.

Greenberg, J., Pyszczynski, T., Solomon, S., Rosenblatt, A., Veeder, M., Kirkland, S., and Lyon, D. (1990). Evidence for terror management theory II: The effects of mortality salience on reactions to those who threaten or bolster the cultural worldview. *Journal of Personality and Social Psychology*, 58(2), 308–18. https://doi.org/10.1037/0022-3514.58.2.308

Greenhough, B. (2011). Assembling an island laboratory. *Area*, 43(2), 134–8.

Greenhough, B. (2012). On the agencement of the academic geographer. *Dialogues in Human Geography*, 2(2), 202–6.

# REFERENCES

Griffiths, P. E., and Wilkins, J. S. (2015). Crossing the Milvian bridge: When do evolutionary explanations of belief debunk belief? In P. R. Sloan, G. McKenny, and K. Eggleson (eds), *Darwin in the Twenty-First Century: Nature, Humanity, God*, 201–31. University of Notre Dame Press.

Grim, B. J., and Finke, R. (2011). *The Price of Freedom Denied: Religious Persecution and Conflict in the Twenty-first Century*. Cambridge University Press.

Grim, P. (2002). Philosophy for computers: Some explorations in philosophical modeling. *Metaphilosophy*, 33(1–2), 181–209. https://doi.org/10.1111/1467-9973.00224

Grim, P. (2019a). Modeling epistemology: Examples and analysis in computational philosophy of science. In *Proceedings of the 2019 Spring Simulation Conference*, 1–12. IEEE. https://doi.org/10.23919/SpringSim.2019.8732892

Grim, P. (2019b). Editorial introduction to the topical issue 'computer modeling in philosophy'. *Open Philosophy*, 2(1), 653–6. https://doi.org/10.1515/opphil-2019-0049

Grim, P., Modell, A., Breslin, N., Mcnenny, J., Mondescu, I., Finnegan, K., Olsen, R., An, C., and Fedder, A. (2016). Coherence and correspondence in the network dynamics of belief suites. *Episteme*, 14(2), 1–21. https://doi.org/10.1017/epi.2016.7

Grim, P., Rosenberger, R., Rosenfeld, A., Anderson, B., and Eason, R. E. (2013). How simulations fail. *Synthese*, 190(12), 2367–90.

Guthrie, S. (1993). *Faces in the Clouds: A New Theory of Religion*. Oxford University Press.

Haarstad, H., and Wanvik, T. I. (2017). Carbonscapes and beyond: Conceptualizing the instability of oil landscapes. *Progress in Human Geography*, 41(4), 432–50.

Habel, P., and Grant, J. T. (2013). Demand for god and government: The dynamics of religion and public opinion. *Politics and Religion*, 6(2), 282–302. https://doi.org/10.1017/S1755048312000570

Hafez, M., and Mullins, C. (2015). The radicalization puzzle: A theoretical synthesis of empirical approaches to homegrown extremism. *Studies in Conflict and Terrorism*, 38(11), 958–75. https://doi.org/10.1080/1057610X.2015.1051375

Hart, P. S., and Nisbet, E. C. (2012). Boomerang effects in science communication: How motivated reasoning and identity cues amplify opinion polarization about climate mitigation policies. *Communication Research*, 39(6), 701–23.

Hasan, R. (2017). *Religion and Development in the Global South*. Palgrave Macmillan.

Hauke, J., Lorscheid, I., and Meyer, M. (2017). Recent development of social simulation as reflected in JASSS between 2008 and 2014: A citation and co-citation analysis. *Journal of Artificial Societies and Social Simulation*, 20(1), 1–24.

Haynes, C., Luck, M., McBurney, P., Mahmoud, S., Vítek, T., and Miles, S. (2017). Engineering the emergence of norms: A review. *The Knowledge Engineering Review*, 32. https://doi.org/10.1017/S0269888917000169

Hecht, J. M. (2004). *Doubt: A History: The Great Doubters and Their Legacy of Innovation from Socrates and Jesus to Thomas Jefferson and Emily Dickinson* (reprint edn). HarperOne.

Hennes, E. P., Nam, H. H., Stern, C., and Jost, J. T. (2012). Not all ideologies are created equal: Epistemic, existential, and relational needs predict system-justifying attitudes. *Social Cognition*, 30(6), 669–88.

Heppenstall, A. J., Crooks, A. T., See, L. M., and Batty, M. (2011). *Agent-based Models of Geographical Systems*. Springer Science and Business Media.

Hirsch-Hoefler, S., Canetti, D., and Eiran, E. (2016). Radicalizing religion? Religious identity and settlers' behavior. *Studies in Conflict and Terrorism*, 39(6), 500–18. https://doi.org/10.1080/1057610X.2015.1127111

Holdsworth, D. (2006). Becoming interdisciplinary: Making sense of DeLanda's reading of Deleuze. *Paragraph*, 29(2), 139–56.

Holland, E. W. (2016). On/Beyond the Anthropocene. *Deleuze Studies*, 10(4), 564–73.

Hoverd, W. J., Atkinson, Q. D., and Sibley, C. G. (2012). Group size and the trajectory of religious identification. *Journal for the Scientific Study of Religion*, *51*(2), 286–303.
Hughes, J. (2008a). *Deleuze and the Genesis of Representation*. Bloomsbury.
Hughes, J. (2008b). Schizoanalysis and the phenomenology of cinema. In I. Buchanan and P. MacCormack (eds), *Deleuze and the Schizoanalysis of Cinema*, 15–26. Continuum.
Hughes, J. (2012). *Philosophy after Deleuze*. A&C Black.
Humphreys, P. (2006). *Extending Ourselves: Computational Science, Empiricism, and Scientific Method*. Oxford University Press.
Hungerman, D. M. (2014). The effect of education on religion: Evidence from compulsory schooling laws. *Journal of Economic Behavior and Organization*, *104*, 52–63. https://doi.org/10.1016/j.jebo.2013.09.004
Iannaccone, L. R., and Makowsky, M. D. (2007). Accidental atheists? Agent-based explanations for the persistence of religious regionalism. *Journal for the Scientific Study of Religion*, *46*(1), 1–16. https://doi.org/10.1111/j.1468-5906.2007.00337.x
Inglehart, R., and Welzel, C. (2005). *Modernization, Cultural Change, and Democracy: The Human Development Sequence*. Cambridge University Press.
Jenkins, M. M., and Youngstrom, E. A. (2016). A randomized controlled trial of cognitive debiasing improves assessment and treatment selection for pediatric bipolar disorder. *Journal of Consulting and Clinical Psychology*, *84*(4), 323.
Jensen, C. B., and Rödje, K. (2010). *Deleuzian Intersections: Science, Technology, Anthropology*. Berghahn Books.
Jervis, B. (2018). *Assemblage Thought and Archaeology*. Routledge.
Johnson, D. D., Lenfesty, H. L., and Schloss, J. P. (2014). The elephant in the room: Do evolutionary accounts of religion entail the falsity of religious belief? *Philosophy, Theology and the Sciences*, *1*(2), 200–31.
Johnson, M. K., Rowatt, W. C., and Labouff, J. (2010). Priming Christian religious concepts increases racial prejudice. *Social Psychological and Personality Science*, *1*(2), 119–26. https://doi.org/10.1177/1948550609357246
Johnson, R. J. (2016). *Deleuze–Lucretius Encounter*. Edinburgh University Press.
Jong, J., and Visala, A. (2014). Evolutionary debunking arguments against theism, reconsidered. *International Journal for Philosophy of Religion*, *76*(3), 243–58. https://doi.org/10.1007/s11153-014-9461-6
Juergensmeyer, M., Kitts, M., and Jerryson, M. (eds). (2016). *Violence and the World's Religious Traditions: An Introduction*. Oxford University Press.
Juergensmeyer, M., Kitts, M., and Jerryson, M. K. (2013). *The Oxford Handbook of Religion and Violence*. Oxford University Press.
Justaert, K. (2012). *Theology after Deleuze*. Bloomsbury.
Kahneman, D. (2013). *Thinking, Fast and Slow* (reprint edn). Farrar, Straus and Giroux.
Kant, I. (1965). *Critique of Pure Reason*. Trans. N. K. Smith. St. Martin's Press.
Kelemen, D. (1999). Why are rocks pointy? Children's preference for teleological explanations of the natural world. *Developmental Psychology*, *35*(6), 1440.
Kenyon, T. (2014). False polarization: Debiasing as applied social epistemology. *Synthese*, *191*(11), 2529–47. https://doi.org/10.1007/s11229-014-0438-x
Kerslake, C. (2007). *Deleuze and the Unconscious*. A&C Black.
Kerslake, C. (2019). *Immanence and the Vertigo of Philosophy: From Kant to Deleuze*. Edinburgh University Press.
King, M., and Taylor, D. M. (2011). The radicalization of homegrown jihadists: A review of theoretical models and social psychological evidence. *Terrorism and Political Violence*, *23*(4), 602–22. https://doi.org/10.1080/09546553.2011.587064
Kinkaid, E. (2019). 'Rights of nature' in translation: Assemblage geographies, boundary objects, and translocal social movements. *Transactions of the Institute of British Geographers*, *44*(3), 555–70.

# REFERENCES

Kinkaid, E. (2020a). Assemblage as ethos: Conceptual genealogies and political problems. *Area, 52*(3), 480–7.

Kinkaid, E. (2020b). Can assemblage think difference? A feminist critique of assemblage geographies. *Progress in Human Geography, 44*(3), 457–72.

Kirchner, D., Benzmüller, C., and Zalta, E. N. (2019). Computer science and metaphysics: A cross-fertilization. *ArXiv:1905.00787*. https://doi.org/10.1515/opphil-2019-0015

Knepper, T. (2013). *The Ends of Philosophy of Religion: Terminus and Telos*. Springer.

Knepper, T. (2022). *Philosophies of Religion: A Global and Critical Introduction*. Bloomsbury.

Ko, T. H., and Berry, N. M. (2004). Agent-based modeling with social networks for terrorist recruitment. *AAAI*, 1016–17. http://www.aaai.org/Papers/AAAI/2004/AAAI04-156.pdf

Koehler, D. (2016). *Understanding Deradicalization: Methods, Tools and Programs for Countering Violent Extremism*. Routledge.

Kosmin, B. A., and Keysar, A. (2013). *Religious, Spiritual and Secular: The Emergence of Three Distinct Worldviews among American College Students* [American Religious Identification Survey]. Trinity College. http://www.trincoll.edu/Academics/centers/isssc/Documents/ARIS_2013_College%20Students_Sept_25_final_draft.pdf

Kossowska, M., Czernatowicz-Kukuczka, A., and Sekerdej, M. (2017). Many faces of dogmatism: Prejudice as a way of protecting certainty against value violators among dogmatic believers and atheists. *British Journal of Psychology, 108*(1), 127–47. https://doi.org/10.1111/bjop.12186

Kramer, S. R., and Shariff, A. F. (2016). Religion, deception, and self-deception. In J.-W. van Prooijen and P. A. M. van Lange (eds), *Cheating, Corruption, and Concealment*, 233–49. Cambridge University Press.

Kruglanski, A. W., Bélanger, J. J., and Gunaratna, R. (2019). *The Three Pillars of Radicalization: Needs, Narratives, and Networks*. Oxford University Press.

Kruglanski, A. W., Jasko, K., Chernikova, M., Dugas, M., and Webber, D. (2017). To the fringe and back: Violent extremism and the psychology of deviance. *American Psychologist, 72*(3), 217–30. https://doi.org/10.1037/amp0000091

Ladyman, J., and Ross, D. (2007). *Every Thing Must Go: Metaphysics Naturalized*. Oxford University Press.

Lambert, G. (2021). *Towards a Geopolitical Image of Thought*. Edinburgh University Press.

Lane, J. (2013). Method, theory, and multi-agent artificial intelligence: Creating computer models of complex social interactions. *Journal for the Cognitive Science of Religion, 1*(2), 161–80.

Lane, J. E. (2021). *Understanding Religion Through Artificial Intelligence: Bonding and Belief*. Bloomsbury.

Lane, J. E. (2023). *How CulturePulse AI Helped Cambridge University Understand Conflict in Northern Ireland, the Balkans, and South Sudan*. https://culturepulse.ai/blog/how-culture-pulse-ai-helped-cambridge-university-understand-conflict

Lane, J. E., and Shults, F. L. (2018). Cognition, culture, and social simulation. *Journal of Cognition and Culture, 18*, 451–61.

Lane, J. E., and Shults, F. L. (2020). The computational science of religion. *Journal of the Cognitive Science of Religion, 6*(1–2). http://dx.doi.org/10.1558/jcsr.38669

Laskowski, P. P., Puga-Gonzalez, I., Shults, F. L., and Talmont-Kaminski, K. (in press). A cognitive model of epistemic vigilance in situations of varying competence, consistency, and utility. In F. Squazzoni (ed.), *Advances in Social Simulation*. Springer.

Law, A. M., and Kelton, W. D. (1991). *Simulation Modeling and Analysis* (2nd edn). McGraw-Hill.

Legg, S. (2011). Assemblage/apparatus: Using Deleuze and Foucault. *Area, 43*(2), 128–33.

Leidner, B., Castano, E., and Ginges, J. (2013). Dehumanization, retributive and restorative justice, and aggressive versus diplomatic intergroup conflict resolution strategies. *Personality and Social Psychology Bulletin, 39*(2), 181.

# REFERENCES

Lemos, C. M., Gore R. J., Puga-Gonzalez, I., Shults, F. L. (2019). Dimensionality and factorial invariance of religiosity among Christians and the religiously unaffiliated: A cross-cultural analysis based on the International Social Survey Programme. *PLoS ONE, 14*(5), e0216352. https://doi.org/10.1371/journal.pone.0216352

Lemos, C. M., Gore, R. J., Lessard-Phillips, L., and Shults, F. L. (2020). A network agent-based model of ethnocentrism and intergroup cooperation. *Quality and Quantity, 54*, 463–89. https://doi.org/10.1007/s11135-019-00856-y

Lenco, P. (2013). *Deleuze and World Politics: Alter-globalizations and Nomad Science*. Routledge.

Lewandowsky, S., Ecker, U. K., and Cook, J. (2017). Beyond misinformation: Understanding and coping with the 'post-truth' era. *Journal of Applied Research in Memory and Cognition, 6*(4), 353–69.

Lewandowsky, S., Ecker, U. K. H., Seifert, C. M., Schwarz, N., and Cook, J. (2012). Misinformation and its correction. *Psychological Science in the Public Interest, 13*(3), 106–31. https://doi.org/10.1177/1529100612451018

Lewandowsky, S., and Oberauer, K. (2016). Motivated rejection of science. *Current Directions in Psychological Science, 25*(4), 217–22.

Lewandowsky, S., Stritzke, W. G. K., Freund, A. M., Oberauer, K., and Krueger, J. I. (2013). Misinformation, disinformation, and violent conflict. *American Psychologist, 68*(7), 487–501. https://doi.org/10.1037/a0034515

Lewis, J. R. (2015). Education, irreligion, and non-religion: Evidence from select anglophone census data. *Journal of Contemporary Religion, 30*(2), 265–72. https://doi.org/10.1080/13537903.2015.1025556

Lewis, J. R. (2017). *The Cambridge Companion to Religion and Terrorism*. Cambridge University Press.

Lewis-Williams, J. D. (2010). *Conceiving God: The Cognitive Origin and Evolution of Religion*. Thames and Hudson.

Lilienfeld, S. O., Ammirati, R., and Landfield, K. (2009). Giving debiasing away: Can psychological research on correcting cognitive errors promote human welfare? *Perspectives on Psychological Science, 4*(4), 390–8. https://doi.org/10.1111/j.1745-6924.2009.01144.x

Lindeman, M., and Svedholm-Häkkinen, A. M. (2016). Does poor understanding of physical world predict religious and paranormal beliefs? *Applied Cognitive Psychology, 30*(5), 736–42. https://doi.org/10.1002/acp.3248

Lindeman, M., Svedholm-Häkkinen, A. M., and Lipsanen, J. (2015). Ontological confusions but not mentalizing abilities predict religious belief, paranormal belief, and belief in supernatural purpose. *Cognition, 134*, 63–76. https://doi.org/10.1016/j.cognition.2014.09.008

Lindeman, M., Svedholm-Häkkinen, A. M., and Riekki, T. (2016). Skepticism: Genuine unbelief or implicit beliefs in the supernatural? *Consciousness and Cognition, 42*, 216–28. https://doi.org/10.1016/j.concog.2016.03.019

Linden, S. van der, Leiserowitz, A., Rosenthal, S., and Maibach, E. (2017). Inoculating the public against misinformation about climate change. *Global Challenges, 1*(2), 1600008. https://doi.org/10.1002/gch2.201600008

Liu, Y., Batty, M., Wang, S., and Corcoran, J. (2021). Modelling urban change with cellular automata: Contemporary issues and future research directions. *Progress in Human Geography, 45*(1), 3–24.

Loveland, M. T., Capella, A. G., and Maisonet, I. (2017). Prosocial skeptics: Skepticism and generalized trust. *Critical Research on Religion, 5*(3), 251–65.

Lundy, C., and Voss, D. (eds). (2015). *At the Edges of Thought: Deleuze and post-Kantian Philosophy*. Edinburgh University Press.

Lysgård, H. K. (2019). The assemblage of culture-led policies in small towns and rural communities. *Geoforum, 101*, 10–17.

# REFERENCES

Mahony, M., and Hulme, M. (2018). Epistemic geographies of climate change: Science, space and politics. *Progress in Human Geography*, 42(3), 395–424.

Maitzen, S. (2017). Against ultimacy. In P. Draper and John L. Schellenberg (eds), *Renewing Philosophy of Religion: Exploratory Essays*, 48–62. Oxford University Press.

Makowsky, M. D. (2012). Emergent extremism in a multi-agent model of religious clubs. *Economic Inquiry*, 50(2), 327–47.

Mandel, D. R. (2009). Radicalization: What does it mean. In T. M. Pick et al. (eds), *Homegrown Terrorism*, 101–13. IOS Press.

Manson, S. M., Sun, S., and Bonsal, D. (2012). Agent-based modeling and complexity. In A. J. Heppenstall, A. T. Crooks, L. M. See, and M. Batty (eds), *Agent-Based Models of Geographical Systems*, 125–39. Springer Netherlands. https://doi.org/10.1007/978-90-481-8927-4_7

Marks, J. (2016). *Hard Atheism and the Ethics of Desire: An Alternative to Morality*. Springer.

Mascaro, S. (2010). *Evolving Ethics: The New Science of Good and Evil*. Imprint Academic. http://hdl.handle.net/2027/inu.30000127033425

Matthews, L. J., Edmonds, J., Wildman, W. J., and Nunn, C. L. (2013). Cultural inheritance or cultural diffusion of religious violence? A quantitative case study of the Radical Reformation. *Religion, Brain & Behavior*, 3(1), 3–15.

May, T. (2000). Philosophy as a spiritual exercise in Foucault and Deleuze. *Angelaki: Journal of Theoretical Humanities*, 5(2), 223–9.

McCaffree, K., and Abrutyn, S. (2020). Big Gods, socio-cultural evolution and the non-obvious merits of a sociological interpretation. *Religion*, 50(4), 570–89.

McCaffree, K., and Shults, F. L. (2022). Distributive effervescence: Emotional energy and social cohesion in secularizing societies. *Theory and Society*, 51, 233–68.

McCauley, C., and Moskalenko, S. (2008). Mechanisms of political radicalization: Pathways toward terrorism. *Terrorism and Political Violence*, 20(3), 415–33. https://doi.org/10.1080/09546550802073367

McCauley, C., and Moskalenko, S. (2017). Understanding political radicalization: The two-pyramids model. *American Psychologist*, 72(3), 205–16. https://doi.org/10.1037/amp0000062

McCauley, R. N. (2013). *Why Religion is Natural and Science is Not*. Oxford University Press.

McFarlane, C., and Anderson, B. (2011). Thinking with assemblage. *Area*, 43(2), 162–4.

McGregor, H. A., Lieberman, J. D., Greenberg, J., Solomon, S., Arndt, J., Simon, L., and Pyszczynski, T. (1998). Terror management and aggression: Evidence that mortality salience motivates aggression against worldview-threatening others. *Journal of Personality and Social Psychology*, 74(3), 590–605. https://doi.org/10.1037/0022-3514.74.3.590

McGregor, I., Hayes, J., and Prentice, M. (2015). Motivation for aggressive religious radicalization: Goal regulation theory and a personality x threat x affordance hypothesis. *Frontiers in Psychology*, 6. https://doi.org/10.3389/fpsyg.2015.01325

McLaughlin, A., and McGill, A. (2017). Explicitly teaching critical thinking skills in a history course. *Science and Education*, 26(1), 93–105. https://doi.org/10.1007/s11191-017-9878-2

McLean, B. H. (2022). *Deleuze, Guattari and the Machine in Early Christianity: Schizoanalysis, Affect and Multiplicity*. Bloomsbury.

Mehryar, S., Sliuzas, R., Sharifi, A., Reckien, D., and van Maarseveen, M. (2017). A structured participatory method to support policy option analysis in a social-ecological system. *Journal of Environmental Management*, 197, 360–72.

Miller, H. J. (2018). Geographic information science II: Mesogeography: Social physics, GIScience and the quest for geographic knowledge. *Progress in Human Geography*, 42(4), 600–9.

Millington, J. D., and Wainwright, J. (2017). Mixed qualitative-simulation methods: Understanding geography through thick and thin. *Progress in Human Geography*, 41(1), 68–88.

Moallemi, E. A., and Malekpour, S. (2018). A participatory exploratory modelling approach for long-term planning in energy transitions. *Energy Research and Social Science*, *35*, 205–16.

Montag, W. (2016). From clinamen to conatus: Deleuze, Lucretius, Spinoza. In J. Lezra and L. Blake (eds), *Lucretius and Modernity: Epicurean Encounters across Time and Disciplines*, 163–72. Palgrave Macmillan.

Morewedge, C. K., Yoon, H., Scopelliti, I., Symborski, C. W., Korris, J. H., and Kassam, K. S. (2015). Debiasing decisions. *Policy Insights from the Behavioral and Brain Sciences*, *2*(1), 129–40. https://doi.org/10.1177/2372732215600886

Müller, M., and Schurr, C. (2016). Assemblage thinking and actor-network theory: Conjunctions, disjunctions, cross-fertilisations. *Transactions of the Institute of British Geographers*, *41*(3), 217–29.

Mythen, G., Walklate, S., and Peatfield, E.-J. (2017). Assembling and deconstructing radicalisation in PREVENT: A case of policy-based evidence making? *Critical Social Policy*, *37*(2), 180–201. https://doi.org/10.1177/0261018316683463

Nail, T. (2012). *Returning to Revolution: Deleuze, Guattari and Zapatismo*. Edinburgh University Press.

Nail, T. (2017). What is an assemblage? *SubStance*, *46*(1), 21–37.

Nelson-Pallmeyer, J. (2005). *Is Religion Killing Us? Violence in the Bible and the Quran*. Continuum.

Neumann, M. (2014). The escalation of ethnonationalist radicalization: Simulating the effectiveness of nationalist ideologies. *Social Science Computer Review*, *32*(3), 312–33.

Neumann, P., and Kleinmann, S. (2013). How rigorous is radicalization research? *Democracy and Security*, *9*(4), 360–82. https://doi.org/10.1080/17419166.2013.802984

Ng, B., and Gervais, W. M. (2017). Religion and prejudice. In C. G. Sibley (ed.), *The Cambridge Handbook of the Psychology of Prejudice*, 334–70. Cambridge University Press.

Nielbo, K. L., Braxton, D. M., and Upal, A. (2012). Computing religion: A new tool in the multilevel analysis of religion. *Method and Theory in the Study of Religion*, *24*(3), 267–90. https://doi.org/10.1163/157006812X635709

Nola, R. (2013). Do naturalistic explanations of religious beliefs debunk religion? In G. W. Dawes and J. Maclaurin (eds), *A New Science of Religion*, 162–88). Routledge.

Norenzayan, A. (2013). *Big Gods: How Religion Transformed Cooperation and Conflict*. Princeton University Press.

Norenzayan, A. (2015). Big questions about Big Gods: Response and discussion. *Religion, Brain and Behavior*, *5*(4), 327–42. https://doi.org/10.1080/2153599X.2014.928359

Norenzayan, A., Dar-nimrod, I., Hansen, I. G., and Proulx, T. (2009). Mortality salience and religion: Divergent effects on the defense of cultural worldviews for the religious and the non-religious. *European Journal of Social Psychology*, *39*(1), 101–13. https://doi.org/10.1002/ejsp.482

Norenzayan, A., Hansen, I. G., and Cady, J. (2008). An angry volcano? Reminders of death and anthropomorphizing nature. *Social Cognition*, *26*(2), 190–7. https://doi.org/10.1521/soco.2008.26.2.190

Norris, P., and Inglehart, R. (2011). *Sacred and Secular: Religion and Politics Worldwide* (2nd edn). Cambridge University Press.

Norris, P., and Inglehart, R. (2015). Are high levels of existential security conducive to secularization? A response to our critics. In Stanley D. Brunn (ed.), *The Changing World Religion Map*, 3389–408. Springer.

O'Sullivan, D. (2008). Geographical information science: Agent-based models. *Progress in Human Geography*, *32*(4), 541–50.

Padilla, J. J., Frydenlund, E., Wallewik, H., and Haaland, H. (2018). Model co-creation from a modeler's perspective: Lessons learned from the collaboration between ethnographers and modelers. In R. Thomson, C. Dancy, A. Hyder, and H. Bisgin (eds),

*Social, Cultural, and Behavioral Modeling*, 70–5. Springer International. https://doi.org/10.1007/978-3-319-93372-6_8

Palmer, J., and Owens, S. (2015). Indirect land-use change and biofuels: The contribution of assemblage theory to place-specific environmental governance. *Environmental Science and Policy*, 53, 18–26.

Paloutzian, R. F., Sagir, Z., and Shults, F. L. (2021). Modelling reconciliation and peace processes. In K. P. Clements and S. Y. Lee (eds), *Multi-Level Reconciliation and Peacebuilding: Stakeholder Perspectives*, 225–42. Routledge.

Parker, W. S. (2022). Evidence and knowledge from computer simulation. *Erkenntnis*, 87(4), 1521–38.

Patton, P. (2002). *Deleuze and the Political*. Routledge.

Paul, G. (2009). The chronic dependence of popular religiosity upon dysfunctional psychosociological conditions. *Evolutionary Psychology*, 7(3), 398–441.

Pazhoohi, F., Lang, M., Xygalatas, D., and Grammer, K. (2017). Religious veiling as a mate-guarding strategy: Effects of environmental pressures on cultural practices. *Evolutionary Psychological Science*, 3(2), 118–24. https://doi.org/10.1007/s40806-016-0079-z

Pedercini, M., Zuellich, G., Dianati, K., and Arquitt, S. (2018). Toward achieving sustainable development goals in Ivory Coast: Simulating pathways to sustainable development. *Sustainable Development*, 26(6), 588–95.

Pennycook, G., Cheyne, J. A., Barr, N., Koehler, D. J., and Fugelsang, J. A. (2014). Cognitive style and religiosity: The role of conflict detection. *Memory and Cognition*, 42(1), 1–10. https://doi.org/10.3758/s13421-013-0340-7

Pepys, R. (2016). *Developing Mathematical Models of Complex Social Processes: Radicalisation and Criminality Development* [PhD thesis, University College London]. http://discovery.ucl.ac.uk/1529407/1/PhD%20Thesis%20-%20Final.pdf

Pew Research Center. (2015). *The Future of World Religions: Population Growth Projections, 2010–2050*. Pew Research Center.

Pickren, G. (2018). 'The global assemblage of digital flow': Critical data studies and the infrastructures of computing. *Progress in Human Geography*, 42(2), 225–43.

Polhill, J., Ge, J., Hare, M., Matthews, K., Gimona, A., Salt, D., and Yeluripati, J. (2019). Crossing the chasm: A 'tube-map' for agent-based social simulation of policy scenarios in spatially-distributed systems. *GeoInformatica*, 23(2), 169–99. https://doi.org/10.1007/s10707-018-00340-z

Pow, C. P. (2014). License to travel: Policy assemblage and the 'Singapore model'. *City*, 18(3), 287–306.

Pretus, C., Hamid, N., Sheikh, H., Ginges, J., Tobeña, A., Davis, R., Vilarroya, O., and Atran, S. (2018). Neural and behavioral correlates of sacred values and vulnerability to violent extremism. *Frontiers in Psychology*, 9, 2462.

Price-Robertson, R., and Duff, C. (2016). Realism, materialism, and the assemblage: Thinking psychologically with Manuel DeLanda. *Theory and Psychology*, 26(1), 58–76.

Protevi, J. (2013). *Life, War, Earth: Deleuze and the Sciences*. University of Minnesota Press.

Protevi, J. (2018). November 28, 1947: How do you make yourself a Body without Organs? In H. Somers-Hall, J. A. Bell, and J. Williams (eds), *A Thousand Plateaus and Philosophy*, 99–114. Edinburgh University Press.

Puga-Gonzalez, I., Shults, F. L., Gore, R., and Talmont-Kaminski, K. (in press). The rise and fall of religion: A model-based exploration of secularisation, security and prosociality. In F. Squazzoni (ed.), *Advances in Social Simulation*. Springer.

Puga-Gonzalez, I., Voas, D., Kiszkiel, L., Bacon, R. J., Wildman, W. J., Talmont-Kaminski, K., and Shults, F. L. (2022). Modeling fuzzy fidelity: Using microsimulation to explore age, period, and cohort effects in secularization. *Journal of Religion and Demography*, 9(1–2), 111–37.

Puga-Gonzalez, I., Wildman, W. J., Diallo, S. Y., and Shults, F. L. (2019). Minority integration in a western city: An agent-based modeling approach. In In S. Y. Diallo, W. J. Wildman, F. L. Shults, and A. Tolk (eds), *Human Simulation: Perspectives, Insights, and Applications*, 179–90. Springer.

Puga-Gonzalez, I., Wildman, W. J., McCaffree, K., Cragun, R. T., and Shults, F. L. (2021). Incredulity in artificial societies. In P. Ahrweiler and M. Neumann (eds), *Advances in Social Simulation: Proceedings of the 15th Social Simulation Conference: 23–27 September 2019*, 81–94. Springer.

Purzycki, B. G., Apicella, C., Atkinson, Q. D., Cohen, E., Mcnamara, R. A., Willard, A. K., Xygalatas, D., Norenzayan, A., and Henrich, J. (2016). Moralistic gods, supernatural punishment and the expansion of human sociality. *Nature*, 530, 327–30. https://doi.org/10.1038/nature16980

Pyysiainen, I. (2009). *Supernatural Agents: Why We Believe in Souls, Gods and Buddhas*. Oxford University Press.

Ramanath, A. M., and Gilbert, N. (2004). The design of participatory agent-based social simulations. *Journal of Artificial Societies and Social Simulation*, 7(4), 1–22.

Ramey, J. (2012). *The Hermetic Deleuze: Philosophy and Spiritual Ordeal*. Duke University Press.

Rankin, K. N. (2008). Manufacturing rural finance in Asia: Institutional assemblages, market societies, entrepreneurial subjects. *Geoforum*, 39(6), 1965–77.

Rink, A., and Sharma, K. (2017). The determinants of religious radicalization: Evidence from Kenya. *Journal of Conflict Resolution*, 002200271667898. https://doi.org/10.1177/0022002716678986

Roberts, T. (2019). In pursuit of necessary joys: Deleuze, Spinoza, and the ethics of becoming active. *GeoHumanities*, 5(1), 124–38.

Robinson, C., Dilkina, B., and Moreno-Cruz, J. (2020). Modeling migration patterns in the USA under sea level rise. *PloS One*, 15(1), e0227436.

Roffe, J. (2015). The concept of the assemblage and the case of markets. In R. Canniford and D. Bajde (eds), *Assembling Consumption*, 42–56. Routledge.

Rogers, D. (2018). Assemblage theory and the ontological limitations of speculative realism. *Dialogues in Human Geography*, 8(2), 244–7.

Roitto, R. (2015). Dangerous but contagious altruism: Recruitment of group members and reform of cooperation style through altruism in two modified versions of Hammond and Axelrod's simulation of ethnocentric cooperation. *Religion, Brain and Behavior*, 6(2), 154–68.

Rolli, M. (2016). *Gilles Deleuze's Transcendental Empiricism: From Tradition to Difference*. Edinburgh University Press.

Rosenblatt, A., Greenberg, J., Solomon, S., Pyszczynski, T., and Lyon, D. (1989). Evidence for terror management theory: I. The effects of mortality salience on reactions to those who violate or uphold cultural values. *Journal of Personality and Social Psychology*, 57(4), 681–90. https://doi.org/10.1037/0022-3514.57.4.681

Rossano, M. (2010). *Supernatural Selection: How Religion Evolved*. Oxford University Press.

Routledge, C., Roylance, C., and Abeyta, A. (2017). Miraculous meaning: Threatened meaning increases belief in miracles. *Journal of Religion and Health*, 56(3), 776–83. https://doi.org/10.1007/s10943-015-0124-4

Ruddick, S. (2012). Power and the problem of composition. *Dialogues in Human Geography*, 2(2), 207–11.

Rybnik, M., Puga-Gonzalez, I., Shults, F. L., Dabrowska-Prokopowska, E., and Talmont-Kaminski, K. (in press). An agent-based model of the role of epistemic vigilance in human cooperation. In F. Squazzoni (ed.), *Advances in Social Simulation*. Springer.

Saldanha, A., and Stark, H. (2016). A new earth: Deleuze and Guattari in the Anthropocene. *Deleuze Studies*, 10(4), 427–39.

## REFERENCES

Scheve, K., Stasavage, D., and others. (2006). Religion and preferences for social insurance. *Quarterly Journal of Political Science*, 1(3), 255–86.

Schilbrack, K. (2014). *Philosophy and the Study of Religions: A Manifesto*. John Wiley and Sons.

Schjoedt, U., Geertz, A. W., Schjoedt, U., Stødkilde-Jørgensen, H., Schjoedt, U., Lund, T. E., Roepstorff, A., and Roepstorff, A. (2011). The power of charisma – perceived charisma inhibits the frontal executive network of believers in intercessory prayer. *Social Cognitive and Affective Neuroscience*, 6(1), 119–27. https://doi.org/10.1093/scan/nsq023

Schjoedt, U., Sørensen, J., Nielbo, K. L., Xygalatas, D., Mitkidis, P., and Bulbulia, J. (2013). Cognitive resource depletion in religious interactions. *Religion, Brain and Behavior*, 3(1), 39–55.

Schmid, P., and Betsch, C. (2019). Effective strategies for rebutting science denialism in public discussions. *Nature Human Behaviour*, 3(9), 931–9.

Schofield, M. B., Baker, I. S., Staples, P., and Sheffield, D. (2016). Mental representations of the supernatural: A cluster analysis of religiosity, spirituality and paranormal belief. *Personality and Individual Differences*, 101, 419–24. https://doi.org/10.1016/j.paid.2016.06.020

Schuurmans-Stekhoven, J. (2016). Are we, like sheep, going astray: Is costly signaling (or any other mechanism) necessary to explain the belief-as-benefit effect? *Religion, Brain and Behavior*, 7(3), 258–62. https://doi.org/10.1080/2153599X.2016.1156558

Seifert, C. M. (2002). The continued influence of misinformation in memory: What makes a correction effective? In Brian H. Ross (ed.), *Psychology of Learning and Motivation*, Vol. 41, 265–92. Elsevier.

Sekerdej, M., Kossowska, M., and Czernatowicz-Kukuczka, A. (2018). Uncertainty and prejudice: The role of religiosity in shaping group attitudes. *European Journal of Social Psychology*, 48(2), O91–O102.

Sela, Y., Shackelford, T. K., and Liddle, J. R. (2015). When religion makes it worse: Religiously motivated violence as a sexual selection weapon. In D. J. Slone and J. A. van Slyke (eds), *The Attraction of Religion: A New Evolutionary Psychology of Religion*, 111–31. Bloomsbury.

Shaver, J. H., Troughton, G., Sibley, C. G., and Bulbulia, J. A. (2016). Religion and the unmaking of prejudice toward Muslims: Evidence from a large national sample. *PLoS ONE*, 11(3). https://doi.org/10.1371/journal.pone.0150209

Shaw, I. G. (2012). Towards an eventalgeography. *Progress in Human Geography*, 36(5), 613–27.

Sheikh, H., Atran, S., Ginges, J., Wilson, L., Obeid, N., and Davis, R. (2014). The devoted actor as parochial altruist: Sectarian morality, identity fusion, and support for costly sacrifices. *Cliodynamics*, 5(1), 23–40.

Sheikh, H., Ginges, J., and Atran, S. (2013). Sacred values in the Israeli–Palestinian conflict: Resistance to social influence, temporal discounting, and exit strategies. *Annals of the New York Academy of Sciences*, 12991(1), 11–24. https://doi.org/10.1111/nyas.12275

Shook, J. R. (2015). Philosophy of religion and two types of atheology. *International Journal of Philosophy and Theology*, 76(1), 1–19. https://doi.org/10.1080/21692327.2015.1041547

Shterin, M., and Yarlykapov, A. (2011). Reconsidering radicalisation and terrorism: The New Muslims movement in Kabardino-Balkaria and its path to violence. *Religion, State and Society*, 39(2–3), 303–25. https://doi.org/10.1080/09637494.2011.604512

Shults, F. L. (2011). De-oedipalizing theology: Desire, difference, and Deleuze. In F. L. Shults and J.-O. Henriksen (eds), *Saving Desire: The Seduction of Christian Theology*, 73–104. Eerdmans.

Shults, F. L. (2014a). Excavating theogonies: Anthropomorphic promiscuity and sociographic prudery in the Neolithic and now. In I. Hodder (ed.), *Religion at Work in a Neolithic Society: Vital Matters*, 58–85. Cambridge University Press.

Shults, F. L. (2014b). *Iconoclastic Theology: Gilles Deleuze and the Secretion of Atheism*. Edinburgh University Press.

# REFERENCES

Shults, F. L. (2014c). *Theology after the Birth of God: Atheist Conceptions in Cognition and Culture.* Palgrave Macmillan.

Shults, F. L. (2015a). Can theism be defeated? CSR and the debunking of supernatural agent abductions. *Religion, Brain and Behavior, 6*(4), 349–55. https://doi.org/10.1080/2153599X.2015.1107251

Shults, F. L. (2015b). How to survive the Anthropocene: Adaptive atheism and the evolution of *Homo deiparensis*. *Religions, 6*(2), 1–18. https://doi.org/10.3390/rel6020724

Shults, F. L. (2016). The atheist machine. In F. L. Shults and L. Powell-Jones (eds), *Deleuze and the Schizoanalysis of Religion,* 163–92). Bloomsbury.

Shults, F. L. (2018a). Can we predict and prevent religious radicalization? In G. Øverland (ed.), *Violent Extremism in the 21st Century: International Perspectives,* 45–71. Cambridge Scholars Press.

Shults, F. L. (2018b). *Practicing Safe Sects: Religious Reproduction in Scientific and Philosophical Perspective.* Brill.

Shults, F. L. (2018c). Strategies for promoting safe sects: Response to Brandon Daniel-Hughes and Jeffrey B. Speaks. *American Journal of Theology and Philosophy, 39*(3), 80–93.

Shults, F. L. (2019a). A germ of tranquil atheism. *Swedish Theological Quarterly, 3,* 183–94.

Shults, F. L. (2019b). Computer modeling in philosophy of religion. *Open Philosophy, 2*(1) 108–25. https://doi.org/10.1515/opphil-2019-0011.

Shults, F. L. (2019c). Modeling metaphysics: The rise of simulation and the reversal of Platonism. *Proceedings of the 2019 Spring Simulation Conference,* 1–12. IEEE. https://doi.org/10.23919/SpringSim.2019.8732897

Shults, F. L. (2020a). Simulating machines: Modeling, metaphysics, and the Mechanosphere. *Deleuze and Guattari Studies, 14*(3), 349–74. https://doi.org/10.3366/dlgs.2020.0408

Shults, F. L. (2020b). Toxic theisms? New strategies for prebunking religious belief-behavior complexes. *Journal of Cognitive Historiography, 5*(2), 18–36. https://doi.org/10.1558/jch.38074

Shults, F. L. (2021a). Evolutionary ethics and adaptive atheism. *Religion, Brain and Behavior, 11*(1), 90–8.

Shults, F. L. (2021b). Theory and data in a computational model of secularization. *Bulletin for the Study of Religion, 50*(3), 98–104.

Shults, F. L. (2021c). Simulating secularities: Challenges and opportunities in the computational science of (non)religion. *Secularism and Nonreligion, 10*(1), Article 1. https://doi.org/10.5334/snr.154

Shults, F. L. (2022a). Progress in simulating human geography: Assemblage theory and the practice of multi-agent artificial intelligence modeling. *Progress in Human Geography,* 03091325211059567. https://doi.org/10.1177/03091325211059567

Shults, F. L. (2022b). The model(ing) philosophy of Wesley Wildman. In F. L. Shults and R. C. Neville (eds), *Religion in Multidisciplinary Perspective: Philosophical, Theological, and Scientific Approaches to Wesley J. Wildman,* 13–36. SUNY Press.

Shults, F. L. (2023). Simulation, science, and stakeholders: Challenges and opportunities for modelling solutions to societal problems. *Complexity,* 1–10. https://doi.org/10.1155/2023/1375004

Shults, F. L., and Gore, R. (2020). Modeling radicalization and violent extremism. In H. Verhagen, M. Borit, G. Bravo, and N. Wijermans (eds), *Advances in Social Simulation,* 405–10. Springer.

Shults, F. L., Gore, R., Lemos, C., and Wildman, W. J. (2018a). Why do the godless prosper? Modeling the cognitive and coalitional mechanisms that promote atheism. *Psychology of Religion and Spirituality, 10*(3), 218–28.

Shults, F. L., Gore, R., Wildman, W. J., Lynch, C., Lane, J. E., and Toft, M. (2018b). A generative model of the mutual escalation of anxiety between religious groups. *Journal of Artificial Societies and Social Simulation, 21*(4). https://doi.org/10.18564/jasss.3840.

# REFERENCES

Shults, F. L., Lane, J. E., Diallo, S., Lynch, C., Wildman, W. J., and Gore, R. (2018). Modeling terror management theory: Computer simulations of the impact of mortality salience on religiosity. *Religion, Brain and Behavior*, 8(1), 77–100.

Shults, F. L., and Wildman, W. J. (2018). Simulating religious entanglement and social investment in the Neolithic. In I. Hodder (ed.), *Religion, History and Place in the Origin of Settled Life*, 33–63. University of Colorado Press.

Shults, F. L., and Wildman, W. J. (2019). Ethics, computer simulation, and the future of humanity. In S. Y. Diallo, W. J. Wildman, F. L. Shults, and A. Tolk (eds), *Human Simulation: Perspectives, Insights and Applications*, 21–40. Springer.

Shults, F. L., and Wildman, W. J. (2020a). Artificial social ethics: Simulating culture, conflict, and cooperation. *Proceedings of the 2020 Spring Simulation Conference*, 1–10. IEEE. https://doi.org/10.22360/SpringSim.2020.HSAA.003

Shults, F. L., and Wildman, W. J. (2020b). Human simulation and sustainability: Ontological, epistemological, and ethical reflections. *Sustainability*, 12(23), 10039.

Shults, F. L., & Wildman, W. (2023). The Methodological Naturalism and Methodological Secularism Scale: Shedding New Light on Scholarship in Religion. *Bulletin for the Study of Religion*, 51(3-4), 92-102. https://doi.org/10.1558/bsor.23700

Shults, F. L., Wildman, W. J., Diallo, S., Puga-Gonzalez, I., and Voas, D. (2020a). The artificial society analytics platform. In H. Verhagen et al. (eds), *Advances in Social Simulation: Looking in the Mirror*, 411–26. Springer.

Shults, F. L., Wildman, W. J., and Dignum, V. (2018). The ethics of computer modeling and simulation. *Proceedings of the 2018 Winter Simulation Conference*, 4069–83. IEEE. https://doi.org/10.1109/WSC.2018.8632517

Shults, F. L., Wildman, W. J., Lane, J. E., Lynch, C., and Diallo, S. (2018). Multiple axialities: A computational model of the axial age. *Journal of Cognition and Culture*, 18(4), 537–64.

Shults, F. L., Wildman, W. J., Taves, A., and Paloutzian, R. F. (2020b). What do religion scholars really want? Scholarly values in the scientific study of religion. *Journal for the Scientific Study of Religion*, 59(1), 18–38.

Shults, F. L., Wildman, W. J., Toft, M. D., and Danielson, A. (2021). Artificial societies in the Anthropocene: Challenges and opportunities for modeling climate, conflict, and cooperation. *Proceedings of the 2021 Winter Simulation Conference*, 1–12. IEEE. https://doi.org/10.1109/WSC52266.2021.9715391

Simpson, C. B. (2012). *Deleuze and Theology*. A&C Black.

Sirseloudi, M. P. (2005). How to predict the unpredictable: On the early detection of terrorist campaigns. *Defense and Security Analysis*, 21(4), 369–86. https://doi.org/10.1080/1475179052000345421

Sirseloudi, M. P. (2012). The meaning of religion and identity for the violent radicalisation of the Turkish diaspora in Germany. *Terrorism and Political Violence*, 24(5), 807–24. https://doi.org/10.1080/09546553.2011.644105

Slone, D. J. (2007). *Theological Incorrectness: Why Religious People Believe What They Shouldn't*. Oxford University Press.

Slone, D. J., and Slyke, J. A. V. (eds) (2015). *The Attraction of Religion: A New Evolutionary Psychology of Religion*. Bloomsbury.

Smith, A. P. (2010). Believing in this world for the making of gods: Ecology of the virtual and the actual. *SubStance*, 39(1), 103–14.

Smith, D. (2012). *Essays on Deleuze*. Edinburgh University Press.

Smith, D. (2018). What is the body without organs? Machine and organism in Deleuze and Guattari. *Continental Philosophy Review*, 51, 95–110.

Somers-Hall, H., Bell, J. A., and Williams, J. (eds) (2018). *A Thousand Plateaus and Philosophy*. Edinburgh University Press.

Sosis, R., Phillips, E. J., and Alcorta, C. S. (2012). Sacrifice and sacred values: Evolutionary perspectives on religious terrorism. In T. Shackelford (ed.), *The Oxford Handbook of Evolutionary Perspectives on Violence, Homicide and War*, 233–53. Oxford University Press.

Speaks, J. B. (2018). Safe and responsible God-talk: Beyond F. LeRon Shults's 'abstinence-only' version of 'the talk'. *American Journal of Theology and Philosophy*, *39*(3), 65–79.

Squazzoni, F. (2009). *Epistemological Aspects of Computer Simulation in the Social Sciences*. Springer.

Squazzoni, F. (2012). *Agent-based Computational Sociology*. John Wiley and Sons.

Squazzoni, F., Jager, W., and Edmonds, B. (2014). Social simulation in the social sciences. *Social Science Computer Review*, *32*(3), 279–94. https://doi.org/10.1177/0894439313512975

Stephens, M. (2014). *Imagine There's No Heaven: How Atheism Helped Create the Modern World*. Palgrave Macmillan.

Stinespring, J., and Cragun, R. T. (2015). Simple Markov model for estimating the growth of nonreligion in the United States. *Science, Religion and Culture*, *2*(3), 96–103. https://doi.org/10.17582/journal.src/2015/2.3.96.103

Stoet, G., and Geary, D. C. (2017). Students in countries with higher levels of religiosity perform lower in science and mathematics. *Intelligence*, *62*, 71–8. https://doi.org/10.1016/j.intell.2017.03.001

Strulik, H. (2016). An economic theory of religious belief. *Journal of Economic Behavior and Organization*, *128*, 35–46. https://doi.org/10.1016/j.jebo.2016.04.007

Subrahmanian, V. S. (ed.) (2013). *Handbook of Computational Approaches to Counterterrorism*. Springer.

Swann, W. B., Gómez, Á., Buhrmester, M. D., López-Rodríguez, L., Jiménez, J., and Vázquez, A. (2014). Contemplating the ultimate sacrifice: Identity fusion channels pro-group affect, cognition, and moral decision making. *Journal of Personality and Social Psychology*, *106*(5), 713–27. https://doi.org/10.1037/a0035809

Swann, W. B., Gómez, A., Dovidio, J. F., Hart, S., and Jetten, J. (2010). Dying and killing for one's group: Identity fusion moderates responses to intergroup versions of the trolley problem. *Psychological Science*, *21*(8), 1176–83. https://doi.org/10.1177/0956797610376656

Tajfel, H. (ed.) (2010). *Social Identity and Intergroup Relations*. Cambridge University Press.

Tajfel, H., and Turner, J. (1979). An integrative theory of intergroup conflict. In W. Austin and S. Worchel (eds), *The Social Psychology of Intergroup Relations*, 33–47. Brooks Cole.

Talmont-Kaminski, K. (2014). *Religion as Magical Ideology: How the Supernatural Reflects Rationality*. Routledge.

Taves, A., Wildman, W. J., Shults, F. L., and Paloutzian, R. F. (2022). Scholarly values, methods, and evidence in the academic study of religion. *Method and Theory in the Study of Religion*, *1*, 1–29.

Teehan, J. (2010). *In the Name of God: The Evolutionary Origins of Religious Ethics and Violence*. Wiley-Blackwell.

Teehan, J. (2013). The cognitive bases of the problem of evil. *The Monist*, *96*(3), 325.

Tobia, K. P. (2016). Does religious belief infect philosophical analysis? *Religion, Brain and Behavior*, *6*(1), 56–66. https://doi.org/10.1080/2153599X.2014.1000952

Tolk, A. (2012). *Engineering Principles of Combat Modeling and Distributed Simulation*. John Wiley and Sons.

Tolk, A. (2013). Truth, trust, and Turing: Implications for modeling and simulation. In A. Tolk (ed.), *Ontology, Epistemology, and Teleology for Modeling and Simulation*, 1–26. Springer.

Tolk, A. (2015). Learning something right from models that are wrong: Epistemology of simulation. In L. Yilmaz (ed.), *Concepts and Methodologies for Modeling and Simulation*, 87–106. Springer.

Torrey, E. F. (2017). *Evolving Brains, Emerging Gods: Early Humans and the Origins of Religion*. Columbia University Press.

Tremlin, T. (2010). *Minds and Gods*. Oxford University Press.

Turker, K. A., and Murphy, J. T. (2019). Assembling community economies. *Progress in Human Geography*, 45(1), 49–69.

Turner, J. H., Maryanski, A., Petersen, A. K., and Geertz, A. W. (2017). *The Emergence and Evolution of Religion: By Means of Natural Selection*. Routledge.

Turpin, H., Andersen, M., and Lanman, J. A. (2019). CREDs, CRUDs, and Catholic scandals: Experimentally examining the effects of religious paragon behavior on co-religionist belief. *Religion, Brain and Behavior*, 9(2), 143–55. https://doi.org/10.1080/2153599X.2018.1439087

Twenge, J. M. (2015). Generational and time period differences in American adolescents' religious orientation, 1966–2014. *PLOS ONE*, 10(5), 1–17.

Upal, M. A. (2005). Simulating the emergence of new religious movements. *Journal of Artificial Societies and Social Simulation*, 8(1), 1–18.

Vail, K. E., Arndt, J., and Abdollahi, A. (2012). Exploring the existential function of religion and supernatural agent beliefs among Christians, Muslims, atheists, and agnostics. *Personality and Social Psychology Bulletin*, 38(10), 1288–300.

Vail, K. E., and Soenke, M. (2018). The impact of mortality awareness on meaning in life among Christians and atheists. *Religion, Brain and Behavior*, 8(1), 44–56.

van Der Tempel, J., and Alcock, J. E. (2015). Relationships between conspiracy mentality, hyperactive agency detection, and schizotypy: Supernatural forces at work? *Personality and Individual Differences*, 82, 136–41. https://doi.org/10.1016/j.paid.2015.03.010

van der Zant, T., Kouw, M., and Schomaker, L. (2013). Generative artificial intelligence. In V. C. Müller (ed.), *Philosophy and Theory of Artificial Intelligence*, 107–20. Springer.

van Eyghen, H. (2016). Two types of 'explaining away' arguments in the cognitive science of religion. *Zygon*, 51(4), 966–82.

Van Heerden, C. G. (2019). *Deleuze and Anarchism*. Edinburgh University Press.

Van Wezemael, J. (2008). The contribution of assemblage theory and minor politics for democratic network governance. *Planning Theory*, 7(2), 165–85.

Voas, D. (2009). The rise and fall of fuzzy fidelity in Europe. *European Sociological Review*, 25(2), 155–68. https://doi.org/10.1093/esr/jcn044

Voas, D., and Chaves, M. (2016). Is the United States a counterexample to the secularization thesis? *American Journal of Sociology*, 121(5), Article 5. https://doi.org/10.1086/684202

Voinea, C. F. (2016). *Political Attitudes: Computational and Simulation Modelling*. John Wiley and Sons.

Voland, E., and Schiefenhövel, W. (eds) (2009). *The Biological Evolution of Religious Mind and Behavior*. Springer.

Voss, D. (2013). *Conditions of Thought*. Edinburgh University Press.

Watson, P. (2014). *The Age of Atheists: How We Have Sought to Live Since the Death of God*. Simon and Schuster.

Watts, J., Greenhill, S. J., Atkinson, Q. D., Currie, T. E., Bulbulia, J., and Gray, R. D. (2015). Broad supernatural punishment but not moralizing high gods precede the evolution of political complexity in Austronesia. *Proceedings of the Royal Society B: Biological Sciences*, 282(1804), 20142556.

Webber, D., Babush, M., Schori-Eyal, N., Vazeou-Nieuwenhuis, A., Hettiarachchi, M., Bélanger, J. J., Moyano, M., Trujillo, H. M., Gunaratna, R., Kruglanski, A. W., and Gelfand, M. J. (2017). The road to extremism: Field and experimental evidence that significance loss-induced need for closure fosters radicalization. *Journal of Personality and Social Psychology*, 114(2), 270–85. https://doi.org/10.1037/pspi0000111

# REFERENCES

Weidmann, N. B., and Salehyan, I. (2013). Violence and ethnic segregation: A computational model applied to Baghdad. *International Studies Quarterly*, 57(1), 52–64. https://doi.org/10.1111/isqu.12059

Weisberg, M. (2012). *Simulation and Similarity: Using Models to Understand the World*. Oxford University Press.

Welch, M. R., Sikkink, D., and Loveland, M. T. (2007). The radius of trust: Religion, social embeddedness and trust in strangers. *Social Forces*, 86(1), 23–46.

Wellman, Jr, J. K. (ed.) (2007). *Belief and Bloodshed: Religion and Violence across Time and Tradition*. Rowman and Littlefield.

Welton, W. A. (2002). *Plato's Forms: Varieties of Interpretation*. Lexington Books.

Whitehouse, H., François, P., Savage, P. E., Currie, T. E., Feeney, K. C., Cioni, E., Purcell, R., Ross, R. M., Larson, J., and Baines, J. (2019). Complex societies precede moralizing gods throughout world history. *Nature*, 568(7751), 226–9.

Whitehouse, H., and Hodder, I. (2010). Modes of religiosity at Catalhoyuk. In I. Hodder (ed.), *Religion in the Emergence of Civilization: Catalhoyuk as a Case Study*, 122–45. Cambridge University Press.

Whitehouse, H., Kahn, K., Hochberg, M. E., and Bryson, J. J. (2012). The role for simulations in theory construction for the social sciences: Case studies concerning divergent modes of religiosity. *Religion, Brain & Behavior*, 2(3), 182–201.

Whitehouse, H., Mazzucato, C., Hodder, I., and Atkinson, Q. D. (2014). Modes of religiosity and the evolution of social complexity at Catalhoyuk. In I. Hodder (ed.), *Religion at Work in a Neolithic Society*, 134–55. Cambridge University Press.

Wichman, A. L. (2010). Uncertainty and religious reactivity: Uncertainty compensation, repair, and inoculation. *European Journal of Social Psychology*, 40(1), 35–42. https://doi.org/10.1002/ejsp.712

Widder, N. (2012). *Political Theory after Deleuze*. Bloomsbury.

Wildman, W. J. (2011). *Religious Philosophy as Multidisciplinary Comparative Inquiry: Envisioning a Future for the Philosophy of Religion*. SUNY Press.

Wildman, W. J. (2018). Reforming philosophy of religion for the modern academy. In J. Kanaris (ed.), *Reconfigurations of Philosophy of Religion: A Possible Future*, 253–69. SUNY Press.

Wildman, W. J., Diallo, S. Y., and Shults, F. L. (2021). Advanced computational methods. In S. Engler and M. Stausberg (eds), *The Routledge Handbook of Research Methods in the Study of Religion*, 136–53. Routledge.

Wildman, W. J., Fishwick, P. A., and Shults, F. L. (2017). Teaching at the intersection of simulation and the humanities. *Proceedings of the 2017 Winter Simulation Conference*, 4162–74. IEEE. https://doi.org/10.1109/WSC.2017.8248136.

Wildman, W. J., and Rohr, D. (2018). North American philosophers of religion: How they see their field. In P. Draper and J. L. Schellenberg (eds), *Renewing Philosophy of Religion: Exploratory Essays*, 133–52. Oxford University Press.

Wildman, W. J., and Shults, F. L. (2018). Emergence: What does it mean and how is it relevant to computer engineering? In S. Mittal, S. Diallo, and A. Tolk (eds), *Emergent Behavior in Complex Systems Engineering: A Modeling and Simulation Approach*, 21–34. John Wiley and Sons.

Wildman, W. J., and Shults, F. L. (in press). *Modeling Religion*. Bloomsbury.

Wildman, W. J., Shults, F. L., and Diallo, S. Y. (2021). Computational demography of religion: A proposal. In P. Ahrweiler and M. Neumann (eds), *Advances in Social Simulation*, 169–82. Springer.

Wildman, W. J., Shults, F. L., Diallo, S. Y., Gore, R., and Lane, J. E. (2020). Post-supernaturalist cultures: There and back again. *Secularism and Nonreligion*, 9, Article 6. https://doi.org/10.5334/snr.121.

# REFERENCES

Wildman, W. J., and Sosis, R. (2011). Stability of groups with costly beliefs and practices. *Journal of Artificial Societies and Social Simulation*, *14*(3), 1–14.

Wilner, A. S., and Dubouloz, C.-J. (2011). Transformative radicalization: Applying learning theory to Islamist radicalization. *Studies in Conflict & Terrorism*, *34*(5), 418–38.

Winkelman, M. (2010). *Shamanism: A Biopsychosocial Paradigm of Consciousness and Healing*. ABC-CLIO.

Winsberg, E. (2010). *Science in the Age of Computer Simulation*. University of Chicago Press.

Wlodarski, R., and Pearce, E. (2016). The God allusion: Individual variation in agency detection, mentalizing and schizotypy and their association with religious beliefs and behaviors. *Human Nature*, *27*(2), 160–72. https://doi.org/10.1007/s12110-016-9256-9

Wohlrab-Sahr, M., and Burchardt, M. (2012). Multiple secularities: Toward a cultural sociology of secular modernities. *Comparative Sociology*, *11*(6), 875–909. https://doi.org/10.1163/15691330-12341249

Wolfram, S. (2002). *A New Kind of Science*, Vol. 5. Wolfram Media.

Xenitidou, M., and Edmonds, B. (eds) (2014). *The Complexity of Social Norms*. Springer.

Yilmaz, L. (2015). *Concepts and Methodologies for Modeling and Simulation*. Springer International Publishing.

Youngman, P. A., and Hadzikadic, M. (2014). *Complexity and the Human Experience: Modeling Complexity in the Humanities and Social Sciences*. Pan Stanford.

Zmigrod, L., Rentfrow, P. J., Zmigrod, S., and Robbins, T. W. (2019). Cognitive flexibility and religious disbelief. *Psychological Research*, *83*, 1749–59. https://doi.org/10.1007/s00426-018-1034-3

Zuckerman, M., Silberman, J., and Hall, J. A. (2013). The relation between intelligence and religiosity: A meta-analysis and some proposed explanations. *Personality and Social Psychology Review*, *17*(4), 325–54. https://doi.org/10.1177/1088868313497266

Zuckerman, P. (2009). Atheism, secularity, and well-being: How the findings of social science counter negative stereotypes and assumptions. *Sociology Compass*, *3*(6), 949–71.

Zuckerman, P. (2010). *Society without God: What the Least Religious Nations Can Tell Us About Contentment*. NYU Press.

# Index

abstract machine, 1, 13–17, 38, 39, 42, 43, 49, 66, 70, 78–80, 85, 188, 190
actual, the, 1, 16, 25, 35, 46, 52–3, 56, 59, 63–9, 71–2, 75, 83, 85–7, 91–2, 122, 166–8, 182–3, 198
Anthropocene, 25, 27, 127, 129, 132, 146–8, 150–1, 172–3
anthropomorphic promiscuity, 30–2, 34, 36–7, 48, 49, 51, 90, 92, 103, 105, 107, 114, 116, 128, 133, 163, 167
anthropomorphic prudery, 37, 43, 46, 115, 142, 164, 169
Aristotle, 7, 9, 53–5, 63, 68, 78
art, 3, 7, 16–19, 48, 189, 191, 192, 195–6
artificial intelligence, 58, 95, 102 *see also* multi-agent artificial intelligence
artificial society, 24, 60, 70, 87, 88, 90–1, 94, 96, 101, 102, 115, 118–9, 124, 149, 166, 169
assemblages, 1, 12, 14–16, 22, 24–5, 32–3, 38–9, 43, 52–3, 59, 64, 66–8, 70–94, 98, 106, 122–5, 127, 130–1, 150, 153, 168, 171–2, 177, 182, 188–9, 193, 198
  atheist, 6, 16–19, 33, 37, 50, 159, 175, 190
  collective assemblages of enunciation, 16, 75, 97
  machinic assemblages, 6–7, 13–14, 16, 37, 75, 159, 177
atheist machine, 1–2, 6–7, 11–13, 16–19, 21, 25–7, 33, 37, 43, 45–8, 51, 69, 93, 125–6, 151–4, 159, 161, 169, 175, 179–80, 185, 190, 193–4, 198
axial age, 27, 33–5, 37, 48, 50, 106–7, 128–30, 140, 157–9, 167
bias, 2, 19, 25, 27–33, 37, 40, 45–6, 92, 103, 106, 127–36, 139, 141, 143–7, 150–1, 153–4, 158–68, 173, 198
bio-cultural study of religion, 2, 5, 19, 25–6, 29–31, 38, 40, 46, 48, 60, 70, 98, 105, 114, 130, 138, 150, 153, 155, 169–71, 198
Body without Organs, 5, 21, 69, 80, 174–89, 192, 194, 197–8
Buchanan, Ian, 77–8

causality, 24, 65, 76, 87, 124, 132, 167
Christ, 4, 152–158
Christianity, 3, 6–7, 9–12, 25, 37, 98–9, 121, 142, 152–4, 156–60, 179
cognitive science, 2, 26, 61, 128, 142, 155, 163
computer modelling and simulation, 1, 20–5, 52–3, 55, 58–61, 67, 69, 73–8, 80–9, 93–9, 103, 112, 115, 123–5, 153, 164–9, 171, 173, 183, 193, 198
confessions, 2, 6, 99, 141, 180, 193

Daniel-Hughes, Brandon, 126, 133–42
DeLanda, Manuel, 22–3, 25, 52, 58–9, 61–71, 73–8, 80–9, 91–2, 94, 97, 122–23, 168

emergence, 1, 24, 52–3, 59–61, 68, 74–7, 80–4, 89–90, 92, 99, 107, 114, 118–9, 124, 168–9, 171, 193, 198
Epicurus, 8, 10, 52
epistemology, 1, 22, 25, 55, 61, 99, 121, 123, 143, 164, 167, 169, 192
ethics, 1, 5, 7, 8, 10, 20, 22, 25, 55, 93, 97, 112, 151–3, 164, 167, 169–71, 175, 178, 180, 194–5

Foucault, 75, 78, 194–5

God, 4–6, 10–1, 20, 26, 34–6, 39, 42, 45–6, 50–1, 140–1, 152, 158, 161–2, 164, 168, 197
  death of, 1, 11, 153, 191
  judgement of, 172, 176–87, 192

Hume, David, 5, 56

# INDEX

immanence, 1, 3, 5, 7, 10–1, 13–15, 17–8, 20–1, 25, 35, 46, 52–3, 56, 58, 60–1, 65, 67, 69, 71, 75, 78–80, 83, 158, 160, 169, 173, 175–8, 180–1, 185, 189–93, 197–8

infinity, 8, 10–12, 18, 33–7, 98, 107, 125, 128, 158, 174, 176–7, 179–80, 194–5, 197

intensities, 14, 21, 175, 177–8, 180–2, 184–5, 187, 189, 195, 197

intensity, 16, 49, 65, 68, 109, 135, 141, 154, 178–9, 187, 197

intentionality, 29, 34–6, 41, 48, 105, 178, 185, 195, 197

joy, 8, 10–12, 18, 154, 174, 176, 180–2, 194, 197–8

Kant, Immanuel, 5, 56, 170

Lane, Justin, 61, 87, 88, 90, 99, 102, 115
Lucretius, 8, 11, 20, 174, 180, 194

metaphysics, 1, 7, 14, 25, 53–6, 58, 60–1, 63–4, 67, 69, 71, 75, 78–80, 97, 122, 126, 164, 167, 169, 175

monotheism, 1, 12, 26, 34–6, 42–3, 46, 49–51, 98, 107, 114, 125, 130, 153, 158–61, 168, 172, 179, 181, 197

morality, 11, 136, 148, 167, 171, 197

multi-agent artificial intelligence, 1, 23, 25, 58, 61, 74, 81, 83, 86–7, 91, 95, 98, 101–2, 113, 115, 122, 124–5, 149, 168, 193, 198

multiplicity, 11–12, 14, 22, 52, 61–4, 67–8, 71, 76, 80, 83, 122–3, 154, 185, 187–8, 198

naturalism, 2, 8, 16, 18–20, 27, 33, 37, 43–6, 50–1, 61, 82, 115, 119–20, 125–6, 132–4, 136–9, 146–8, 159–60, 164, 167, 169, 174, 198

neolithic, 28, 33, 48–9, 51, 99

Nietzsche, 2, 4–5, 8–11, 20, 52–3, 56, 123, 153–4, 174, 178–81, 190, 194

nomads, 2, 4, 7, 13, 21, 40, 42–3, 45, 49, 51, 80, 126, 175, 178, 186, 189, 195

Oedipus, 4–5, 11, 13–14, 18, 40, 42–3, 154, 174, 177, 182, 187–8, 190, 194, 197

ontology, 1, 22, 52–3, 61, 66, 68–9, 71, 78, 84, 169, 198

philosophy, 1–13, 15–23, 25, 33, 44, 48, 52–5, 58–61, 64–5, 73–9, 81–3, 86–7, 95, 98–9, 121–5, 128, 142, 151, 153, 161–2, 164–9, 171, 174–80, 184–5, 189–94, 197–8

philosophy of religion, 12, 25, 44, 153, 161–2, 164–7, 169

Plato, 9, 15, 53–7, 59, 63–4, 68, 71, 167, 190

Platonism, 9, 14–15, 18, 25, 52–3, 55–8, 61–2, 64, 69–71, 73, 75, 78–80, 83, 85, 121, 168, 174, 185, 189, 195

priests, 4–6, 10, 12, 29, 34–7, 39, 42, 50, 61, 130, 133, 158–9, 164, 175, 178, 181, 190

radicalisation, 98–9, 102, 106–14, 117

schizoanalysis, 1, 4–5, 13, 18–19, 46, 51, 154, 174

secularism, 2, 16, 18–20, 27, 33, 37, 43–6, 50–1, 61, 100–1, 114, 119, 125–6, 132–3, 137, 146–9, 160, 164, 167, 169, 198

serenity, 1, 3, 11, 25, 125, 175, 193–8

simulacra, 8–9, 15, 18, 56–8, 70, 79, 97, 121, 125, 174, 185, 197

singularities, 16, 63–8, 71, 79–80, 836, 88–92, 97, 123–4, 160, 168, 183, 195–8

sociographic promiscuity, 37, 41–3, 46, 106, 115, 132, 142, 164, 169

sociographic prudery, 30–2, 34, 36–7, 42, 48, 50–1, 91–2, 103–4, 106–7, 114, 116, 128, 131, 133–4, 163, 167

sorcery, 7, 175, 184–9, 193, 198
Speaks, Jeffrey, 126, 133–8, 140–2
Spinoza, 2, 5, 8, 10, 20, 52, 174, 178, 180–1, 194

spirituality, 147, 175, 192–3, 196
state, 3, 15, 18, 38–40, 43, 47, 180, 186, 188

Stoics, 5, 9–10, 52, 57, 170, 195
sustainability, 25, 72, 77, 88, 92–3, 95–6, 125, 127, 146–8, 150

theism, 7, 12, 16, 25, 27, 33, 37, 46, 98, 100, 102, 106, 114–15, 117–19, 121,

126–7, 129–30, 142, 152, 161, 172, 175, 177, 179, 194
theist machine, 6–7, 107
theogonic reproduction theory, 2, 26, 29, 31–2, 37, 40, 42, 45–6, 103, 114, 127, 133, 140
theology, 6–8, 10, 12, 18, 35, 44, 99, 133–4, 138, 157, 161–2, 164, 166, 168, 171, 174, 185
transcendence, 1, 3–4, 10–11, 18, 35, 39, 46, 52–3, 56, 58, 61, 65–6, 83, 97, 133, 158, 167–8, 180, 185, 192, 198

virtual, the, 1, 16, 25, 52–3, 59–60, 62, 64–9, 71–2, 79, 83, 85–8, 91–2, 94, 97, 122–3, 182–3, 193, 198

war machine, 2, 4, 13, 15, 21, 27, 38, 40, 42–3, 51, 80, 186
Wildman, Wesley, 44, 48, 50, 59–60, 99, 101, 135, 137, 161, 170

EU representative:
Easy Access System Europe
Mustamäe tee 50, 10621 Tallinn, Estonia
Gpsr.requests@easproject.com

www.ingramcontent.com/pod-product-compliance
Lightning Source LLC
Chambersburg PA
CBHW051122160426
43195CB00014B/2304